To Charles

Thank you for your
kindness, generosity &
support in 2015.

I do hope you enjoy
this book.

All the very best for
2016

THE BLUE ARENA

THE BLUE ARENA

Squadron Leader
BOB SPURDLE
DFC and Bar

CRÉCY BOOKS

First published in 1986 by
WILLIAM KIMBER & CO LIMITED

This revised edition published by
CRÉCY BOOKS LTD 1995

© R. L. Spurdle, 1986, 1995

ISBN 0-947554-58-0

Typeset by Ann Buchan (Typesetters), Surrey
Printed and bound in Great Britain by
Bookcraft (Bath) Limited,
Midsomer Norton, Avon BA3 2BX

Contents

List of Illustrations

List of Illustrations in the Text

Dedication

I wish to dedicate this book to a WAAF whom I never met – Mrs Anne George, wife of a fighter pilot. And to the mothers and sisters, the wives and lovers who agonised in our moments of peril. She wrote:

> We lay in the ditches and watched the dog-fights and cheered on our warriors and laughed and danced and sang with them in the evenings. And we saw them off the next day with the tight fist of fear knotted deep in our insides. And more and more fell – and all of them so young. I mourned for them then, now and forever.
>
> They held our lives, our happiness and our heritage in their strong, young hands.

In the springtime of our lives it was an adventure – not many of us realised what it meant in heartache to those who loved us.

Foreword by
Group Captain E. P. WELLS DSO, DFC

It is a great pleasure for me to say a few words about such a stout wartime companion as 'Bob' Spurdle, the author of this book.

He started his operational life as a Spitfire pilot in No 74 Squadron, RAF, commanded by the famous 'Sailor' Malan, based first at Kirton-in-Lindsey and later at Biggin Hill from where he took part in the Battle of Britain.

Bob completed one operational tour then, 'taking a break', a second tour, this time with the Merchant Ship Fighter Unit on Atlantic convoys. Back in England he completed his third tour before returning to New Zealand where he set up the fighter gunnery school at Ohakea. Getting bored with this he joined 16(F) Squadron and flew against the Japanese in the Solomons, completing his fourth tour of Ops.

On being returned to the UK, I had the pleasure in recommending him as squadron commander of the 80 Squadron with which he completed his fifth tour. As if this wasn't enough excitement he joined the 6th Airborne Division crossing the Rhine by glider and then finished the war in an 11th Armoured Division tank on the Elbe river.

Bob, or 'Spud' as he was nicknamed, destroyed eight enemy aircraft, probably five more and damaged at least fifteen others.

Leading 80, 'Spud' was responsible for destroying or damaging scores of MT, Locos, flak posts, shipping and all the enemy targets he could find. In the Solomons, his expertise in anti-shipping sorties was demonstrated when, with a companion, he destroyed three Japanese motor torpedo boats.

After the war he started his own engineering business in Wanganui, New Zealand, where he built his diesel-powered *Whai*, the first surveyed catamaran in New Zealand. In *Whai* he motored to Japan and back with a crew of other keen divers. This adventure is related in his first book *Into the Rising Sun*.

All in all, he has had a full and adventurous life and I would like to say:

'Well done, Bob!' and to wish this new book every success.

Edward Preston Wells,
Lt Capt (retd.)

Acknowledgements

My thanks to the many friends who assisted in researching and verifying facts for this book.

Mrs Lesley Gair; Dr David Clouston (ex-485 pilot); Mr Kenneth Wynn (historian); 'Titch' Mynard (ex-91 ground crew); Flying Officer Leslie Withers (ex-80 Squadron Administration Officer) and flying comrades Bobby Oxspring, Roger Hall, Louis Graham-Smith, Douglas Greig, Frank Lang, Noel Pirie and Max de Denne.

My thanks also to the ground crews, men and women who kept us flying. Working tirelessly, often in appalling conditions and living rough, they soldiered on unsung. During hundreds of hours of flying I never suffered a mechanical failure due to negligence. To you, and my Talisman Lady Luck – Bravo!

Lastly, my deep appreciation to Toni, loved companion, who suffered hours of enforced silence whilst I struggled to forge these words together.

Introduction

Over the years many books have been written by experienced fighter pilots who usually got a prominent air force personality to write a foreword. This tends to put a seal of approval on the author's work. I don't know that I can get such an accolade because in this book many toes will be trodden on and not everybody will wear a white hat.*

I am intensely proud to have been an RAF pilot. So proud in fact, that at the end of the war I wouldn't apply for a permanent commission in case it should be declined. This would have broken my heart.

Yet it has taken me nearly forty years to conquer the bitterness instilled in me by the war. Not a hatred for an ancient enemy but that engendered by members of our own RNZAF and the shortcomings of our American allies. If some facts in this book are hard to accept, then imagine how hard it was for us – experienced, battle-tired, veterans. Many of us were not much more than callow youths when we set off on the Great Adventure. On our return to New Zealand our reception turned some of us into cynical rebels.

Today, as far as I know, the RNZAF is a service of which we can all be proud. The cunning ones have long gone, or lost their teeth.

The Americans? They claim they won World War I and II. What happened to them fighting a peasant Vietnam? No, it is men, not machines, that count when the chips are down.

Readers will, no doubt, criticise generalisations – but please remember that the war was so huge, so complex, that to deal in specifics alone would be impossible. This is my story as seen through my eyes and as it happened to me.

* You could always tell the good guys from the baddies in the early cowboy movies – the goodies wore white hats.

As I write these pages, memories come flooding back; the vapour trails fading in the high thin cold air of time reform; the plane's roar, the ripping tear of cannons and machine guns and, more poignantly, the shouts of my comrades' laughter I hear again.

R. L. 'Bob' Spurdle
DFC & Bar, MID,
S/Ldr. RAF 44230

CHAPTER 1

'I'd sooner fly than march!'

Held together by its rotting flying suit and torn helmet, crucified on spears of broken bamboo, the skeleton grinned down at me.

It was deathly quiet in the jungle; only the soft cooing of bush doves and the occasional dry rustle of palm fronds intruded into this silent place. I backed away, gaze locked on the Japanese flier suspended above me in the bamboo thicket and dried into a ghastly scarecrow. There would be three or four more like him nearby and suddenly the urge to find the wrecked bomber died in me.

This was my first dead human seen at close range. It could have been me! Up till now, death in the air had been that of machines. Machines that grew fiery comet tails, machines which existed, then exploded with violence to fall as debris. Or disappeared in mighty splashes or cratered the earth. One didn't die! One just didn't return to the Mess, home and comfort. But here death himself creaked and rattled, beckoned with outstretched arms, and I felt appalled, vividly aware for the first time of my mortality.

Here, in Guadalcanal's steaming miasma, the youth who so cheerfully signed up for war now faced the other side of the King's shilling – the side that pictured payment in full.

At nineteen, I had no clear ideas or plans for the future – driving cars fast, experimenting with drink and girls took up all non-working hours. I was a storeman-cum-warehouse assistant for an engineering firm and among my friends was a young man who had just been accepted for a short-service commission in the Royal Air Force. I admired John Gard'ner – he was a rather smooth type and he gave me the score on joining up.

'You sign on for five years. You get a gratuity of £100 for each of the last four years. At the present rate of exchange it means you'd come back with five hundred quid.'

And so I applied to join the RAF. I had enough brains and

ambition to know I'd need capital one day and this was a project that appealed; real adventure and escape from the hum-drum. Also, it was obvious that World War II was on its way and I'd sooner fly than march.

Along with several others, I was interviewed by a flight lieutenant pilot from RNZAF Headquarters, and examined by a medical officer. The pilot was a Kiwi, thank God, or I would never have made it. The sum total of my educational achievements was the Proficiency Certificate from primary school. In all my four years of secondary schooling, I occupied alternatively bottom and second to bottom place in the form. My mind was lazy and hated any form of mental exercise unless it produced immediate material results.

'So, you went to the Wanganui Collegiate! You'll be OK. What sports do you play?'

My mind scrabbled around – tertius cricket was scarcely a recommendation, so bluffed it out with, 'Oh, the usual – footy, tennis, cricket, swimming.'

And thanks to the old school tie, I was in!

Having been accepted as likely officer and gentleman material, I was now medically examined. My height was recorded, then, seated on the floor, back to the wall, I had my legs measured. With relish, almost, the MO said, 'I don't think you'll make it – your legs are too short.'

The RNZAF had obviously never heard of adjustable seats and rudder bars! However, I could still qualify for air crew as an air gunner or wireless operator, so wasn't immediately discarded.

The official acceptance came after some anxious weeks, while overseas, Hitler made more and more noises and our forces slowly geared up for the coming conflict. The mail brought a list of peace-time clothing and toiletries to be bought before embarkation. This nearly sent me broke with the buying of expensive sports clothes so I wouldn't be an embarrassment to myself or the RAF. I had to have visiting cards – engraved – ('Don't get them *printed*, old man! You can always *feel* the difference!')

War was declared and a letter arrived from the RNZAF. It said, God help me, that, 'Now a state of war is extant, perhaps you might like to reconsider your joining the RAF.'

No alternatives were offered. I wish I'd kept it as a souvenir and not heaved it in disgust and unanswered into the fire. The RNZAF formed in 1937, was a little naive and even 'Mickey Mouse' in some respects. On the outbreak of war, it largely expanded from an old boys' network, members of the Rongotai Aero Club and other clubs like it. The regular RAF officers and technicians had mostly filtered back to the UK by the time war was declared. A core of first-rate territorial volunteers were inducted and the RNZAF quickly expanded into quite an effective training organisation.

My orders were to report to No 11 Course, Rongotai Airport, Wellington, for Ground School with 'Tiny' White as officer commanding. Twenty-two of us turned up and, after milling about for a few days, we were measured en masse, for uniforms and each issued with a large mimeographed collection of 'traditional' service songs. As officers, albeit, acting pilot officers (a low form of life), we were supposed to receive our uniform allowance in cash and select our own tailors, but some racket was worked and we ended up looking like untidy dustmen in ill-fitting uniforms while our commandeered allowance disappeared like magic. This was the beginning of a distrust in senior brass which grew over the years. We were introduced to the hated 'button stick' and brasso. The new buttons took many hours of spit, polish and curses to rub into the required brilliant glow.

A sing-song was organised at which, shamefacedly, we stood around and went through the farce of mouthing the 'songs'. Later of course, at parties we roared out obscene ditties with gusto and laughter, but that night we felt ashamed and degraded. We were all very green.

From Rongotai, after hours of drill and ceremonial, we were sent to a new 'drome at Taieri, out of Dunedin. This was our Elementary Flying Training School – bleak and raw, with builders still grunting around. We were introduced to the Tiger Moth and to our flying instructors. I had three changes of instructor due to organisational problems, and, after thirteen hours' dual instruction, was nearly washed out as a no-hoper. The CFI (Chief Flying Instructor) studied my reports and looked me over. At last he took me up himself; after a careful circuit and bump he said those magic words, 'Go ahead – and don't prang it.'

There are no words, however magic, to describe completely the thrill of having, for the very first time, a whole aircraft to oneself. The absence of that rasping, chiding voice of the instructor in one's ear, all troubles a mile below and the shining wings slipping through the whispering air. And the sky – that huge beautiful arena.

From Taieri we were sent to Flying Training School, Wigram, the RNZAF's biggest 'drome, not far from Christchurch City. Here we were to fly Fairey Gordons (which had seen service on the North-West Frontier of India) and the big Vickers Vildebeeste torpedo bombers. At Wigram some of our numbers were converted onto twin-engined Oxfords. Most of us, of course, wanted to be fighter pilots, but to our consternation, we were told our fate was to be light bombers. Bloody Hell!

Days of swotting, hours of flying in the open cockpit, oily biplanes. Bombing, navigation, (I cheated a little in this exam for my wings and the one filched answer was wrong! I got 98% and wished I'd kept my eyes to myself!) and aircraft recognition, morse code, ground signals, air-to-air and air-to-ground firing, drill and ceremonial, the stripping of Lewis and Browning machine guns, and so on. The practical stuff was fun, but the theoretical nearly finished me.

In our spare moments we relaxed with escapades as wild and irresponsible as those of university students. One pilot passed out at a party and was carried, bed and all, to the middle of the airfield. He awoke in broad daylight with planes trundling around and a furious CFI bearing down on him. 'Ardy' Ashworth (later to win the DSO), while fooling with a Very pistol, accidentally fired it inside the control tower. The blazing magnesium projectile rocketed from wall to wall and finished up coming to a rest on a book which happened to be entitled *Heat, Hell and Humour*.

At night in the Mess we crowded the bar and signed away our paltry pay as fast as we got it. Faster sometimes, and one pilot disappeared from the station. We understood he wouldn't pay for his Mess bills; got himself removed from the Air Force and war service. And what happened to Ward Phelan, a Canadian volunteer who affected a Meerschaum pipe and went riding in riding-breeches and his uniform jacket, (very, very dashing, but most irregular)? He was a real character, a pilot in civilian life, who had a fantastic scrapbook. There was Ward as a freedom fighter in Bolivia – he had a machete scar (so he said) on his back – and Ward as a sky diver stunt-man. Why did he just disappear?

Lloyd Parry, an Australian, paired up with me, and, flying as a team, we bribed the crew of a drogue-towing Gordon to let us fly alongside the drogue to machine-gun it at 50 foot range. This gave us impossibly good scores. We deliberately scattered our practice bombs hundreds of yards from the ground targets. We hoped to influence our chances of becoming fighter pilots; in fact we were very nearly discarded, along with our results, but by now so much money had been invested in us that we were too valuable to scrap.

The thrill of flying became an obsession; the wonderful feeling of freedom in the open skies with mosaic fields far below. One felt as a God must feel, and this God complex was dangerous, particularly after about one hundred hours' flying. You knew you were hot stuff and became impressively cocky. Some of the fledglings became impressed on the ground, which sobered soaring ideas and required Courts of Enquiry and accident reports.

At this time I was drinking pretty heavily and as a consequence, while our course was waiting embarkation leave, I was sent to hospital passing blood and barbed wire in my urine.

'Knock off the Wizards, you young fool, or you'll be out on your ear,' admonished the MO. For those who haven't met 'the Wizard', it comprises one and a half brandies and three drops of bitters whisked up in lemonade. After six or seven of these you feel wizard all right!

My course went away without me. At the time I felt my heart would break – these were my mates and I'd let them down. They went on to England and light bombers. Eleven went on to death. Only five out of the original sixteen who gained their wings survived the war and of these, two never saw action, being relegated to ground duties due to personality weaknesses.

On leaving hospital I was in a sort of limbo and with my mother went for a long extended tour around the North Island. In Gisborne, I met Florance, a beautiful girl and got engaged – a stupid, impulsive and selfish thing to do and one which eventually caused us both much unhappiness. She was lovely and we fell in love.

I was posted to the UK being attached to No 13 (War) Course and on 7th June 1940 our group sailed on the *Rangitata* for England via the Panama Canal.

Twelve days at sea – the bloody scene was the same as on the first day! Except that the sea was now deep blue instead of green. Shoals of flying fish exploded in showers of flashing diamonds away from the creaming bow wave, skittering across the ocean swells; they would dip their long caudal fins into the sea and with rapid beats surge off again to glide still further from us. Sometimes bo's'n birds trailing long red tails circled the ship and screamed harshly to one another. At night the completely darkened ship thrummed through the velvet blackness and our tall masts slowly described circles against the magnificent canopy of glittering stars.

Early one morning a neutral ship passed across our bows. It was ablaze with lights and as we surged secretly by, the smokers amongst us cursed and envied the distant sailors puffing unconcernedly away.

On deck a swimming pool was erected and under the beating sun we lay around yarning; grew brown and lazy. The ship ran out of grog two days from Panama and tempers got short in the oppressive humidity. I was officer-in-charge of a large group of observers, fresh from their training, all sergeants and stroppy with Kiwi disregard for authority.

It was my first taste of giving orders and I didn't like it. Hell! I'd been to school with some of them – others could give me five years.

At night we lay on deck in windrows of sweating, tossing, cursing insomniacs. Unless it rained to force us into overcrowded cabins. Then we tried to sleep under crude air-conditioning made by hanging damp towels in front of the cabin-blowers.

On board the *Rangitata* were about twenty women. Why? Who were they? They were not nurses or trained war-workers. The older ones retreated to quiet enclaves of deck chairs to cluck about the younger ones having the times of their lives. Even the plainest girls were subject to pressure from a hundred opportunists trying every type of approach known to man.

Panama at last! Slowly we were winched and tugged into and along the mighty locks. US soldiers armed with automatic shotguns patrolled the passages and gangways. We gave them hell.

'When are you guys going to start fighting? When are you? Are you windy?'

We weren't allowed into Panama City but at Balboa and Colon we stirred things up in the sleazy bars and honky-tonks festering the back alleys.

On again – on to colder weather. The pool was dismantled and thick jerseys appeared. Our duty roster of lookouts was increased now we were in Atlantic waters and everyone took a turn.

When we reached New York a convoy was formed and the slow slog over the Atlantic began. Being a trooper and food ship, we were placed about half-way along the convoy. Several days out, a tanker was torpedoed and we watched the horrible struggles of two crewmen literally cooked to death in the steel pot of their crowsnest. To our great excitement, a Sunderland flying boat sank the U-boat responsible, in full sight of the convoy.

The radio told us of France's collapse and of Dunkirk. Our flying careers were being re-directed; new decisions being made as to our use. It was Britain's need for fighters, immediate and urgent, which changed our futures. Churchill's magnificent fighting speeches were the only encouraging note in those desperate days. His speeches and the fact that we were young and fit as buck rabbits, made us thirst for the great adventures ahead. We couldn't get there fast enough; the enormity of events was beyond our comprehension.

Off the coast of Scotland, a Dornier 17 'Flying Pencil' bomber on reconnaissance, circled round and around the convoy. Where were our fighters? Every now and again a destroyer let off a few shots, forcing Jerry to keep his distance. Long after it had left, a deep soft purring sound brought us out on deck and there, in the crystal sunlight, I saw my first Spitfire. A strange thing happened. My palms sweated and my heart thumped; breathing hard, I followed the streamlined beauty with longing eyes. It was a form of love at first sight and one which never left me.

We landed at Methil in Scotland and immediately entrained for London and Uxbridge, the big RAF ground station. It was late at night when, tired after the long slow train ride, we entered the Uxbridge Mess. While waiting for beds to be allotted, refreshments were available and Wally Churches (Auckland, NZ) and I gazed in awe at tables piled with legs of lamb, salads, ham on the bone, trifles and cheese boards of fantastic variety. For a country at war it was astounding but then we had never experienced the luxury of an RAF peace-time establishment. The stark realities to come could only be imagined in those early days.

'We have two New Zealand officers to join you, sir,' the batman said as he ushered us into a bedroom.

'Bloody coloured troops,' the occupant grunted, and he climbed out of bed, piddled in the handbasin, and fell back into his tumbled sheets.

Wally and I looked at each other. We discussed the situation in whispers – would we thump the bastard? But what was his rank? We decided to forget it for the time being. In the morning he left before we woke.

We were given a week's disembarkation leave. Whacko! Seven days on the tiles in London with money in our pockets and lechery in our hearts! Being newly engaged and on the straight and narrow, I envied my carefree cobbers. Each night the chaps who hadn't found a bed, or who retreated from one for a breather came back to Uxbridge. Here, every night, were the fantastic piles of goodies – the great hams, the cold shoulders of mutton, pickles galore, the cheeses, jellies and trifles. This was Britain at war!

We couldn't understand it. We couldn't understand either, why we hadn't been rushed off to our OTUs immediately on landing in the UK. After all, we'd just spent the laziest six week holiday at sea and were raring to go!

Came the parting of the ways. The *Rangitata* contingent was split up, air gunners and observers to training camps, the pilots to various OTUs, Bomber Command, Coastal Command etc.

Single-engine pilots, we learned, were being sent to No 57 Spitfire OTU in Wales and our cheers could be heard for miles. The unfortunate twin-engine pilots, so smug in their previous lordly status, now looked at us with envy.

That night, we had a fearful thrash and in the morning left the station with splitting heads, for Hawarden airfield, on the Welsh border. It was still hard for us to believe our fantastic good fortune. Spitfires!

*

We were paraded in front of the Station Commander, who had already viewed our log books.

'I'm Hallings-Pott, your CO. Here at Hawarden you'll learn to fly the Spitfire. Firstly, you'll do a quick conversion on the Fairey Battle, then the Miles Master, to get the feel of modern aircraft and familiarization with our countryside. You'll find the Master faster than anything you've flown before. It's made of wood and it's easily broken, so watch it. Any pilot who prangs is automatically off fighters: we can't afford to lose Spitfires to ham-handed oafs! Any questions?'

We shuffled and stared past him at the sleek aircraft dotted around the airfield's perimeter.

'Right. Let there be no misunderstanding. The Empire is fighting for its life and you men are urgently needed. The Adjutant will now take charge of you; good luck, Gentlemen.' He strode off and the Adj took over.

'What aircraft were you New Zealanders trained on?'

Chorus: 'Tiger Moths, Fairey Gordons and Vickers Vildebeestes.'

'Good God! Are they still flying?' and with those cheerful words we were sent off to collect Sidcot suits, flying helmets, gloves, goggles, boots and parachutes. Some English pilots joined us as well as the odd Australian and Canadian.

We were divided into small groups, about six per instructor, and started cockpit drill. Flaps, retractable undercarriage, two pitch propellers! In the old crates one just trimmed the tail plane, opened the throttle and took off. Now we learned by mnemonics the correct order of cockpit check.* There were dozens of different 'taps', switches and instruments, levers and gadgets in the Battle's cockpit. They turned out to be ponderous affairs – old gentlemen's aircraft.

The Masters were delightful aircraft with 585 hp Kestrel motors in the Mark 1's and Wasp radials in the later 11's and 1V's we flew. Being made of plywood and very light, they took off like homesick angels. They were said to have the fastest acceleration of any machine and one was literally pressed back into the seat on opening the throttle. Soon we were ready for the Spitfire. One or two pilots had been washed out as temperamentally unsuited for fighters and

* Included in Appendix

had disappeared off to other commands. One or two actually volunteered for bombers and these, too, were whisked out of sight. Incredible.

*

'Climb in,' said the instructor and I clambered up the steeply slanted wing, over the little flap door and let myself down into the Spit's tiny cockpit. So much for the NZMO's short-leg nonsense – the Spit had two rudder pedal levels – the lower one for comfort and the other to combat multiplication of 'G' forces draining blood from the head in high speed turns. The seat could be raised or lowered to accommodate the correct eye level for the optical-type gun sight.*

'Now remember what you've been told; do two circuits and on getting the green light, come in and land. For God's sake, be careful and watch for swing on take-off. Watch the height of the nose too – we don't want you decapitating daisies or digging in. And,' he said, fairly glaring at me, 'if you feel it shaking, for God's sake give it full throttle and ease off the stick. It can fall out of the sky in a high speed stall. The Spit is the easiest thing to fly – it gives you plenty of warning of incipient stalling; it starts to shudder. Your biggest problem is the sensation of speed. Just take your time. The aircraft has absolutely no vices. You'll be OK!' And with that he hopped down onto the grass.

I checked the trim wheel and flaps and signalled the mechanics to lie on the tail plane for running the motor up full bore. Soon the Merlin was roaring and the whole machine shook with its power. Grass and dust whirled past, stinging the backsides of the unfortunate erks (ground staff) lying across the tail plane surface.

---

* This sight replaced the old 'ring and bead'. It had an inclined glass plate on which was superimposed a ring and dot of light. The pilot looked through the glass plate at his target and the dot represented the focal point his eight machine guns harmonized in a 'cone of fire' at 250 yards range. There were two horizontal moveable arms of light which could be adjusted to the wing-span of a target. For instance, an Me 109's wing span was 32 feet and a Ju 88's, 60 feet. Knowing the target's wing span a pilot could set his 'arms' and when the target's wing tips coincided with the inside tip of the 'arms' the target was exactly 250 yards away. These arms were useless in the average whirling mix up of air combat but they gave an indication of sorts as to the correct range.

Each mag switch tested OK, no rev. drop and I throttled back. The airmen ran to the chocks and I waved them clear.

Opening up the throttle a little, the Merlin's coughing changed to a deep purr. More throttle and with a hiss from the released airbrakes, we were off, rumbling across the grass to the runway.

Everything about the plane was strange. The tiny confined cockpit, the complexity of instruments, levers, switches – the very power at instant command and, thrill of thrills, the potent gun button on the split spade-type joystick. And the reflector gunsight not a foot from my excited face. This was it! The dream come true! I looked out across each beautiful elliptic wing, camouflaged green and brown, with its roundels shining in the sun. The plane rolled forward at a faster pace than seemed safe, the throttle so sensitive to the slightest movement. The radio warmed into crackling life and the control tower gave me the okay for take-off.

Open radiator flap, full fine pitch; a quick glance to the side and I turned her into the wind, the air brakes hissing in spurts as I lined up on the runway. A last look around and I steadily pushed the throttle forward. The big flat-topped engine cowling cut out all forward view and it was a question of judgment to keep the plane running true until the nose slowly depressed with the tail coming up. Fantastic! I eased back the joystick, and up we lifted – the speedo leapt; 90 – 100 – 150 mph. Things flashed past; trees, buildings, pylons and we were under the cloud base before I remembered the wheels.

These were Mark I Spitfires with hand-operated undercarriages. One had to pump the wheels up by moving a lever up and down. This tended to induce a sympathetic movement in the pilot's other arm – the one holding the joystick. Hence, until the pilot got the hang of it, his Spitfire tended to fly as on a switchback – a curious undulation. These Mark I's were being phased out as quickly as possible, mostly by the German Air Force and the far superior Mark II's were replacing them. The II's had the new variable pitch Rotol propellers and the hydraulic power-operated undercarriages. They also had increased the horse-power by one hundred and forty five, to 1,175 hp.

Magically the speed leapt faster and I throttled back to 2,500 revs. The speed increased to over 200 mph before I started to turn. The nose dropped slightly. Quick! Top rudder; open the throttle more!

The whole thing took too short a time; too many emotions of delight, pride, fear and complete out-of-this-world strangeness blurred the flight. I was alone as never before; alone with a thousand horsepower and this beautiful little aeroplane. All too soon I had to line up for the landing and sweated as I came down on a low-powered approach. The Spit seemed to float and float across the 'drome. The far boundary was rushing towards me when with a whoosh she sagged down and started to roll at over eighty miles an hour. The nose came up and I couldn't see ahead. Yellow marker boards flashed past; the rumbling of the plane's wheels reminded me of the airbrakes. Too hard! The nose dipped and I had visions of arsing over on my prop. There was only one thing to do – ground loop – and around we went, scattering grass until I saw we'd still plenty of room ahead. I straightened out my direction and remembered to go into fine pitch. The flaps! I had forgotten them! So I put them down and taxied around to the dispersal.

'You bloody half-wit! Lift your flaps when taxiing. You came in much too fast! Didn't I tell you to come over the boundary at about ninety-five? Now go and do it again and for Christ's sake remember!'

With the wonderful euphoria dampened, I repeated the performance but remembered to lower my flaps after putting down the undercarriage.

Luckily the instructor hadn't noticed my peccadillo, for an extraordinary accident had occurred as I was coming in the first time. Jim Falconer (a primary school chum of mine) had landed much too hard and his starboard oleo-leg had collapsed. The plane careered around in a huge curve, kicking and bucking as each blade of the propeller hit the ground and shortened itself. Poor Jim was on the train that night – destination, a Bomber OTU.

We crammed in flying hours. Someone asked if we'd ever done fixed front gunnery. 'No? What! Not any?' And so we were told to go and have a squirt at a sandbank off the coast. Some seagulls got a hell of a fright! This was the *total* extent of our training with live ammunition and fixed front guns. The next time my guns were fired the enemy was the target.

*

It was a grand day and I was on sector reconnaissance (officially) but for the fun I was hurtling up and down the brown tussock-clad hills of Wales. Low flying, strictly forbidden, is the most marvellous thrill but here there were no houses or roads, so no one to report me. But what's this? A long line of army types in line abreast struggling up a slope. Let's add some realism to the manoeuvres; so around we go, my Spitfire and I, in a tight bank, white contrails peeling back from each wing tip. It was a most satisfactory beat-up, with the 'brown jobs' throwing themselves down enthusiastically each time I roared over.

But back at Hawarden the Wing Commander had me on the mat.

'If you weren't so badly needed I'd have you thrown out! Do you know what you did?'

'Yes sir! Beat up some brow . . . er, army exercise, sir.'

'Did you, hell! That was Lord. . . [I've forgotten] grouse shoot you ruined. Now get out of here and don't put a foot wrong again in my command!'

Wing Commander Hallings-Pott DSO, DFC was a terrific guy – he had led the famous bombing raid on Sylt early in the war and I felt very ashamed to have caused this stink. Later I was to cause a much bigger stink and be punished for it by this same officer.

The day came for our posting to operational squadrons. We were split up; there was a small choice given to cobbers so that they might stick together, but no choice of squadrons. It was 20 August 1940, and Wally and I were posted to 74 'Tiger' Squadron, based at Wittering. We were fortunate – 74 was a famous World War I and postwar squadron commanded by 'Sailor' Malan. Its motto was 'I fear no man' and its logo a tiger's mask.

The squadron was impatient to get back into the huge air battles presently raging over Kent and London. Earlier in the fierce fighting around the Dunkirk perimeter, the Tigers had proved a crack squadron. Later, at the beginning of the Battle of Britain, the squadron had destroyed twenty-nine, and probably a further seven, and damaged fifteen enemy aircraft in just two days' fighting on 11th and 12th August.

They were withdrawn to Wittering to re-form and train new pilots – replacements of the fallen.

*

Wally and I stood outside Euston Station looking for a cab. One drove up; the cabby touching his cloth cap.

'We've got our suitcases in the left-luggage. Hang on to these while we get them.' And we bundled our hand luggage into the taxi. A London bobby, tall in his great helmet, sauntered over.

'You can't park here!' he admonished the driver.

'I'll just go round the corner,' shouted the cabbie to us as we hurried off for our cases. And he did – and kept on going – we never saw him or our gear again. We were furious. The bobby took details and majestically moved off while we looked for another cab. I'd lost my NZ log book and toiletries, but poor Wally lost most of his good woollen underwear.

'God damn! And right in front of a cop too!' snarled Wally.

'Yeah. Do you think they're in on it together?'

But the idea of a British bobby being a petty racketeer was too much to swallow and that was that.

CHAPTER II

The Tigers – 74 Squadron

Wally and I stood before Sailor Malan and gazed at our new CO with deep respect. 'You pilots will be trained hard in the next few weeks. Your life expectancy will be in direct ratio to your ability to learn. Spurdle, you are being put into 'A' Flight – your commander is Flight Lieutenant Freeborn. You, Churches, are in 'B' Flight with Mungo Park. This is a famous squadron and I expect you both to remember it. In the last war Major Mannock won the VC flying for 74. He shot down 73 enemy aircraft. Soon you, too, will have plenty of targets. I'm sure you'll do well!'

Sailor was to become the RAF's leading ace, a position he held for several years. We couldn't have joined a better squadron.

Then Flight Lieutenant Mungo Park, tall, slim and dark, came in followed by the shorter, florid Freeborn. We were introduced, then led out to meet the others.

'More coloured troops! Are we scraping the bottom of the barrel already?' someone hooted. Sheepishly we sat in a corner to keep a low profile. A couple of other 'new boys' joined us and we felt less conspicuous.

This was our first experience of the dispersal hut in an operational squadron. Pretty spartan with unlined wooden walls, metal-framed beds to rest on, old knocked-about chairs, cast-iron fuel burning stove, a couple of tables.

At one end of the hut was the 'readiness' board giving the state of aircraft serviceability for each flight and the pilots to man them. Each section, usually of four aircraft, would be allocated a colour; thus, say, pilots A,B,C, and D would be Blue or Red section etc. and be referred to over our aircraft's RT (Radio Telephone) as such, prefixed by the squadron's call sign. 74's at this station was 'Dysoe'.

This board, and others like it, was to be the focal point of my life for the next five years. On them the names of hundreds of comrades and the identification letters of aircraft would be chalked up. After each operation the boards were wiped clean and flight commanders would reorganise again the teams on whom our country's fate depended. A prosaic thing, but, when my turn came to select fighting units, the full and heavy responsibility made me pause as I faced the board.

We learned the operational technique used in running a squadron on the ground. There were three stages of readiness: 'standby' (two minutes to get in one's machine), 'readiness' (five minutes to get kitted up and assume standby) and 'available'. 'Available' was usually in the Mess playing cards or billiards. Or, if the billets were close enough, asleep. 'Released', of course meant that your name wasn't on the board for that day and you could leave the station, get tanked up or whatever.

Each pilot knew the evening before if he'd be required the next day. From his listing on the board he knew with whom he was teamed, the colour of his section and the aircraft he'd be using. Each pilot tried to have his own aircraft – but with more men than machines, only the CO, Flight Commanders and some of the more experienced chaps could hope to monopolise a favourite plane.

Flight commanders chose their teams with care. If the CO wasn't flying, usually the senior flight commander led the squadron and a deputy led his flight. It was not uncommon for a Sergeant Pilot to lead commissioned pilots of less combat experience.

Our phone was manned twenty-four hours a day by airmen in relays and was a direct link with the sector operations room. When a scramble came through, the operator called out our instructions, at the same time pressing the 'panic' button. With the klaxons wailing, pilots jumped from their card games or snoozing and ran for their machines. Often ground crews had the motor running by the time a pilot reached his plane. He'd be helped up, strapped in, the little side door snapped shut and the chocks manned ready to pull away. Squadrons not off the ground and formating within three minutes were in for a blister from Group.

Along with Wally and myself, three more new boys arrived – Pilot Officers Ricalton, Boulding and Franklin. Being English and not cursed with our Kiwi nasal whine they were more readily assimilated. 74 was gaining strength and rapidly becoming operational again. We were busy firstly doing circuits and bumps, then a sector reconnaissance to familiarise ourselves with the local scenery, then two practices at air drill. That same night a signal came through that the squadron was to go to Kirton-in-Lindsey and early next morning the lucky ones flew down south in their Spits. The rest of us groaned off in overloaded three-tonners along with the ground crews, aeroplane spares and rations.

Some of the pilots owned cars or motor cycles and made their own way – the squadron 'Spy' (Intelligence Officer), Doc, engineering and transport officers used squadron transport – the flight vans, CO's car etc. A real circus, winding along the country lanes with stops for 'egging' or the odd pint in picturesque pubs.

At Kirton, we started battle-formation-flying and fighter tactics in earnest with blooded leaders. 74 had a tremendous élan in the air but was a curiously divided and unhappy unit on the ground. With Malan we would have flown anywhere against anything, but 74's curse was, in my opinion, the presence of several Auxiliary Air Force types, who affected longer than regulation hair and who tended to treat menials and pilot officers as they must have treated fags at their public schools. But they knew how to fight. It was too bad that their ragging smacked of the fazing I'd suffered as a 'new bug' back at Collegiate in Wanganui.

In a subtle way we 'Colonials' and the new young British recruits, unless 'well connected', were largely excluded from this kind of old boys' club and felt it keenly.

Soon we learned how to fly in really tight formation. Malan was a first rate flyer trained in peacetime. His delight, when coming to a strange 'drome with large runways, was to land the whole dozen machines at once in echelon starboard. This was pretty hair-raising and most spectacular. It was discontinued when a couple of machines ran into filled-in bomb craters with soft ground. Wally and I, green and completely obedient, began to be selected by Sailor, alternating as his number two's. The No 2's flew as partners to section, flight and squadron leaders. Their job was to stick with and support their leader. To stick with meant just that even in the midst of a dog fight. Later we were to find that No 2's tended to swan off on their own if a tempting target presented itself, or if their leader acted like an oaf. But Wally and I were dead keen and we worshipped

Malan. He realised he had two dependable pilots capable of sticking with him and he used us almost exclusively.

We used to go 'egging' for fun and food when off duty. We'd climb into someone's car with the odd pet dog underfoot and the squadron's skeet-guns to hand. Anything that could go into the pot was legitimate game. We'd bag pheasants, ducks, rabbits and hares. We'd go to farms and dicker for eggs and butter. Rationing became more and more a fact of life and we needed to augment the declining meat rations with black market food and game hacked down with the shot guns.

*

One day we motored into a quiet little village, with its common-green surrounding a duck pond. Large oak trees shaded the edge of the village main street. Old timbered cottages, and ducks quacking on the pond. How pretty!

'Out, Kirk! Get some of those ducks,' ordered Freeborn, and the hapless sergeant was bundled out with the shotgun. There was an almighty bang, a duck flopped over, and the rest flapped away, quacking loudly, as the village burst into startled life.

'Quickly, you clot,' roared Freeborn, and drove the old Talbot forward. Kirk ran to the edge of the pond and frantically started to take off his shoes.

'Forget your shoes! Get into the water, you bloody oaf!' shouted Freeborn, but seeing the oncoming village bobby, he calmly drove off.

Two days later poor Kirk was released from the lock-up and returned to the station. It slowed our egging not a jot, but we looked at Freeborn with a new kind of respect. We realised here was a leader to whom fate was kind.

New pilots arrived, keen and eager: Sergeants Glendinning, Freese and Morrison, and Pilot Officer Howard.

More formation flying, air drill, dog fighting, Ciné camera gun attacks and DF homings. On the 28th, Wally and I went on our first real patrol but nothing happened – we just stooged around excited and ecstatic with great expectations. More and yet more ciné camera practice (some of the Spits had cameras mounted in the wings and we'd practice mock attacks, 'firing' the camera at the 'target' plane. Later the films would be assessed and faults pointed out).

Deflection attacks, blind flying in formation through heavy cloud (this was something! You had to concentrate on your leader and that was all. He could see his, and so each man flew in his particular place and so the whole lot flew as one.). We flew in tight 'Vic' (vee) formations of three aircraft with a fourth 'in the box', i.e. immediately below and behind the squadron leader. The next flight leader would fly immediately below this aircraft with his Vic around him, and so on. Thus twelve aircraft with no more than twenty feet separating each individual aircraft could fly blind through cloud or rain without getting separated.

Pilot Officer Armstrong joined on 28th August and, on the 30th, while practising head-on attacks, Wally collided with Sergeant Skinner, cutting off Skinner's tail plane. A shaken Skinner baled out OK and Wally landed dead-stick in a field not quite sure how it all occurred.

We flew in naval AA (anti-aircraft) exercises and once we actually flew for the *March of Time* movie producers. Then the war caught up with us in earnest. We were fully operational again and began regular patrols and scrambles (emergency take-off for enemy interception).

September 1940: Flight Lieutenant Freeborn called me into his office.

'You're to take a replacement Spit to Hornchurch. They're running out of machines. The place is often bombed and strafed, so fly low and don't fool around. I'm getting rid of 'L' – it's the last of the hand-pump undercarriage kites.' I pitied the unfortunate pilots who would use this outmoded model.

As I approached Hornchurch I listened to the staccato commands of a squadron engaged somewhere way up above in the twisting smoke trails over London. Ack-Ack bursts just ahead warned me of approaching trouble.

Hornchurch was a mess – bomb craters, shattered brick walls and empty, gutted hangars. No sooner had I landed, low on fuel, than a bombing raid started and, taxiing furiously, I just made it to an empty revetment and into the shelter of its anti-blast walls before the first of the bombs came whistling down. Leaving my parachute in the cockpit and with the prop still spinning, I leapt out and rushed for the nearest shelter.

Clouds of dust and acrid stinking smoke! Hammer blows on the ears and chest! Crumping blasts with bricks and pieces of wood jumping in unison off the ground. The black hole of a shelter gaped at my feet and I fairly skipped down the steps, to pause panting in the dark doorway. A long line of dully gleaming steel helmets and shadowy forms were pressed up against each dank wall. Nobody spoke. Everyone too occupied with sombre thoughts as outside the Bofors coughed and the large AA guns cracked and banged away.

More bombs fell; their rising whistling shrieks drove me into the shelter proper, and I stumbled over boots and equipment to a gap in the frightened figures. I stretched out my hand and, gently waving it from side to side, groped for a seat. And groped, instead, right up a WAAF's skirt.

I felt a proper fool – I don't know what the WAAF felt like because at that moment everyone was ordered out to refuel and rearm fighters landing in the middle of it all. Some erks had to be forced out at gunpoint by officers determined to keep the fighters in action. I was pleased to catch a train back to my squadron and leave Hornchurch to its torment.

September 9th: Yet another move. This time to Coltishall, a 12 Group station, and a little closer to the real conflict. We were flying as a wing of two squadrons with 242 commanded by the flamboyant Bader.

Bader had lost both his legs in a flying accident back in 1931 and had been invalided out of the RAF. Tied to a desk job with the Shell Company and driven almost beserk at the thought of being useless in the coming war, he enlisted the aid of his old Commandant, Air Vice Marshal Halahan. A promise was exacted that, should he be found physically fit, he'd be given the chance to fly again.

Eight years after his accident Bader did just that, becoming an ace with over twenty Jerries to his credit before being taken POW near St Omer after bailing out of his crippled Spitfire.

At Coltishall we flew with the Duxford Wing, brain child of Air Vice Marshal Leigh-Mallory. The idea was to clobber the Hun with bigger RAF formations. Unfortunately, the wing always arrived too late and we were only involved in minor skirmishes.

The 11 Group squadrons, directed by the brilliant tactician Air Vice Marshal Sir Keith Park, were battling it out, often outnumbered ten and more to one. Park had to fight not only the Germans but bitter opposition from Leigh-Mallory. However, the New Zealander was supported by the C–in–C Fighter Command, Air Marshal 'Stuffy' Dowding, and the soundness of his strategy is a matter of record.

To our delight the new Mark II Spitfires were being introduced and the old I's flown off to OTUs or back to the factories for modifying into II's.

September 14th 1940: On my fifth operational patrol Flight Lieutenant Freeborn, my section leader, Sergeant Kirk and I were vectored on to a Bogey (unidentified suspect aircraft) which turned out to be a Heinkel 111K medium bomber approaching the coast. The radio advised the E/A was to our port, and suddenly, with 'Tally Ho! Turning Port!' Freeborn dived hard left and there it was! Fat and mottled greeny-grey with sunlight flashing on its perspex snout.

I switched on the reflector sight and tucked myself in under my leader. Yellow sparkles flickered from the front of the bomber as it seemed to float up towards us. Things banged and clanged off my plane's wings and even off the windscreen. I was frozen into following my leader. I was formating under him far too closely and suddenly I saw the streams of empty cartridge cases spewing out of the vents under his wings and flashing all around me. I couldn't fire for fear of hitting the jinking, diving machine so close in front and we flashed past the bomber to climb and curve back and dive again in a quarter stern attack. This time I was left behind and well out to one side: mouth dry, palms wet, heart pounding. The rear-firing gunners in the Heinkel hosed their weapons at me, but I felt quite safe behind a ton of engine and two inches of bulletproof glass. I clearly saw the lower gunner in his blister as I flashed past and below. But he'd quit firing; the flickering red bursts of our de Wilde ammunition had silenced him.

Around again and the Heinkel disappeared into a cloud bank.

It was gone – the starboard engine trailing black smoke. For the first time I really smelt the gun fumes in my cockpit. For the first time had really felt the thudding hammer of the plane's eight Brownings and felt the whole aircraft hesitate from the recoil of each burst. There was another smell – hot and oily. The engine temperature was way up and a thin stream of grey vapour streaked back below my starboard wing.

'Hallo, Red Leader, Red Leader. Red Three returning to base, engine trouble, Over.'

'Hallo, Windrush, Red Three to Windrush. Please give me vector for base return urgent. Over.'

'Windrush to Red Three, Red Three, steer 260, repeat 260. Over.'

'Red Leader to Red Three. Shut up! Red Leader to Windrush. Any sign of bandit (enemy aircraft)? Over.'

'Hallo, Red Leader. Windrush. Vector 68, five miles, Angels five.'

But the Heinkel had staggered off, hidden in a cloud, and I limped back to Coltishall with a cartridge case from Freeborn's plane jammed in and puncturing my radiator.

It was a valuable experience – I learned a lot from it. Not to slavishly follow my leader so closely; that other things than enemy fire can damage a plane. And that it wasn't I who was of prime importance – I was expendable.

*

The IO (Intelligence Officer) had to hover on the outside of the circle of excited pilots and glean, bit by bit, the results of our scrap. For the first time I saw and, indeed, had to use the 'there I was' technique of planing hands to describe air combat. How else can one paint the crazy picture of wheeling wings and complex speeding curves? For the first time I realised how each pilot saw a different picture; a different angle to the same hectic event.

The IO wrote the information down, later it would be sifted over and analysed. Had we made best use of our training? Were the enemy's tactics unusual? Its armaments? Did the enemy air-crew display any special tenacity, aggressiveness? Was it just a probing flight to test our alertness? Or did it have a specific target?

More and more we started to run into hit and run raiders – probing bombers and the odd Hun fighter forays testing our defences.

September 24th: A bad day – Sergeant Ayers had to bale out over the sea off Southwold and was drowned. On the 28th Pilot Officers

Chester, Buckland and Pearce joined us and on the 30th, Pilot Officer Smith arrived. Sergeant Soars celebrated this day by being shot up for the third consecutive day by Me 109s giving rise to many appalling puns and much work for the ground crews. 'Aren't you sore? That's three times you've had it up the arse!'

Pilot Officer Smith joined on the 30th bringing us up to full strength again.

October 4th: Sergeant Ayers' body was recovered from the sea and on the 9th, a horrible accident occurred when Pilot Officers Hastings and Buckland collided and were both killed.

In drizzling rain the squadron mustered for the funeral. Muffled drums, reversed rifles, best blues, the lot. As I stood by the gaping earth and listened to our Padre trying to console the weeping women, I knew it must be bad for morale. In the short time I'd known Hastings we had become friends and now they were firing a salute over his coffin.

The tears, the opened earth got to me. I never went to another burial. Not even for my own boys later in the war. I just got drunk, got angry. If I could arrange it I flew out on a strafing mission against the damned enemy, preferably alone.

I decided it was too demoralising for aircrew and not to be endured. In fact, later, as a commanding officer of a squadron, I refused to detail aircrew to attend funerals leaving this chore to non-flying types. This made them a little less stuffy over our fliers' excesses and the realisation that it was 'us' who paid the terrible price for our more glamorous lifestyle. If a pilot's particular friends wished to attend OK – but no enforcement.

October 15th: At last! Orders to go to Biggin Hill – the centre of action. We were off to 'Biggin on the Bump' and the whole squadron was excited at the prospect of really getting 'into it'. Everybody tore around packing kit. The flight commanders chalked up the pilots detailed to fly and the others, moaning at having to go by road and rail, sorted out their transport. It was goodbye to Kirton and its pleasant environs.

Wally and I were lucky to be flying and, clapping each other on the back, made our way out to our Spitfires. We carried little bundles of over-night toiletries as the ground party might take over twenty-four hours to catch up with us.

With a roar each section tore down the field and slid up into the sky. 74 formated in tight Vics and headed for the real thing. With Sailor leading, the Tigers droned over the green fields far below.

We were a strong, well-trained and competent squadron and we were led by the best.

CHAPTER III

Biggin Hill

October 15th, Sortie 33. 1.05 hours duration

We taxied to our new dispersal points and immediately the petrol bowsers started pumping in fuel to top up our tanks. The CO was being briefed by a Spy who crouched on his wing and gesticulated at the pilots now clambering out of their machines. A runner came tearing over.

'Get back in – you're off as soon as refuelled' and away he went to the next kite and the next. Ground crew collected the small toilet bags that the pilots had with them and in a few minutes we taxied out and formed up for take-off. Hell, that was quick, I thought. Whacko!

Malan looked right and left at the Spits on either side, raising his gloved hand. Thumbs up! We acknowledged in the same way. The CO lowered his arm and with exaggerated nods of his head indicated to open throttles. As one, our flight of four aircraft rolled forward faster and faster, with marker boards zipping past and clouds of grass particles and dust billowing behind us. 'A' Flight and 'B' Flight followed to form up on us as we climbed towards the north-west.

'Angels 20 Maidstone,' the RT crackled, and Malan's laconic 'Dysoe on the way' brought things into perspective.

This was it! The real thing! I felt sick with excitement. Far off in the cold blue to the south we could see tiny white contrails heading our way. My palms grew slippery with sweat and I wiped them on my Sidcot suit. I wouldn't wear gloves as they inhibited me – I'd take my chances if the plane caught fire.

Now we settled down in 74's standard formation of three sections of four aircraft flying in line-astern forming a Vic on the leader*.

* This gave great flexibility and ease of control to the Squadron Leader but it was only good for gaining height or position in the shortest possible time. Later it was used slavishly by some units on offensive sweeps over France. After several notable 'bouncings' by German fighters, the leaders brightened up their ideas and adopted the German 'four finger' formation or variations introduced by enterprising COs.

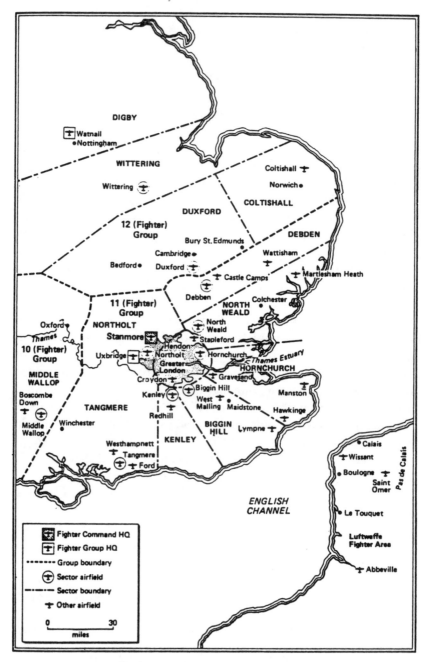

*Deployment of Fighter Command in the
Battle of Britain*

Up, up we flew, radiator flaps wide open, temperatures reaching danger levels. Oxygen on at 13,000 feet. Now the CO turned back towards Maidstone. Short snatches of information came through.

'Fifty plus snappers (enemy fighters) to your starboard, Angels 20.'

'Forty plus snappers Angels 26 over Dungeness coming your way.'

But all we could see were our twelve Spits alone under the blazing sun. Far below, green and brown fields slowly shrank as we climbed still higher and to the south the Channel curved around in a great green arc.

'Blue Leader here. I think I see them two o'clock below.'

'Hurricanes.'

'Okay.'

On and up; now each aircraft trailed white streamers which appeared as if by magic. Water vapour from the hot exhaust gases were condensing and giving our position away. Malan dipped the squadron until the 'tadpoles' disappeared and then levelled us off. The Jerries' smoke trails had disappeared – they too, had dived below the condensation level and hoped to hide their presence as we had. But all the time our directions kept coming through – the magnificent Observer Corps and radar stations all feeding sightings into underground operations rooms. Here the reports were correlated and interceptions planned.

'Tally Ho! Bandits one o'clock above!' and with that a cloud of silver arrows appeared, each tipped with a little black speck. The Jerries had seen us and were climbing to gain height advantage.

'Dysoe aircraft through the gate.'*

Good! I'd always wanted to do it! I pushed the throttle around past its notched slide, breaking the sealing wire. The Merlins' heavy purr became a harsh roar and brown smoke poured from the exhausts. The Spitfires leapt forward.

'Spread out and good hunting!'

I saw the flight on either side of us slide away and each flight split into two pairs. Stephen and his No 2 lifted from below and behind me and climbed out to our port. I rechecked that my gun's safety catch

---

* This put excessive strain on the motors and could only be used for about five consecutive minutes.

was off. The gun-sight graticule glowed clearly and I lowered my seat a notch. Malan curved to meet the Huns head on and all at once we were into them.

Yellow spinners, stiff square-tipped wings with sparkles of light flickering. I tried to follow my leader around but, being fascinated by the enemy aircraft, somehow lost him. All at once I felt alone and frenzied with excitement. I couldn't find a single Jerry. Twisting and turning, I couldn't see a damned aircraft! Nothing! The sky was clean and bare. Far off, white contrails curved lazily this way and that. But I couldn't watch *them*. Where had everyone gone? It was no use horsing around up here, twisting from side to side, looking up, back and around, frantic with disappointment.* I dived for the deck – orders were to go straight back if separated and there was no fight in one's vicinity.

At 10,000 feet I formated alongside a Spit with its gun patches gone and smoke-stained wings. It was the CO! He looked at me and shook his fist. Automatically I lowered the undercarriage and, as the plane humped nose-down, Malan just turned away and slowly shook his head. I felt an awful fool but the clenched fist shaken (slowly and regularly) meant wheels down. Oh, we were well trained and obedient! Back at Biggin I was on the mat.

'Where the hell did you get to?'

'Sorry, sir, I lost you in a turn.'

'Clot! – there were lots of targets! Better pull your finger out!'

*

At Biggin Hill we were quartered in Holly Cottage, a requisitioned house outside the 'drome's perimeter. The flight commanders each had a station-wagon for the transportation of pilots to and from the mess and dispersal points. Our batmen soon got things organised so there was a degree of comfort at night. Not that we spent much time in our own beds if we could help it – every night was a search for excitement – every night a search for relief from the day's pressure.

---

* This phenomenon was quite common – most newcomers to aerial dogfighting got 'lost' and often didn't even see the enemy aircraft at all after the initial flurry. Nor any other aircraft for that matter. The dog fight would wheel away in three dimensions and it was now that the green pilots faced their moment of truth. This was the moment when they could be picked off by cool experienced killers hunting for just such as they.

We grew to hate the blue sunny days and to welcome the chill grey fogs which sometimes crept over Biggin Hill and cancelled flying. One of the squadrons (No 92) at Biggin had draught beer on tap in their dispersal and girls living in their quarters. Morale was high in the air but on the ground their discipline was lax and no longer enforced. They considered it didn't matter as long as they were effective in combat – but it did.

Fighter pilots on leave could be seen wandering London's streets in flying boots and jackets, no tie, buttons undone. Senior officers crossed streets or looked the other way rather than have confrontations as several ugly clashes had occurred between pilots psyched-up and reckless by too much pressure and those not actively engaged in the air-fighting.

Long white contrails snaked and coiled over London and Kent as air battles erupted. The fighter pilot, living on the razor's edge, just didn't give a damn. He would go up, often several times a day, always against superior numbers, fight, and come back to lie around awaiting the next scramble. But at night, it was off to the pub and oblivion in alcohol or soft arms. I don't think the average pilot could have run a hundred yards without panting or feeling sick. At dispersal points the big easy chairs and beds got more use than those in our quarters.

By now I'd been involved in several air battles. As Malan's No 2, I had seen enough to have the greenness bleached a little – I knew what it was all about. Had shot and been shot at. Had puked my guts out before getting into my Spit and flown almost automatically until the call Tally Ho!

Then the mouth would dry up and the heart start pounding. Then the plane seemed to lose its power and felt like an airborne greenhouse and about as safe. With the enemy in sight and identified, another change would come over; a kind of elation. A quick check of the safety ring on the firing button, a quick squirt to blow the muzzle patches off and test the guns. Gun-sight graticule glowing, prop in fine pitch, the manoeuvering for battle began. A sort of frenzy to get started would grip you – the circling for height or the long dive in attack were almost a formality – something to be got over. But quickly.

New pilots came and disappeared. Old names, regulars on the

readiness board, were rubbed out forever. Gradually the squadron changed in calibre as all active squadrons must, and repressed tensions erupted in excesses. Excesses in the air and on the ground, in the messes and in the bars and night clubs where most of us sought frenetic release from the unnatural pressures on us.

Men with wives or sweethearts at home were under an added strain. With life so demonstrably short, who could censure those who lived it to the full? No wonder many of us put our home life into limbo – something to be treasured and thought about in solitude with love.

The bar girls and night club hostesses only lightly brushed our lives; casual couplings forgotten in the light of day. Some pilots ratted around and found digs near their 'dromes for wives. Some girls, not yet collared for war work, formed liaisons with loved ones and filled their days in anxious limbo.

ATA pilots would pop in and out like startled rabbits leaving replacement aircraft for the depleted squadrons. It was an incredible moment when I met a Wanganui girl, 'Grub' Hunter, clambering out of a Spitfire she had just delivered. Somehow it knocked my arse in and the elite complex was diminished. A girl flying a fighter?

More new pilots and still more. They arrived excited and keen. Sometimes we never knew or remembered their names. Straight from their OTUs they were thrown into squadron life without a sector reconnaissance and often without even squadron air-drill or formation flying with their new units.

Sometimes their names were erased from the board on the same day they appeared; even before their bags were unpacked.

*

There were few combat aircrew who didn't wear a lucky scarf, carry mascots or indulge in some cranky pre-flight ritual like slapping their aircraft's fuselage. I suppose Roman Catholics genuflected – I patted my Tiki medallion, fiddled with my scarf.

Religion was another matter.

In the still lonesomeness of an early dawn I found myself contemplating the future and finding it grim. I concocted a prayer which I used just once. It went something like this: 'Oh God! When it happens I won't have any time to ask for your help. I'll be too busy. Please accept this prayer now, once and for all time.'

Then I stalled. What to ask for? For the same help and safety as the enemy did? It was stupid to expect greater favours just because I was British!

I decided then and there not to be a God-botherer; that it was just as sensible to pray to Lady Luck, and she became my talisman. I loved Lady Luck and she must have loved me. Must have, when I look back at all the hairy escapades and the sheer good fortune which kept me unharmed.

Religion, to me, became incomprehensible as I saw both friends and enemies wounded or killed in unspeakable torture. Our daily life was occupied with inhuman cruelty and acts of wickedness inflicted on other human beings. If there is a mighty overall plan, a reason for this dreadful exercise, are we, the chief actors, to be used in some celestial role? It's nonsense; it's sheer egoism bred into our species as we have crouched around a million camp fires and wondered at the lonely stars.

Our egoism has rejected the unthinkable idea of finish – of nothingness. Our egoism has bred hope for the immortality of our life-spark and that hope has created religion.

And yet . . .

And yet there must be something more than a mindless nothingness. Something more than yeasty spawnings and final oblivion. How else are acts of love and understanding, or self-sacrifice to protect another to be explained? Moments of truth when, to aid a comrade, a man would voluntarily interpose himself against deadly odds and become himself in mortal jeopardy.

We have not set out the ground rules, we can only do our best to be caring, decent creatures and to hope.

In the meantime, my job was to kill Germans and on this unsatisfactory note I put religion, per se, behind me for the duration.

October 22nd, Sortie 37. 1.00 hour duration: Sure enough, the warning wailed as we tore back to dispersal after a hasty lunch. George put his foot down and the brake (station-wagon) howled round the perimeter track. We could see the white fog-trailers weaving fantastic clouds far above us. I felt dead inside; it was our third scramble of the day. How long would this keep up? How long could it?

We clambered out before the Humber had rolled to a stop and ran to our lockers. Yellow Mae Wests on; the tapes were difficult to tie with nervous fumbling hands; Helmets and gloves snatched up. No one spoke, we knew we'd be on the next patrol.

The board was being filled in. Good show; I was No 2 to the CO and Wally Churches was No 2 to Mungo in Blue Section.

The telephone rang; the operator repeated aloud: 'Maidstone 20,000.' We didn't wait for more, but shot out of the door, the scramble-buzzer hideous in its haste and urgency. The brake was rolling slowly down the track and we flung ourselves aboard. One of the new sergeants gave an excited laugh, but heaven only knows what there was to laugh about. Wally dropped off and ran to his kite – then Bill Armstrong, Roger and I. The car kept rolling, the pilots leaping for their machines. I was feeling dreadful; each scramble seemed that it would be my last and I was honestly afraid.

Sergeant Soars' parachute was loose, the straps fell off my shoulders but the Sutton harness was good and tight and held them up. I was using his 'R', too, a plane harsh but fast. Soon it was – 'Chocks away, crew away.' The green turf rolled under smoothly and I taxied for the runway. I switched on the radio and its slow warming-up drone covered the engine's rumble.

Sailor was in position and I rolled up to his starboard. The runway stretched before us. Steve and his No 2 slid to Malan's port and we roared off down the field. 'R' swung a bit, lifted, bounced once and slid into the warm air. Behind and below, twenty feet away, I could see Steve* sliding into line astern. I half-laughed; as if a flyer like Steve would chop off my tail . . . but Sailor was haring along, and climbing like a rocket.

Up, up, oxygen on, air-scuttle open – slowly the blue sky turned a deeper shade and at 23,000 feet faint trails of mist formed, thickened, and streamed behind like comet's tails. The radio nattered away to our supporting squadron.

Far off we could see the trails of our adversaries – a 50-plus, according to Operations. They were higher than we, but ten to fifteen miles away. We climbed on, up and up in great circles. Now we were above them. We spread out into sections of two in a rough

*Flight Lieutenant H. M. Stephen, DSO, DFC.

line abreast, and we could see their yellow spinners, Me 109's. One after another the yellow-nosed devils were peeling off for the deck – the usual trap for the unwary; follow one down and five more are on your tail.

A strange thing happened. We were some 700 yards away and closing head-on at astounding speed, when a cloud of them rolled for the deck. Then it turned to a rout without, as yet, a shot being fired. 109's are breaking in all directions. I see Johnny* and his section zoom up after seven or eight which climb towards the sun. Steve is whipping round after a dozen or so that overshot to starboard. It is going to be a real show.

I hared after Malan. A tinkling sound of empty cartridge cases bounced off my bullet-proof screen and scratched 'R's' wings. Malan had fired at a 109 crossing ahead of us. It rolled lazily on its back, hung there dead and ugly. A puff of black smoke and it disappeared in a dull, red flash. Something black and ragged fell away. Someone calls 'Look out!' Malan's 'Shut up, you fool!' brings a warped grin. I am sweating hot, choking with a dry mouth; I don't seem to be getting enough air to breathe. I feel reckless; impatient to squirt at one of the devils. Suddenly there doesn't seem to be a machine in the air; just a lot of crazy white cords lacing the blue above. 'R's' belly seems horribly bare and vulnerable and I roll her on to her back and look down. Sure enough, there's a 109 just a couple of hundred feet below. It sees me and rolls on its back and dives.

I heave the stick back, black out, recover and glance at the altimeter – 27,000 feet. The 109 is diving vertically. I grin and open 'R' full-bore, fine pitch. The airspeed winds up and up; it passes 450 miles an hour and the red patch denoting top permissible speed. I can't depress the nose sufficiently to get the gunsight on the Hun. I push at the stick and wind on full tail-trim. I go into coarse pitch and 'R' drops like a rock.

Now the slip stream is screaming and wailing past the hood and the whole machine is taut and quivering like a violin. Three hundred yards in front, the black 109 seems to be slowly drifting up as the Spitfire draws down on it. Below, the chequered fields are lazily expanding. I swallow and my ears clear with a popping sensation.

* Flight Lieutenant J. C. Freeborn, DFC and Bar.

The 109 is beneath me somewhere still dropping vertically. I twist the stick over and roll 'R' round her axis and the 109 reappears and the joy-stick starts to judder in my grasp.

Wham! A blast of solid air hits me. 'R' flicks into a spin like a mad thing and the stick threshes round the cockpit. Everything goes brown but I can see a horrible space where the starboard wing should be. I heave and struggle to get out. Something is holding me down. My hands are cut and bleeding where I grip the shattered perspex above my head. I pull and pray. Then, with fatalistic calm, I remember the Sutton-harness. I pull out the pin. Now for my helmet. I fumble with my neck-strap. Get out! Get out!

How much height is there left; but I can't read the blur which is the 'unwinding' altimeter. My hands are sticky with a clear slime which evaporates as I gape at them. A whining scream. Something black whips past and I struggle up and, like a cork, popped out of the spinning wreck.

I'm out! It isn't like falling at all! I shut my eyes and there is no rush of air, no sound. It is quite peaceful – a marvellous sensation. I take several deep breaths. 'Count ten', someone had said. Count ten! My fingers scrabbled at the rip-cord's metal ring and I heaved it out a foot. Nothing happened! Mad prayers and thoughts. I opened my eyes. Then my head nearly snapped off and pain cut into me; I felt as if I'd been knackered.

There is a white saucer hanging over me and everything is quiet except for little rustling sounds as the silk flexes. The chute seems small; the silken cords rigid, straining. I look at the ground. How funny not to have wings and a motor and yet fly! I look for the other boys but can't turn my head as the harness, loose in rest, has ridden up and squeezed my Mae West about my ears. I 'brown out' through lack of oxygen. It is dreadfully cold; my boots have been torn off. The ill-fitting harness is cutting into my crotch. One of my testicles is being crushed. I wound the steel rip-cord round the harness release-plate and put my foot in the ring, standing up. If I can't release my weight and free the leg-straps, I'll go crazy; the pain is so awful. The cord, slipping, unwinds the quick-release plate. I sag back into the harness. The freed cord falls, turns slowly, grows smaller and smaller and vanishes thousands of feet below. I hang there in terrible fear; the slightest jar on the release-plate and the chute will be jettisoned and I'd fall like a stone.

Something whining shrilly streamed past and I saw strange twisted white lines drawn as into infinity. More of them and weird rushing sounds. I appeared to be the centre of a mad, wind-blown spider's web. Amazed, I heard the crackling, tearing sound of cannon-fire like a giant ripping canvas, and then a high whistling shriek. Something big and black tore past me – a 109E.

It climbed right in front of me, turning for another go. I cursed and wriggled frantically in the harness trying to draw my revolver.

There was a deep purring roar and 'P' flashed by, followed by 'S' – Steve and Wally! I laughed with relief. Boy, what a grandstand view! The Hun half-rolled for the deck and I watched him twist and turn beneath me. It seems that I can almost stand on him and my chute above quivered and rippled at the machine-gun fire as Steve got on the Hun's tail. Now he's had it! Ha! Ha! A good show, Steve! The Jerry staggered, slipped and fell, crippled and smoking into a wood. I saw rows of hop poles below me and the ground seemed to have come much closer all of a sudden. It is rushing to meet me. I got ready for the landing and fiddled with the harness but I can't make the thing manoeuvre as I want to. Loud and clear the rending crash of the Hun came up. Serve the bastard right!

The landing was just as they said – like a jump off a 12-foot wall. I lay still on the warm earth and panted. Hell, but my hands and feet were cold! I shut my eyes and relaxed on the soft ploughed field. I heard someone running over the uneven ground and next minute a huge farm-labourer threw himself on me.

'Get off me, you stupid oaf!' I screamed. 'Don't you know your own bloody side?'

He reared up, fist ready to smash me down. Slowly comprehension dawned.

'Be you RAF, sor?' he asked with a beaming smile.

'No, I'm a fucking angel! For Christ's sake, let me up!'

Then he heaved me to my feet and put his arms around me. I suppose I look scared, shivering with fear, and he started to pat me and tried to stroke my head.

'I'm not scared! I'm bloody cold. Leave me alone!'

By this time there must have been a hundred hop-pickers surrounding us, all smiling and shouting, 'Good for you!' 'Up the RAF' and other nice things; all, under the circumstances, quite inappropriate. There were some real dolls among the crowd and, looking into their eyes, I could see I had it made. But what can you do in socks, ankle deep in ploughed soil, bloody hands and a whole village watching?

A bobby arrived and took me in charge. Soon I was having tea and cake in his kitchen while he phoned Biggin for a squadron car to pick me up.

Three scraps in one day, a parachute descent and Peter St John dead. It had been quite a day.

The squadron Doc looked at my bruised legs, patched my torn hands.

'You were pretty lucky!'

'I feel pretty pissed off! That's one Spitfire confirmed for only a third share in a damaged bomber so far. I don't even know why the bloody wing came off!'

'The engineer officer tells me the tail unit was found ten miles from the fuselage, with you about in the middle!'

'Yes, I was fairly motoring when it happened – we've worked out that the speed must have been well over 650 mph.* I thought you could do anything in a Spit. It was a lesson to me! The funny thing is my boots landed in the same field with me, even though it took twenty minutes for me to come down from over 20,000 feet!'

'Right, now! We're sending you off for five days' leave. Take it easy on that leg and make the girls do all the work!'

The MO fancied himself a bit of a lad. It could be an idea – the wounded hero and all that jazz. Besides, I'd have to check my gear out!

So I took off to London, checked into the Regent Palace Hotel and whooped it up. For five glorious days I lay in bed sleeping, venturing out only in mid-afternoon to visit the huge Kensington Science

---

* This was approaching the speed of sound and the phenomenon of 'buffeting' an extreme situation not at that time really studied or fully understood. In this situation the Spitfire literally shook itself to pieces.

Museum, Madame Tussauds, the Tower and all the usual tourist traps. At night, the clubs, famous and infamous relieved me of everything I had until, exhausted, I'd stagger back to the hotel.

By day, the contrails formed huge loops speeding across London in graceful arcs as squadrons fought it out thousands of feet above. At night shrapnel spanged from concrete ledges and struck sparks from rubbly roads. Bombs screamed down to crump around us. Glass crashed and tinkled in the streets. In the south-east glaring fires and waving searchlights made a spectacular backdrop for the AA guns banging away in the parks. I felt a bit of a waster and wanted to get back to the squadron and my friends.

It was while on this leave in London that my early disenchantment with Top Brass became even more acute. I was becoming a rebel in some ways. It was not conducive towards promotion but then I had no ambitions other than that of being a section leader and then, if Lady Luck smiled, a flight commander. In fact I became so bolshie as to distrust anyone over the rank of wing commander and he had to be an operational pilot at that!

I had read Air Vice Marshal A. G. Lee's great book *No Parachutes* (Arrow Books Limited) written about World War I air warfare. The colossal stupidity of those in high places who refused to allow British aircrew parachutes in case 'they would jump to safety rather than fight' was beyond belief.

And here I was in Lady . . .'s (I've forgotten) warehouse of officers' uniforms trying to get a free replacement for my outfit damaged in the parachute descent. These uniforms were mostly donated by the families of aircrew killed in combat and, through this organisation, made available free-of-charge to brother officers in need of uniforms lost or damaged due to enemy action.

One of the charming volunteer workers brought out an air vice marshal's uniform for my inspection. It was not of the approved barathea cloth nor even true air force blue. Five or six rows of fruit-salad* complete with rosettes and oak leaves adorned it. How could this sort of thing be given out to a facility such as this? It was of

---

* Decorations – in this case mostly honorary things given out for dancing attendance in the corridors of power.

no use to anyone – just a senseless exhibition by a vain and obviously flawed personality. Just for fun I tried it on – had it fitted I would have taken it and worn it at parties.

Later I was to see another example of this incredible type of egoism – the 'PS' initials worked in the concrete balustrades and carved woodwork at Port Lympne, a magnificent mansion built for Sir Phillip Sassoon, Under Secretary of State for Air, and taken over as billets for aircrew operating from Lympne airfield.

My antipathy for higher authority was ill-hidden and didn't advance my air force career!

On my return I found that Sergeant Scott had been killed.

Drinking at the bar in the Mess, the chaps were ranting about my being machine-gunned while hanging helpless from my parachute.

'You're nuts! The Hun was right!! I'd do exactly the same if over their territory and one of the bastards was getting away. He's only going to come up again and it could be my turn the next time.'

But the argument went back and forth; I was dumbfounded at the mawkish 'It's not cricket' attitude.

'God damn it! I'd shoot up an ambulance or their bloody women to help win the war!'

And, in time, I did exactly that.

The Irvin Parachute people sent me a letter informing me of my inclusion in their Caterpillar Club and with it a little gold tie pin. It was in the form of a silk worm. Engraved on the back was my name; it had little ruby eyes. But we couldn't wear the unofficial trinket so I posted it home to Florance in New Zealand.

CHAPTER IV

Got Him! At Last!!

October 30th, Sortie 38. 1.30 hrs duration

It was my first flight since baling out eight days before. We were at 33,000 feet and the cold made my left leg ache. The bruising was one long hurt from knee to ankle. The Jerry formation of some fifty fighters was about a mile ahead and we had the jump on them by several hundred feet. About a dozen peeled off and dived away towards the Channel. Then twenty or more! It's a rout!

Malan called, 'Get them boys! Go!' and 74 split into pairs, spread out and were after them in whistling curves.

I couldn't follow. Suddenly I was a mass of jangling nerves hanging in space. A terrible fear gripped me. Oh God! I'm stuck up here! I can't go down! And now about five of the yellow-nosed 109s were heading for me, guns flashing and sparkling. I was on my own.

*

'What happened, Spurdle?' Malan had me in his office. 'I couldn't dive, sir. I found I couldn't follow the others down! Then the Jerry top cover got stuck into me and by the time I'd shaken them off, I was down to about 16,000 feet. I was all right then.'

'Did you get any of them?'

'No, sir. I know I damaged one, but every time I got into a firing position, two or more would latch on to me.'

'Well, you'll just have to get over it. Keep your eyes fixed on your No 1 and stick with him.'

*

The same day, Sortie No 39. 1.25 hours duration

Again, the bell rang. We'd only been down an hour! The boys started and looked towards the phone. The telephone orderly grabbed the receiver. Breaths were held – a faint pop-pop-popping of a battery charger in the distance – the orderly stiffened and looked towards us, repeating, '30 plus Maidstone – 20,000 feet'; the klaxon blared out. There was a great rush for the door, the boys grabbing their helmets and gloves as they dashed out. The inevitable stooge pilots started their loud barracking and bemoaning at being left out of the flap. Pure bluff!

Outside mechanics and riggers, warned by the scramble buzzer, race madly towards their machines. Soon the roar of the first Spitfire shatters the warm afternoon sky and rooks rise raucous from the field. Harnesses are being buckled and chocks being pulled away; over at the far edge of the dispersal some unfortunate pilot is still running to his kite – his is the furthest from our hut; he must have missed the brake. Christ! He'll get a trimming from the CO.

Now they are taxiing away from the field towards the runway, the ground crews standing by their fallen chocks, their arms slack and a strange longing in their eyes. Poor devils! They don't know the thrill of smooth wings, the rushing eager power surging underhand. No Merlin's magic for them – theirs is the dirt and the mud and the oil; they can only trudge away, forgotten until the machines return.

Thirty-plus Maidstone – 20,000 feet: the familiar old call! My breath came hard as I reached my kite. Christ, but I'm out of training! My knees were weak and trembling – silly jerky thoughts flashed through my mind – Florance – Mum – my tiki. I patted it. Practised hands and automatic movements got me into the cockpit. 'Good luck,' the rigger shouted – I grinned in answer, but the face mask gave him no sign. I waved and winked; Bill saluted – a good guy – the sucker wants to be a pilot.

Air pressure low – never mind, it'll build up, radiator temp – oil pressure, gun sight, tail and rudder trim – OK. Oxygen? Christ, it's a bad bottle – I'll kill the bastard. The radio warming – crackled into life – yes, old slow coach is copping it – Jeez, but the CO is tough. Must remember that phrase – nice for a party. I'm scared I'll funk diving again when the time comes. God! It's an awful feeling.

The ground bumped by under my wheels, and some oaf in 'T' nearly ran into me. That's Nelson – or is it? I can't remember but cursed him mentally. I saw the first three zoom off down the runway – that's the CO with his Nos 2 and 3. Now I see Mungo taxiing into position, his 2 and 3 rolling either side of him. With a bellow and a cloud of dust they roared down the path and slid into the blue. I rapidly rechecked my taps – everything is OK and I saw Steve with his head in the office. The two No 4s take off – I hear Malan cursing his for being slow. There is no reply – they are bucking in the second section's slip stream – guess he can't take his hand off the stick to answer.

Where the hell's our No 2? I slewed my kite around a bit and saw him. He'd pranged it – he'd gone over on his nose; must have struck a soft patch in an old bomb hole. He is green – I laughed into my mask – he's a cocky oaf. Steve has seen it and raised his hand – thumbs up! I raised mine and opened the throttle as Steve's kite rolled forward. We tore down the runway and staggered into the air.

Up wheels, alter pitch, I felt the Rotol bite and throttled back a bit, the rev counter was fluctuating – I'll kill that mechanic! He hasn't checked that cable yet! The CO was calling up Ops and getting more dope. Curse 2 – now I'll have to take zero* and miss some of the gen. Christ! 30-plus at 25,000 feet and another bunch of 20-plus crossing the coast. I glanced around the squadron – 11-strong. I wriggled in my harness and could just see the tips of 4's wings. With Steve's 2 missing, that left only three in our section. I decided to stick to Steve; become his No 2 and 4 can tag along.

Higher and higher we climbed. The glycol temperature was nearing the danger point, the oil temperature was off the clock. Air pressure built up OK. Somebody's wheels weren't fully retracted and I called him up. I raised my voice till it sounded like the fancy boys at the Running Horse – (it transmits better) – 'Your wheels are down, Yellow leader' – and I heard a laconic 'OK'. The wheels jerked into place.

Altimeter reads 13,000 feet – time to turn on the oxygen – Jeez, but it's foul – must be an old bottle – Hallo, Ops say, the Jerries have joined together and are heading north. 50-plus to 11! Bloody hell, just about the decent proportion for a good scrap. I switched on my gun sight and firing button. I closed the radiator flap a little. Oil from

* The Identification 'Friend or Foe' radio device was switched on by one of the No 2's detailed for this chore. Its intermittent transmission interfered with RT use on that particular machine.

Steve's kite was spotting my windshield and I slid out to one side a bit. Hell's Bells, but it's getting cold – the fresh air scoop was jammed open and I cursed myself for not reporting it before. It's always the same and each time I come down I forget it. My mirror was streaky too – that's a kick for someone!

Things were now getting pretty active; above us, and towards the afternoon sun, there were several vapour tadpoles forming, streaking along – they were turning towards us too. All of a sudden the few turned into a cloud. Tallyho! someone shouted and Malan turned the squadron towards them. As usual my mouth dried, the palms of my hands got moist, the engine seemed to lose its power and the CO seemed to have gone off his head. He's turning towards the Jerries' port. They were about ten miles away and in two minutes we will be into them. I prayed and cursed silently. Christ! We haven't got a show. There seemed to be hundreds above us too – the CO is mad – why doesn't he climb? Now we were going at full bore just to their port. I saw long trails of white vapour streaming back from the black devils. We were smoking too and I slid under Steve's tail and got between his smoke trail and the Jerries – I can watch the bastards better. Hell! they're streaking along – I can see their yellow noses now. Oh! cunning move, cunning move! The CO turned left sharply, says, 'Oh Kayee!' We split up into pairs. I stuck to Steve's tail like a leech – God! If I could only have a drink!

Something's died in my mouth. Fierce thoughts surged through my mind and black thoughts too: Ricalton and Hastings, my friends – dead. Kirkie too – all right you bastards! Come and get it! Steve headed straight towards a bunch, a dozen or so, and I slid further out to one side and drew a bead on the starboard 109. I saw great streams of tracer twisting past my port wing and could see the wicked flashes from the Jerry's guns. My eight Brownings spluttered and the acrid smell of burnt charges filtered into my mask.

I held my fire on the Hun as we screamed together and, as I saw the smaller details of his kite, I heaved back the stick. My face dragged down and strained on my skull, my mask nearly broke my nose and everything went brown, then black. I held the stick hard back and kicked on left rudder – that'll fox the bastard. The black-out faded and for an ageless instant I couldn't see a single plane. Then I spotted a lone Me 109 on my starboard and, turning towards him, I crouched forward, my head nearly touching the gunsight. Damn my harness – now, now – allow plenty of deflection, quick now, give him a squirt. Hell, the bugger is made of iron! No! I've hit him – yes, yes – Christ! What's that? A great stream of solid fire screamed past my hood, I got a fleeting glimpse of four 109s diving on me, a wicked flickering at their ugly noses. Right rudder – stick hard over, and full back – I half rolled and cut in underneath them. Something flashed past my nose – I flew through the black cloud that streamed behind. Hell, that was close, my heart was banging and I felt sick. Nearly collided. I gave myself more oxygen. Thwack! Something hit my kite. Sounded like a pickaxe on an iron roof. Hell, I've been hit – my hand shot up in reflex to the hood release and with a curse I realised that I'm a fool – bail out indeed! Yes, there's a hole down by the starboard flap panel. Where are those bastards? I turned and twisted – couldn't see a thing. I felt as big as a glasshouse. There's a hell of a lot of nattering on the RT – sounds like a party – Christ! If only I had a drink.

I saw Jerries below and again it happened! Again I couldn't dive. I was trapped in a ghastly nightmare, a horrible mental barrier which held me in the icy blue while far below the others caught up to and mixed with the enemy. Again there were a few Huns who stayed high and now turned their attention onto me. This time it's almost a relief not to have to face descending. In a few moments we met head-on, to zoom past and climb again. Aircraft are very sloppy in the rarified air and tight turns are impossible. The 109s with their higher wingloading couldn't out-turn me. This time they stuck together more or less and soon I managed to get on one's tail.

The Teutonic twit! The fool's changed his mind! He's turned the other way and now I've got him in my sights. A quick glance at the others now away to my port. They're diving for the ground.

The Brownings spluttered and white tracer bullets streamed away in thread-like spirals to envelop the enemy. De Wildes sparkled in tiny red flashes on fuselage and wings. He's lifting, lifting; white contrails streamed back from both wing tips as his G's built up into a high speed stall and he fell onto his back. More strikes! A puff of black smoke from his motor. A shower of sparkling perspex and he flashed past and behind, spinning down inverted.

I can't descend! In a trembling fury I watched the German plane falling out of sight still inverted, until he disappeared through a thin cloud layer miles below. Now the problem of getting down to the 'drome. Obviously I'll come down when the gas runs out.

Slowly, oh! so slowly, I throttled back, turning the plane to head north away from the battle area. By watching the far horizon and just keeping the plane above stalling speed, we sank down to the warmer air below. By watching the horizon and not my instruments or the land beneath slowly expanding, an illusion of level flying was achieved. Gradually confidence came back and soon I managed to pull myself together and began to fly again. The old Spitfire magic returned and we became as one.

I wondered how the boys were – was that a Spit I saw go screaming past me with the fiery tail? God, I hope not. Ah! here's the 'drome – funny how easily I've found it – usually have to fly north a bit, then west a bit along the railway till I come to the quarry. Silly half-lucid thoughts flocked through my mind. Has the wind changed? Where's that kite of Johnny's? Oh yes; there are the obstruction flags around it.

My knees were trembling with reaction and my mouth was like a kiln. That's funny, I was one of the last back – seemed to be a lot of kites at our dispersal. I shoved the radiator lever open and dropped the undercart. The wheels locked with a solid click and I saw the green lights flash on. Down flaps then alter pitch, then turn in to land. A little motor, steady; now she drops down with a last rush and sigh, and I'm braking her to a roll. Up flaps and I taxied around to my pen.

Bill rushed up as I switched off. The Merlin coughed to an unwilling stop and I heard the faint clicking of the cooling exhaust manifolds. Funny how quickly they lose their heat.

'Any luck, sir?' Bill asked the old question. I could see he was thinking of a Swastika on F's sleek sides. I pointed to the hole in the wing; Bill grinned, the mechanics clambered up and started to re-fuel; armourers already creeping over the wings, unscrewing gun panels with practised speed.

My hands trembled, fumbled and Bill pulled out the harness-locking pin. It dropped away and I lifted myself out. The oxygen hissed loudly in the empty cockpit; I let it run out – Christ it was foul!

'Any luck sir? Any luck?' I shook my head. 'Can't say; I damaged one, probably won't get home. We'll soon find out – maybe damaged a second.'

The armourer corporal called out, 'Your starboard No 2 gun has a stoppage, sir.' 'OK let's know the cause.' No more holes in my kite, thank goodness, so I climbed into the waiting brake. 'Any luck, sir?' 'Hallo George. Yes, I think I got one, damaged a second.' 'What were they?' '109 bastards.' 'Oh.' 'Is everyone back yet, George?' 'No. Mr Nelson and Mr Chesters and Sergeant Soars aren't – you're one of the last, sir.' 'OK.'

We drew up at the hut and I stumbled out of the car, my mouth wet now but dry scum crusted my lips. I scraped at it with an oily finger – Jeez! but my hands are dirty. I suddenly felt very tired. Inside the hut the din was terrific and the air blue with smoke from freshly lit cigarettes. Old Sandy, our adjutant, was there grinning like a cat. Must be good news – A successful scrap? The Intelligence Officer was getting annoyed – he wouldn't get much sense out of the boys just yet!

Everyone is laughing except the stooges and Soars' friend. Wally Churches came over. 'Christ – I got a bastard. Blew him to hell.' He pushed through the crowd. I felt pleased for him.

Suddenly the 'phone rang and the orderly called for silence. The CO was quietly chatting in the corner with Sandy – I heard 'seven destroyed, four probables and a couple damaged.' I moved over to the Intelligence Officer to say my piece – the orderly called out that Sergeant Soars has crash-landed at Manston – he is OK but the machine is a write-off. We all wondered where Nelson and Chesters were. They should have been back by now – that is, if they are alive.

Again the phone – Nelson's OK and will be back after refuelling at West Malling. Flight Lieutenant Freeborn's stooge, Chesters, is the last. Again; the phone! Fantastic! We've just heard Chesters shot up a Hun and escorted the crippled machine to a belly-landing at Penshurst Field. Then he landed by it to supervise the pilot's capture!

November 1st 1940: Five scrambles today! Five hours thirty-five minutes in the air with three wild mixed-up whirling scraps from thirty-odd thousand feet to the deck. No real results for me. I've decided to discount the odd hit on a E/A. Unless something actually comes off it or there is smoke or fumes, it wasn't damaged as far as I was concerned. However, each flight brought more confidence and a more professional outlook. Flying became absolutely second nature, my machine and I one entity. But each take-off was a conscious effort of the will, the butterflies in my stomach not at all keen to formate and fly.

Sergeant Soars got shot again and, this time, wounded; he should be taken off fighters. Flight Sergeant Burnard, too, but my friend Flying Officer Nelson got himself killed. He was an American who had joined the RCAF for the adventure. Or was it because he believed in freedom and was prepared to die for it?

November 2nd, Sortie 45. 1.20 hours duration: I got him! I got him! The Spy has just told me my Jerry crashed near Ashford and is woodened out. Oh! Bloody marvellous! My first Hun confirmed and my lost Spitfire now squared for. There were eleven of us and over forty of them. My confirmation as Flying Officer came through and to round off a wonderful, wonderful day, I scooted off to the Mess bar, shouted the crowd, had a batman sew on my new broad rings and drank myself unconscious.

Wizard! The Spy has got me souvenirs from my Hun – he was Oberfeldwebel* Fritz Noller, holder of the 1939 Iron Cross 2nd Class. On him was the photo of a woman, ration coupons, odds and ends.

The photo gave me pause, but Wally got quite excited, waved it about and shouted, 'Don't be a clot! It could have been you! Remember! They started it! Now let's get onto the plonk and it's your round.'

*

Autumn drew to a close. The trees were bare and evening mists curtailed flying much earlier. The Jerries sent over great waves of fighters to escort fewer bombers than previously. The fighting was hard and only the occasional bouts of bad weather released us from ops. It was a relief to be stood down; to leave the 'drome and hare off to the nearest dog track or pub; or just to slouch around in the Mess

---

* Equivalent rank to our warrant officer.

playing cards or billiards or snooze in front of a fire. Wally and I spent hours in the Link trainer or banging away skeet shooting to keep our eyes in.

In flying weather a constant state of readiness kept us on our toes and we could expect to fly almost every day. New pilots had to be trained; these chaps first doing a sector reconnaissance to familiarise themselves with Biggin's environs and later practising dog fights for assessment as to ability.

November 14th, Sortie 55. 1.10 hours duration:
Sailor was on leave and Mungo leading the squadron.

At last! After weeks of trying and waiting; after dozens of fighter versus fighter interceptions, we caught a large formation of the hated Ju 87s flying in to attack Dover. They were under a cloud layer at about 16,000 feet in tight vics, tier upon tier. About fifty of them and their escort of 109s had stupidly gone above the cloud layer! And with Mungo's 'Tally Ho' we got stuck in.

In a few seconds there were machines all over the sky. Timid Huns broke for home but the leader and many others bored on regardless and these brave men were cut to pieces. Eventually they too, broke and with all semblance of air discipline gone, the Stukas turned and fled jettisoning their bombs – some diving for the deck and France; some climbing trying to reach the clouds and safety.

Flaming bombers fell out of the grey sky trailing red comet-tails to crash and burn on the Channel's cold waters. The Stukas were painfully slow and awkward things, bigger than I had expected. Or perhaps with our overtaking speed of nearly a hundred miles an hour, they loomed large in our sights in a matter of seconds, causing us to squirt hastily at them and break away to avoid collision.

We ignored the few 109s that joined in trying to head us off – the wonderful targets spread out too temptingly and a mad exhilaration gripped us. Guns thudding away, 74 and its companion squadron No 66 cut them down as they dived and ran for France, each man for himself.

It's swimming up towards me – now! The Brownings hammered and pieces flew off to flick past and away. His rear gun stopped firing and stuck up vertically, waving slowly from side to side as the gunner sagged down. I throttled back, went into fine pitch and the Spit slowed but not enough and I was forced to slide below and out to one side. I didn't trust the rear gunner being completely harmless and out of it. Full bore again and around and back in a screaming 'S' turn. This time there was no return fire and I saw my De Wildes winking along the Hun's fuselage and wheel spats. Its motor belched puffs of smoke and the propeller windmilled slowly. It's finished and I dived on the next.

Again the rear gunner opened up and again my eight Brownings enveloped the diving Hun. Bits jerked off and I left him to go on to yet a third and pour all my ammunition into it from the rear. There was a shower of fragments and the whole of the enemy's canopy came away. A quick turn and back onto his tail. I could see the pilot, helmet off, bent forward in his cockpit and to keep behind him I lowered my flaps. The Spit heaved up and I forced its nose back down and drew a bead on the stricken plane ahead. Only one gun fired! I was out of ammo! Of all the bloody luck!

Slowly, like a wounded thing, the Ju 87 rocked its wings up and down. I tried formating on it – I wanted to force the pilot to turn around; I'd wonderful visions of getting it back to Hawkinge 'drome complete. But the pilot was leaning forward, head almost on his panel as if trying to read the instruments. It was no good and Jerry escorting fighters started to interfere so with a last look around I headed for the coast and home. Behind me a fantastic sight – at least eight towering exclamation marks of black smoke from wreckage burning on the sea. The most marvellous funeral pyres! Dozens of planes wheeled and dived with tracer streaming in all directions.

> And hast thou slain the Jabberwock?
> Come to my arms, my beamish boy!
> O frabjous day! Callooh! Callay!
> He chortled in his joy.

and I laughed all the way back and landed in huge delight.

At the dispersal the Spy was having a hard time. Ops wanted to know how we got on but we were far too excited to settle down and milled about laughing and clapping one another on the back. Wally had a flamer, a 109; Mungo Park, who had led us, got an 87, while Stephen got three! One by accident, as it was downed in a collision

The last New Zealand volunteers for the RAF short service commissions. The 'war' courses then started. All, with the exception of Smith, Ashworth and the author, were killed in action. Kean left the RNZAF after gaining his wings and his war service is not known to the author. *Back row, left to right*: the author, R. D. Daniell, A. B. Smith. *Front row*: D. C. Mackenzie, L. E. F. Parry, W. G. Gasquoine, A. Ashworth, N. R. Mansfield.

One of the Fairey Gordons which saw service on the North-West Frontier in India before the RNZAF took them over.

Taken from a *March of Time* documentary filmed 31st August 1940 at Kirton in Lindsey. *Left to right*: Wally Churches, myself, Flight Lieutenant Freeborn, Sailor Malan, Sgt Freese, Pilot Officer Scott.

Ben Draper, 'Steve' Stephen, and Sailor Malan with Peter, Sailor's famous terrier, at Biggin Hill.

A gift from Burma for Sailor Malan. Biggin Hill, 1940. *From left to right*: Flying Officer Franklin, self, Sailor Malan, Flying Officer Armstrong.

The deadly pair. H. M. Stephen and Mungo Park at Biggin Hill.

(*Right*) Poor 'F'. Biggin Hill, 2nd December, 1940.

(*Bottom left*) Darkie and myself.

(*Bottom right*) Taken from the body of Fritz Nöller, shot down 2nd November 1940.

(*Left*) Myself at Manston, April 1941, while with 74 'Tiger' Squadron (*Right*) 'M' with the cannon shell hole in a propeller blade. Manston, 6th April 1941.

My ground crew at Manston, April 1941.

Atlantic convoy: Catafighter
at readiness.

MSFU. FDO's and myself.
Left to right: self, Bruce
Patterson, Doug McNair and
Charles Morbey.

MSFU: rocket-propelled
catapult launch of Mk I
Hurricane.

(*Left*) Billy Orr, 'B' Flight Commander, 91 Squadron, Hawkinge.

(*Below*) Three of the 91 Squadron ground crew stalwarts at Hawkinge. These men, like thousands of others and the WAAF, laboured on expecting no special rewards or privileges to keep us in the air. Bravo! *Left to right*: Pip Norton, Titch Mynard, Fred Lord.

(*Left*) 'Demo' — Jules De Molenes, Free French; and (*right*) 'Heapo' — Flying officer J. R. Heap, both of 91 Squadron.

'A' Flight of 91 'Nigeria' squadron at Lympne. *Left to right:* Scotty Downer (NZ), 'Demo' De Molene (FF), Ron Ingram (UK), Billy Orr (UK), 'Heapo' (J. R. Heap) (UK), Squadron Leader Bobby Oxspring, our CO (UK), Frank Silk (UK), 'A' Flight Commander, self (NZ), the Adj, Johnny Edwards, Sammy Hall (UK), John Lambert (FF).

(*Left*) 91 Squadron pilots at Port Lympne. Note 'P.S.' worked in concrete balustrade. *Left to right*: 'Demo', Doc, 'Heapo', Billy Orr, John Lambert. (*Right*) A typical 91 Squadron Sunday morning hangover! Doc (hand on knee), our popular MO, suffers with us. Port Lympne.

91's recces were dicey things.

with the 87 he was firing at! My friend Ben Draper destroyed three 87's* and damaged a 109. Franklin got an 87 and Sergeant Glendinning, two flamers and a damaged. Sergeants Skinner and Freese each bowled a Nazi while another of my special cobbers, Flying Officer Armstrong, despatched two more 87's before stopping a cannon shell from a 109 in his motor and being forced to bail out.

Up the Tigers! They had driven off the dreaded Stuka; it was never to fly against England again. It was a poor thing in fact, and only effective when completely protected by massive fighter support.

December 2nd – Operational Sortie No 67.

Uh-ooh! The bloody undercarriage lever's stuck! I bashed away at it with my clenched fist. We'd been in a pretty hairy scrap and on returning to base I couldn't lower the undercart.

'Red Three to Red Leader, my wheels won't come down; will orbit Angels Two awaiting instructions.'

'Red Leader to Red Three, try steep dives and high gee pull-outs.'

'Red Three to Red Leader, I will get out of circuit and try it.'

But it was no good; the wheels were locked solid and no number of pile-inducing pull-outs would shift them.

'Red Three to Base. Will fly past tower. Please advise if wheels hanging down and give instructions for crash landing.'

This could be quite exciting, and with my squadron of butterflies formating in my stomach, I prepared for a wheels-up landing.

The rest of the squadron put down one after the other and a fire engine and ambulance started up, positioning themselves near the workshops. I motored slowly across the 'drome in fine pitch and with flaps down at about a hundred and twenty miles an hour. I could see the faces of ground staff staring hard at the underside of my machine.

'Tower to Red Three. Your legs are fully up. Come in on grass, clear of the runway.'

I flew around again and lined 'F' up for the nearest out-of-the-way position as near the hangars as possible where it could be salvaged more easily and not interfere with squadron take-offs and landings.

---

* One of these was half mine. Ben only required one more E/A to qualify for a gong and as he was getting married this was my gift to him. We arranged that his next would be part mine. Ben got his gong, got married and got killed.

Lower seat, lean right back until the Sutton harness clicks, locking firm; coarse pitch, flaps down, radiator closed, throttle closed, mags off; and hold off – off – off –. The motor just windmilled without power. Slipstream moaning past. 'F' sagged on to the grass with a sigh at 85 miles per hour.

Bang! Clouds of earth! Bits of propeller flying away – a tearing rasping screech of tortured metal. 'F' heaved and lurched trying to nose over while I pulled the stick back into my stomach and tried to keep the tail down.

Rumbling and bucking, the unfortunate Spitfire slid to a stop, to drop back onto its belly with a thump. I had felt every piece of paint come off, I swear! The fire tender and ambulance rushed over and many hands pulled me out and away. But it was OK, and 'F' was repaired to fly again.

*

The Luftwaffe very rarely sends bombers now except by night. They're using 109s on hit-and-run raids sometimes in formation but more often in small units; even solitary aircraft on days with suitable cloud cover. They zoom in to scatter small bombs indiscriminately over London and then hare back across the Channel. But it is still too dangerous to gain height by climbing over the Kentish fields and so, to gain altitude, we flew north, climbed and then headed back south to the arena when we were over 20,000 feet high.

The newspapers began to blurb about the merits of our 'superlative' fighters and to draw comparisons between Spitfires and Hurricanes. Hell! Don't they know the Jerries' nickname for Hurricanes is 'Tired Birds'? Of course, the Hurricanes have had greater successes – there are more of them; and we Spit boys' priority was to take on the Jerry fighter escorts, leaving the lumbering bombers to the slower Hurribirds. In actual fact, a Hurricane was of a better design from a fighter pilot's point of view, having a downward sloping nose allowing full-deflection shooting in tighter turns than the Spitfire. A Spit's broad flat engine-cowling could actually blank out-of-sight an E/A in a very tight turn.

Another thing which browned us off were the faults which had shown up in our machines. The peacetime pilots must have really goofed off – and we had to ask if they ever fired their guns way up high in the icy cold. Did they ever test the bloody things to see if they'd work? On one of our first high-altitude battles we, 74, had only nine machine guns fire out of 96 (eight to a kite). The oil had frozen, locking breech mechanisms solid. Now, all guns were lubed with refrigerator oil, then wiped almost dry.

And we asked, why did no one report that windscreens, over two inches thick and bulletproof, would freeze over, becoming opaque shields through which nothing could be seen? This occurred on diving fast from great heights to the warm moist air below. What was wrong with those weekend fliers? A classic incident (on 5th December, Sortie No 69, duration 1.30 hours) underlined the windscreen problem.

We'd scrambled to well over 30,000 feet and had a whirling confused scrap down to almost sea level near Dungeness. My windscreen was completely frozen over and as fast as I scraped the frost off the inside, it re-formed. It was impossible to see ahead except obliquely through the small perspex side screens. The gun sight was useless to me. Ahead two fighters patrolled about 60 yards apart and I flew between them to join forces thinking they were ours.

Hell! They're 109s! Into fine pitch, throttle back, slide to starboard behind the nearest Hun. I can't see him! Just a grey blur in the middle of a white mist. There is only one thing to do – spray ahead and hose in a wavering circle, hoping for the best. The Jerry to my left turned towards me but he wasn't slowing quickly enough and was overshooting! Another squirt fired in anger rather than hope. It's madness to stick around – all I'd be was an Aunt Sally for these aroused bastards. And so, in sheer rage and frustration, I dived for the deck. It wasn't for twenty minutes more that the blasted windshield defrosted. Absolutely furious, I landed and taxied to dispersal. The engineer officer was sorry – everyone was sorry – but hell! They'd had years to find this out and rectify it and now our men were being handicapped and the bloody enemy getting away, all because unthinking jerks fiddled in peacetime. Oh yes, they produced clear plastic screens stuck on the inside and fluid squirters on the outside. And then (successfully) air jets on the inside. But why wasn't this sorted out in peacetime?

'You got it, Spud! The Army reported one of your 109s came down in the sea fives miles off Dymchurch!' But it wasn't the same. There was no thrill – with the confidence of several successes and promotion to section leader, I had begun to enjoy, albeit nervously on occasions, the fantastic excitement of legalised mayhem. But to drop a Hun and not see it hit was unsatisfactory. For the first time, I realised what the German ace Major Helmuth Weick had meant when he bragged, 'I choked with glee'* when he downed an adversary. We were becoming creatures, inhuman.

Winter's icy fingers crept slowly over sodden fields to touch, then grip, trees and grass in frigid bondage. Skeins of grey mist wove cold blankets covering Biggin Hill and dimmed the sun with clammy folds. The unfortunate ground crews, up long before dawn, squelched around in gumboots with their overalls flapping and clambered over aircraft slippery with freezing dew. Motors had to be checked, radios tested; the DI's done.

As each Merlin coughed into roaring life, rooks rose and sailed away like pieces of torn black paper whirling and twisting, to be caught in the bare branches of ancient oaks.

Inside the chill dispersal huts, pilots on standby crouched around tiny glowing stoves, playing cards – or trying to sleep, lay huddled under prickly, grey blankets on iron beds.

Back in the messes the aircrew on readiness queued up for food and got ready to relieve those on standby. In billets or boudoirs the lucky lay snug, released for the day, forgetting the past and ignoring the future. Like the very poor, with nothing else to look forward to, we sought sex and drink as an anodyne. For tomorrow, if we were unlucky, the sun would be shining and we'd be facing the board again.

* Propaganda report by Dr Goebbels on GAF fighter pilots' statements.

CHAPTER V

The Old Jail Inn and off the Narrow Path

I discovered The Old Jail Inn when out walking along a meandering country road. Inside it was warm and cheerful, with ack-ack gunners, airmen, land-girls and Waafs knocking back half 'n halfs with the locals.

One night during a big air raid, one of the girls with whom I'd struck up a friendship, asked me to take her home as she was frightened. Outside, under the cold glitter of a million stars, we saw the probing searchlights and heard the warbling beat of German bombers. Things swished down, pieces of shrapnel, empty incendiary cannisters, all sorts of hardware, to clatter and thump on frozen fields. Dozens of incendiary bombs lay hissing and spluttering, the glare of their magnesium cores reflected from clouds of fuming smoke and steam. The noise was incredible. Sticks of bombs fell with rising multiple screams to crump in dull red flashes across the fields. But most unnerving was the eerie parachute mine, an evil monster which drifted down, silent as a nightmare, to detonate with a frightful roar.

Everything for hundreds of yards was flattened; the ground shook as from an earthquake.

Louie held me tight.

'Please don't leave me – I'm frightened!'

'But where are your folk?' I asked, my mind on my fiancée and possible complications. This was not a sought-after affair.

'In the Anderson Shelter – they practically live there.'

In the morning I awoke to the sounds of tea cups chinking.

'Hell! It's your old man!'

'Not to worry – he's OK.'

And with that, Dad came in with a breakfast tray and a cheerful smile. I think he'd seen all this before.

'Cor, what a night! Never slept a wink!' and he winked at me.

I began to spend more and more nights in the tiny village and often, rather than stagger back to the billets, used to share a huge double bed at the inn with Louie and the barmaid. The unfortunate barmaid would get off to sleep as best she could. But it must have been lonely and frustrating for her!

One of the Old Jail habitués was a sly poacher. In his dirty and tatty coat he had sewn extra pockets, deep and hidden. Ferrets with beady eyes and sharp teeth lived in their dark smelly interiors. One night he offered to sell me a muzzled greyhound. Nahlin had been her track name but she'd grown too aged for racing and too old to learn the poacher's tricks. Sorry for the lovely creature, I bought her for a quid. She'd been speyed I was told, useless for breeding and had the bad habit of yipping with excitement while coursing for hares and rabbits. It was my quid or a knock on the head.

I renamed her Darkie and she became my constant companion on long walks around the 'drome perimeter. I preferred to be alone when confined to the airfield's environs as one clique in the squadron indulged in stupid horseplay which infuriated me.

Hares, startled into jinking flight, were easily outrun by the speedy animal and she got me many a tasty meal. But in her frenetic chasing she showed complete disregard for the barbed wire defences and suffered horrid tearings as she followed her prey at full tilt through the rusty coils.

At day's end, as the sun slipped below the darkening horizon, our Spitfires were covered for the night and we were released until the morrow.

Then the banshee warbling of the sirens would start up one by one and a carpet of sound would unroll towards London. Soon the beat of German motors, deliberately unsynchronised to foil the sound-locators of the anti-aircraft batteries, started throbbing and we'd know another night of fear and frustration was being inflicted on us.

Now came the hour of the night fighter and Defiants, scattered around the perimeter, were started to warm their motors in preparation to do battle.

But there were far too few of them and some of our day fighter pilots, trained in night-flying, had duralumin plates bolted on their Spitfires' sides to shield their eyes from exhausts' red glare. Not being equipped with radar like the Defiants, our machines had to be vectored around by ground control; we could only be used on the brightest of nights when the moon silvered the fields of Kent.

Sergeant Freese crash-landed at Detling and was killed but Roger Boulding that same night shot down a Heinkel bomber! In the morning, Freeborn, Boulding and some others not on duty drove over and examined the wreckage. But the brown jobs had been their first and stripped it of all souvenirs, much to their disgust. You had to be very quick or very lucky!

One cold night, staggering back to Biggin from the Old Jail, I was caught in a bad raid. The flash and crump of bombs, the falling debris unnerved me. Feeling dreadfully alone and surrounded by empty fields I put my arms around the trunk of an ancient oak. It was alive! Clinging to it, kneeling in the grass, I drew comfort from its great strength.

It had been here when my forebears had set out for New Zealand; it had been here when German Zeppelins had droned over on their way to London in the First World War.

I was suddenly intensely aware of the abominations in the air above, of the insult, of the sheer disgusting invasion of our homeland, and, in getting furious, my rage overcame my fear. This night and this wonderful old tree changed my entire outlook and attitude towards the war. Up to this moment war had been a fantastic if scary adventure. Now it became a crusade against the evil things Hitler's Germany had spawned.

*

After the Battle of Britain, odd things happened in 74. The CO was up at Group for endless conferences. Rumours were that he was being promoted to Wing Commander and I started feeling alarmed that my Flight Commander, with whom I did not get on, would be the new CO. No way was I going to stay if this occurred. All manner of directives were coming through from Group and some experienced pilots were posted to bolster up weak squadrons or to provide the nuclei of new ones being formed.

Pilots due for a rest were being lent to the Air Transport Auxiliary for ferrying new and reconditioned aircraft to squadrons based all

over Great Britain. Some pilots were sent on refresher courses,
gunnery courses or on leave. I was a fool – I should have gone on the
gunnery course. I was a lousy shot.

Demands on squadrons to release experienced pilots for the
Middle East became cynical excuses to get rid of incompatible or
dud fliers. We often wondered what happened at the other end when
the cast-offs could be coupled with some of the more outdated Desert
Air Force planes.

The Hun attacks on England had basically changed from day to
night bombing. Day raids by fighter bombers in pin-pricking hit and
run forays were really of nuisance value only. It was a strange time; a
hiatus in the air war, while all manner of modifications in tactics
evolved. The specialist night fighters came into being and their
exploits replaced those of the day fighters in the newspapers.

February 8th: Sent on 'rest', I got a posting to the ATA at White
Waltham to ferry single-engined aircraft. The job lasted only a
month and I was pleased to leave it – most of my flying time seemed
to be spent in returning to our base in draughty old Ansons, winding
up the ruddy undercarriages, which took ages, cranking away while
the ferry pilot bumbled about in mist and rain. I flew a Tomahawk
which I put down in disgust after twenty minutes. The Yanks would
have to do better than this. I pitied any squadrons unfortunate
enough to be equipped with them.

Back to 74 and sure enough Malan was leaving. It looked as
though Freeborn was out of the running and 'B' Flight Commander
Mungo Park would take over. Feeling better, I sauntered down to
the dispersal hut to get the gen on what else was new.

Wally had shared in destroying a 110 with Sergeant Morrison
who, two days later, went missing over the Channel. A new pilot, a
Pole, Sergeant Rogowski, crashed near Eastbourne and was
hospitalised.

A new flight commander, Flight Lieutenant Tony Bartley from 92
Squadron was taking over 'B' Flight and Mungo would be acting
CO, while Sailor stayed on at Biggin as Acting Wing Commander
awaiting confirmation of his new job – I had myself transferred to 'B'
so I could fly with Wally.

The RAF had begun sweeps over Coastal France to stir up the

Jerries and bring them to combat. These were pretty tentative affairs at first. There were rumours of Hun movements – whole squadrons and groups being withdrawn into Germany. It was an uneasy time; Hitler's Germany ruled all the Continent, but Britain, protected by the Channel, was isolated and alone. Brave words from Churchill cheered us but the future was unclear and uncertain. Young and careless, we just flew as required and left the tomorrows to fate and the top brass.

March 4th, Sortie No 85:   It was the day after my twenty-third birthday and wearing a monumental hangover I walked out to 'T'. I felt sick; not only from the grog, but because this was to be my first sweep and I wasn't looking forward to it. At 4 p.m. we took off and circled, climbing to formate with the other squadrons, heading south-east. We were still climbing steadily as we crossed the French coast. It was a lovely blue day and far below light cumulus clouds drifted over the green fields of the Pas de Calais.

A small formation of aircraft flew over us, going the opposite way, and I clearly saw the duck-egg green bellies and black crosses. I expected them to turn and dive on us: I expected our leader to 'Tally Ho!' and climb to attack. Somehow they missed being seen and in a moment they'd be behind and in a perfect attacking position. So I pulled out of formation, gave 'T' full boost and heaved the stick back in a climbing loop which brought me under the leader. My fire went straight into the Hun's belly and there was a flash and burst of flame. My Spitfire shuddered violently, stalled and fell. I let it go and radioed, 'Bandits behind and above Knockout!'

It happened so fast and here we were spinning below the circling machines. After falling about 5,000 feet, I pulled 'T' out and started climbing again. More Jerries, this time in front of me, diving away in a shallow curve. Nose down, once again through the gate and with thin brown smoke pouring out of the exhausts it was only a few minutes to overtake the 109s which didn't seem aware of the danger.

I opened fire, this time on the rearmost aircraft. Faint white mist came out from under the wing roots and the Jerry half rolled for the deck. The others started turning, diving or climbing in confusion. I had to break off – it was impossible to keep an eye on all of them – and so I put my nose down and headed flat out for the coast.

When well over the Channel, about a mile in front of me, I watched a 109 stalk and close on a lone Spitfire. There was nothing I could do other than call, 'Lone Spitfire look behind! Bandit on your tail!' But the warning wasn't heard and the Spitfire was soon trailing glycol and smoke. The Jerry turned away from his victim back towards France. He hadn't seen me and, opening fire, I closed to point-blank range almost head-on. Clouds of black smoke! Flames! The Hun fell down out of the sky like a flaming torch.

I overtook the crippled Spit and weaving slowly behind it, escorted it towards Ramsgate. The pilot looked OK and even waved once. Soon its prop stopped and the smoke died away. Glycol streamed in a grey fog from under the oil-streaked fuselage. It was obvious the glide couldn't be stretched as far as Manston 'drome and I suggested he bale out; there was no acknowledgement so I assumed his RT was damaged. I radioed a full May Day just in case and we continued down until, with a spray of grey sand, the Spitfire slid to a stop on the mined beaches of Ramsgate. The pilot emerged and nonchalantly walked across the deadly sands while soldiers on duty there bellowed at him to stay where he was.

It was Squadron Leader Wood, a pleasant chap, supernumerary in our 74 Squadron, who explained later, 'Forgot about the mines – had the twitch at the time, old man.'

We spent hours on convoy patrols along the Channel coast, guarding shipping from hit and run bombers. Margate to Folkestone was the danger area and minesweepers in particular had a rough time, being unable to make quick changes off course in the sudden attacks.

By this time I was a section leader and with Sergeant Dales had two exciting encounters. On 24th March we caught a Ju 88 and claimed a probable – the E/A just holding off with its port engine stopped and smoke and glycol pouring out. We were out of ammo and were merely waiting for the Hun's end to claim it as destroyed. The flak batteries of Dunkirk gave us a pasting and drove us away from our victim. 109s came out to interfere so we didn't see its finish.

We also caught a lone bomber on another occasion, this time actually on its bombing run over a minesweeper. As I gave the 'Tally Ho!' and bent forward to adjust the gun sight graticule, I realised to my horror that the silhouette I took to be a plane turned away was, in fact, a Do 215 turning in to face us! I just had time for a quick squirt, to see some strikes, pull the stick back and, as my kite heaved up, the bomber roared between us actually passing below me and above Sergeant Dales. As it passed we were both hit by bullets from its front gun – both our planes had a bullet hole in the starboard wing! By the time we'd pulled ourselves together and turned, the cocky Hun had escaped in a cloud bank and we were left flying around with red faces. And we'd only fired a few rounds doing very little damage.

Something ugly occurred. Four of us were high up, over 33,000 feet, and our contrails formed thick behind us. Ahead and below were four or five 109s and the section leader was hell bent on getting one.

'Red Leader, Red Four calling. I'm being attacked from behind!'

No answer from Red Leader. I screwed around in the tiny cockpit and peered back over my shoulder. There were about twenty bandits! Diving, the lead aircraft was already firing on Red Four, the last machine in our section.

'Red Leader, Red Leader, this is Red Four! Am being attacked!'

Again no answer.

'Red Leader, Red Four calling! Am breaking away!'

And with that, Red Four half-rolled for the deck with several Huns in hot pursuit. The others lifted their ugly yellow snouts and started to overhaul Red Three. At this altitude there is little lift from the rarified air and violent action only results in a high speed stall with subsequent spinning down out of control until flying speed is regained.

Now it was Red Three's turn to call in vain.

'Red Leader, Red Three. I'm being fired on!'

Still no answer. We were overhauling the Jerries in front; very soon we'd be in a position to open fire.

'Red Three breaking away.' This was becoming really serious for me – I was the next to be paid attention and already the lead aircraft had started firing. Yellow flashes from his wing cannon were quite distinct, then the twin cowling machine guns flickered as he got closer into range and tracer spiralled around my machine. I knew what was happening and, furious at being so grossly made use of, half-rolled for the deck. Let Red One get his Hun if he can! But not at my expense!

Back at the base the three of us were ordered into the the Flight Commander's office. The section leader was there and red with rage but we were also mad and united against him. It was a miracle none of us had been killed and we let him have it. Perhaps his radio had been u/s but we doubted it.

Sailor came in and eyed us in silence. The air was electric with the violence of our feelings.

'I don't know what this is all about and I don't particularly want to,' said Malan. 'I suggest you go back to dispersal' and with that we stalked out the door.

April 6th 1941, Sortie No 114. 1.20 hours duration: Cursing the war and frigid dawn with bitter hatred, I stumbled out of bed and across to the electric heater. The switch was cold and stiff snapping over with a loud click; slowly the filament reddened as I bent shivering over it, dully making supplication for a successful day's hunting.

Darkie yawned and stretched, looking at me with indifferent eyes. I'll put you on the floor tonight, I vowed; no more sleeping on top of the bed for you! Her legs were too long, her paws too hard; besides, she would try to push me out of bed and got quite peevish when I heaved her down to the foot.

I peeked a look under the black-out curtain at the weather – low cloud and a little fog. Good for sneak-raiders; didn't look too thick a cloud-layer either. The fleece-lined flying boots were damp with the perspiration of yesterday's hot work (God! I was lucky) and I pulled them on with distaste, tucking a map down into the side of my right boot.

Outside the stars were still twinkling coldly and the distant roar of warming Merlins shivered the frosty stillness. Darkie trotted along beside me, stopping as usual by the sunken garden, later rejoining me in the mess. Here it was warm and friendly, the smoke from last night's cigarettes still scenting the empty hall. Flight Lieutenant Tony Bartley (the new 'B' Flight Commander), and Wally were in the kitchen, rustling toast and tea. As usual, there was no coffee and furtive cockroaches scuttled about by the warm stove.

We talked shop till the others came in. Baker was last again, with reddened eyes and tangled fair hair. He would be left behind, still guzzling tea and buttered toast. Darkie had wandered off somewhere, grubbing for scraps I guessed – she was always hungry with her worms and I asked Baker to bring her over when he came. We rumbled off in the dispersal brake to the sergeants mess and collected the NCO pilots.

Tony Bartley tore a strip off young Dales for being scruffy – I felt very ashamed of my two days' growth of beard and pulled my Goon-skin higher. The brake was cold and the wind blew through the stuck side window. The icy blast chilled us and the brake's broken exhaust made the air foul. Nobody talked.

The guard at the gates didn't bother to stop us – he must have been browned-off, poor devil. When we reached the dispersal the fires had only just been lit and the hut was like an ice-box. Wally and I jointly moaned at the telephone orderly who, tired after his all night vigil, mumbled a surly excuse. It seemed it was the guard's fault, etc.

I rang up Ops: 'Anything on the board?'

'Not a sausage,' was the answer and, disappointed, we curled up on the beds still warm from the guards' stolen sleep. Young Dales paced around, restless. He's new and not content with waiting for trouble.

At twenty past eight, the 'A' Flight boys trouped in, waking us with rude horseplay. We rolled from our beds, cursing and groaning; they seemed quite proud of their being twenty minutes late. The usual questions sped our leaving. 'Anything doing?' 'Nope.' 'What's the news?' 'Been asleep.' 'Hell! That's all you bastards ever do!'

We rushed out the door, scrambling, clawing our way into the brake. Smithie missed out and had to lie along a mudguard, one arm over its headlight. He looked frozen as the brake roared around the perimeter; we made corny jokes about his discomfort. We lucky seven pushed and shoved around inside the brake, suddenly alive and warm. The windows misted over but we could still see Smithie's red scarf flying stiffly in our wind. We laughed. Life was good.

The sun was hidden by the dull clouds and the planes stood sleek and silent on the wet grass. Most of the duty crews were at breakfast and the relief boys were busy sitting around jawing. It was getting warmer now and the wind had died a little.

Wally and Tony yelled something at each other about doing a Rhubarb sweep and we all started speculating on the conditions. It certainly looked a grand day for one, clouds about 1,000 feet, little wind and very clear visibility under a firm cloud-base. Wally and I had a violent argument about who would go with Tony. Being slightly senior I got my way and, as we sat at our breakfast, Tony briefed me for the trip.

Tony suggested going in over Gravelines and having a look at the aerodromes further inland – say St Omer. I'd been wanting to go on a 'personal' sweep for weeks now and here it was. I was lucky to get 'M' the squadron's fastest kite and decided to take my revolver and some chocolate. I couldn't eat my food and felt squirmy inside. My heart pounded away and there was a great expectancy and tension in the air. *Couldn't the others feel it?*

I tucked myself close to Tony as he dived on the dispersal hut and together we screamed down on the boys, their upturned faces showing flat and pink against the brown walls. Just for a blurred second we could see the smiles and waves and then they slid under and behind us as, with a lovely climbing turn, Tony headed for Margate and the sea. We kept strict radio silence; no need to alert the Hun.

I slid out to port and began the old routine, checking oil pressure, rad. temperature, revs. and mags. 'M' was purring along effortlessly – funny how some kites are better than others; this one was a peach and took weak mixture just as cleanly as rich; easy and smooth on the controls too. And yet it was the scruffiest looking machine in the squadron with oil and carbon streaks and flaking paintwork.

A warm exhilarating feeling came over me. Christ! How I loved Spits! The clouds were getting lower now and more broken, cutting out the horizon and forcing us down near the lashing waves. I could see spray flying before the freshening wind and frequent rain-squalls forced me to close in on Tony's bucking machine. Now and again a brown puff would stream back from his exhausts as a particularly rough drop would surge his fuel. 'M' was being buffeted a bit too; the heavy cloud base was a mass of powerful air currents and thin spots. I glanced at the clock – eight minutes flying from our coast – my mouth started to dry up and my heart to thud.

Only another two minutes before we cross the French coast. I started weaving across Tony's tail. Ops are still droning on:

'Hullo Red Leader, Red Leader, Tandem calling. We have no information for you – listening out.'

So far so good. My palms grew moister and my mouth drier – I gave myself some oxygen and kidded myself I felt cocky. The grey waves are more tumbled now, spray flying in whirling skeins. We are flying at less than thirty feet.

Ah! There's the coast – just a line of white foam and sombre sand-dunes. Tony turned north-east and we stooged up the coast edge about half a mile out to sea. I felt terrible – knew something was going to happen. Suddenly Tony turned starboard and, opening up, roared towards the coast. The white surf-line grew and we swept across it and up and over the sandy slopes. I felt a great weight lift from my spirits and the old cockiness returned.

No flak yet – God! How I hate it! Gee, how green the grass and how flat are the fields! There's a windmill and another, another. Several farm houses silently sweep under as we flash low across the unhappy countryside. I can't keep my eyes on the deck as I'd like to – this tail-protecting weaving racket is a stooge's job and I grow impatient to lead. Next time I'll come alone to poke about. I imagined I heard a change in 'M's' steady purr and fussed about with the magneto switches. Christ! I nearly took Tony's tail off as he waggled his wings frantically. I slid up to him and he gave me the line astern signal. My heart leapt and I felt a bit sick – wonder what he has seen? Damn my nerves! We have stumbled on an aerodrome and as Tony banked around it we were only at three hundred feet and I'm scared stiff! Green and red fire streamed between us; machine guns. I skidded along, hoping to fox the gunners. Oh! Hell! Some cannons have opened up – their tracer shells flashed past my port wing, vanishing into the clouds. Tony was flying fast – I had to thrash 'M' to keep up. I was on the inside of his turn and at such a low level it was very dicey, as I was often in the line-astern position.

We stooged away from the 'drome. There were no kites on the deck – the dispersal pens must be camouflaged in the woods. I breathed easier and opened the air-scoop fully to cool the cockpit. My neck got sore with the continual stretching and twisting around. Suddenly, Tony did a steep bank to the left and I looked frantically for what he had spotted.

It was a 109 on its belly in a field! A forced landed kite!

The light mottled greys and greens of its camouflage clashed sharply with the sodden turf on which it had skidded to a stop near a farm cottage. Tony circled around and around, sometimes almost hidden in the clouds that hung heavy and low over the dreary farmlands. Suddenly he swooped down, satisfied of no flak trap, and I followed, excited and hungry for the splutter of my guns even if only against a harmless 109.

The Brownings flamed and flickered their wicked light; I could see Tony's explosive bullets flashing all over the wings and fuselage of the unfortunate 109 and a great brown haze rose from the plastered machine. Following, I too sprayed the little devil and pulled out from my dive only in time to clear the building. It was stupid of me to have forgotten to switch on the gun-sight but the tiles splintering and dancing on the farmhouse roof were spectacular! Some of my bullets had hit the Hun, however, and, happy, I lifted 'M' up and around under Tony's tail again.

We flew on, hunting something to beat up – anything. I'm feeling grand and not at all tense. We came upon St Omer and roared low over the houses and a waterway. I can see Froggies looking up and once I spotted a Hun uniform. A machine gun flickered into life but jerked to a stop after a few futile bursts, its bullets silently streaming through the air, the tracer smoke leaving white patterns against the sombre clouds.

St Omer vanished behind us and on we swept, farms, windmills, sheep, cows, all drowned in the roar and rush of our Spitfires' passing. What looked to be a big ammunition dump – little huts segregated behind high grassy walls – appeared before us, the rigid squares like a giant's chessboard. More flak from hidden machine guns. Tony zoomed up to the cloud base which had lifted a few hundred feet and I cursed him silently – it would be much safer if we kept hedge-hopping – and more fun! Again and again I was forced to fly directly behind my leader and then it happened.

Krang! There was a terrific jar and shudder through the crate. A great stream of rushing red balls streamed past my cockpit, snaking as from a hose, vanishing in the clouds beyond. While pulling the stick back in instinctive reaction, a mass of startling clear thoughts flashed across my mind.

Warn Tony – no time – the first time I'd heard a hit such as this! Christ! I've had it. Turn on the bastard!

I caught a fleeting glimpse of Tony zooming crazily for the clouds with the horrid red shells flicking past his machine. I banked 'M' vertically, heaving on the stick in a climbing turn to port. My mask crushed down on my nose, I could feel the very flesh on my face dragging down as the G's built up. My stomach sick with fear and straining as the great blood vessels filled. A red haze fogged my eyes and my head sank on my chest as everything went brown, then black. Your mind still works in a blackout. Too much so!

Something hit behind my head and exploded by my left elbow. Whack! Whack! Horrible jerks wrenched 'M's straining body, the jars violent through the joystick. Amazed at being hit in such a tight turn, I eased the stick forward and rolled her back and up into the cloud as my vision cleared.

I saw it – an Me 110 still firing. Then the cloud wrapped its mantle around me – safe.

Safe! At barely one thousand feet and with all my instruments gone crazy? Oh, Christ! The hood's jammed – I can't open it – if I spin now, I've had it.

The airspeed was dropping. Shaking and sweating, I eased the stick forward. Curse the gun sight! I had to drop the seat a few notches so I could see the artificial horizon more clearly. It was careering madly and the gyro compass spinning fast as a top. I caged it. I eased on left rudder to stop her swinging; immediately the turn and bank indicator showed a fierce right-hand skid, the turning needle swinging wildly. The airspeed crept faster and faster and the slipstream began to shriek through a jagged hole behind my head. I eased the stick back and held the rudder bar central. The compass started circling slowly so uncaging the gyro, I held 'M' steady on the reading.

God only knew where I was. I tried to compose myself but ridiculous thoughts cluttered my mind: 'Don't fly straight and level – flak will get you.' I started weaving gently, trying to think of a compass course to get me home. 270°? 290°? *Can* I get home? 'M' shook like a live thing with St Vitus Dance; harsh vibrations seemed to be tearing the engine out. Must have had a bullet in the motor or a piece off my prop. Perhaps my tail unit was damaged? I managed to force back the hood and the white cloud mists felt clammy on my hot face. My mask stifled me – tear it off – ah! – I throttled back gently; the vibrations got worse – terrible – must be the prop – I increased the revs and at 2600 revs found the shaking not too bad. Oil pressure and temp, rad-temperature, revs – all OK. I tested the mags and thanked God. Being a prisoner didn't appeal to me at all! 'M' seemed strangely sluggish on the ailerons; there was a jagged hole near the port flap panel – cannon shell, nothing else on the port side. I scanned the broad wing on the starboard side; I could see another hole, round and neat, down by the radiator – machine gun this time. Couldn't see any Glycol leaks. Jeez! I was lucky!

It was impossible to think clearly while cloud-flying so I decided to come out and find out where I was and beat it for home. On again with the gun-sight, test the guns, they spluttered dully in the clouds, their flashes brilliant in the white fog. One cloud 'confirmed'; I managed to laugh – poor Peter St John and his clouds! 'M' and I burst through to green fields and a sleek grey shadow sliding along below.

Hell's bells! A 110! Just three or four flashes from the rear gunner before 'M's' leaden hail smashed down – the De Wilde's bursting red and winking over the squared wings. I held the gun button down and a crazy pattern of torn earth streamed along, around, behind and beneath the Hun. The 110 lifted, dipped, and flew right into the deck.

A wild exultation surged over me. Got the bastard! Got him! Three black trails of churned earth trailed behind like a speedboat's wash as engines and fuselage skidded over the flooded fields. Puddle water steamed on its motors and small bushes flattened in its wake.

I heaved around in a steep bank using full aileron. The plane was very sluggish and felt queer in manoeuvering back to attack the now stationary Hun.

Hah! The gunner's out and scrambling off for the woods. The spray from my eight machine guns enveloped him and left him writhing in the grass.

I felt hot and churned up inside and began to shake with reaction – I had the twitch all right! Putting 180° on the compass verge-ring I climbed for the clouds. I wanted to call base just to hear a friendly voice, but was scared to in case the Jerries might get a fix on me.

Rad, oil, mags all OK. Here and there the cloud broke into layers and I climbed frantically to the next level and switched on my IFF. I decided to take a chance. Cloud cover would be easy to reach if I were intercepted again.

'Hullo Tandem, Tandem – Knockout Red Two here. Can you give me a vector please.' And back it came, clear, prompt and concise – 'Red Two steer 225 Angels 2.'

Getting on course, I gave it five minutes, checked that the IFF was off and called up again. 'Hullo Tandem – Red Two – confirm vector please' – and again that magic voice – 'Tandem – Red Two steer 230 let down five minutes.'

Down I came as instructed to find the wrinkled grey waters of the Channel below me. In the distance Dungeness beckoned. Dymchurch, Folkestone, Dover and Deal slid past and then we were in the Manston circuit.

Test flaps – OK. Undercarriage OK. I stirred the stick around – sluggish in the ailerons but elevators and rudders OK. Manston like a large green farm stretched before me and I could see the boys outside the disperal, faces uptilted.

'Hullo Tandem, Knockout Red Two – in sight of base – have sustained damage. Will land when reception ready.' I stooged around and around with the rad flap wide open until the ambulance and fire tenders rolled out on the field. If a tyre is blown they could be needed! Here goes!

The boys rushed over and helped me out of the kite. Tony had not returned. 'What happened?' and soon we were looking at the various holes and the Spy taking down my report.

'Look at it! Just look at the bloody thing!' The engineer officer was browned off. I felt like a naughty boy. 'Oxygen bottle burst, port aileron gone, cannon hole through prop – look at the goddam holes!'

Tony turned up much later having landed at Hawkinge where 92 were stationed, and was on the mat before Mungo. 'Why didn't you report in? We were worried sick!' A few days later Tony was posted away on sick leave with eardrum trouble and a supernumerary Squadron Leader P. Wood, took over his flight.

My replacement Spitfire came next day all shiny and new. The ground crew were pretty chuffed. When there was no one around I sneaked into a hangar, climbed a ladder and sawed off 'M's' damaged blade for a souvenir.

Poor 'M'! So quickly replaced but I'll never forget our adventure together.

At this time several of us were agitating for a change in our battle formation. The old line-astern system was the best for rapid climbing in interceptions or manoeuvering into attack but once at height we thought it preferable to spread out. This open formation was used by the Jerries and was most effective for mutual defence. I made myself very unpopular by getting too heated on the subject; I became more and more dissatisfied during the hiatus when Sailor was away.

There were one or two in my flight who delighted in ragging others who, because of their nature or physical size, couldn't retaliate. It was useless to resist – in no time, despite frantic struggling, the unfortunate victim's pants (or more) would be off and flung into a tree or onto the dispersal's roof. The scragging became worse, bitter and even rank was pulled on occasion to force submission.

It was fun for them but became hell for the victims. Several of us joined forces and there were many quite violent scuffles. It got beyond a joke; our flight was not a happy one.

One day one of our chief tormentors shot down a Jerry from over 30,000 feet, and misjudging his height, did a Victory roll right into the parade ground. I paddled in the fire-fighter's foam and the unburnt oil; kicked debris around and rejoiced. Ashamed of myself, nevertheless, I faced facts. We were becoming stark realists – sentiment and sorrow were for friends only and I had hated the oaf. Feeling better, I went off to the mess, whistling.

Things had changed from my early days with 74 and it had become an unhappy divided squadron for me. I had never been at ease with Freeborn, but, protected to a degree by the awesome Malan, it had been a rude shock to learn that Sailor was indeed promoted wing commander and was to lead the Biggin Wing. So I had put in for a posting to another squadron, choosing 91 as it had been recommended by Malan and sounded exciting. Malan thought its particular role more suited to my temperament than that of a conventional squadron.

The posting came through and Wally and I said goodbye. We'd

shared the high honour of flying as Malan's No 2's almost exclusively. There had been intense, good-natured rivalry between us and we were at even scores as to Huns shot down.

'Good luck, Spud, I bet I'm a flight commander before you! Bet I get more Huns too!'

I said goodbye to my especial friends in the squadron; to my ground crew, batman, phone operators, engineer officer, Spy and the squadron doctor, the drivers, mess orderlies – a host of chaps to whom I owed my comfort and safety.

Malan and the men of 74 had been my teachers. From each, batman to the CO, I'd learnt something. As green as grass on arrival, I left this famous squadron equipped, and very well equipped, to look out for myself.

With Darkie in tow I was on my way. It was now over to Lady Luck and the fortunes of war as far as I could manipulate them.

From time to time I heard news of the Tigers' exploits. And so, from time to time, heard the price the squadron had to pay to achieve its many successes. Brzezina was to die. And Wally. And Mungo Park the new CO and Ben Draper, Glendenning, Howard, Morrison, Mould, Stevenson and many, many others too; replacements of the fallen.

One in four of 74's pilots were killed in the Battle of Britain.*

Wally's death was hard to take. We'd flown together some eight months – a long, long time by a fighter pilot's reckoning. I remembered the good times, the wild parties, the pub crawls, egging expeditions; but most of all, the shared ecstasy of watching soft dawns creeping over sleeping fields as our Spitfires circled higher and higher to greet the golden sun.

No point in ranting against their fate – in mute and terrible agony of mind and spirit one could only curse the Hun and promise revenge.

---

* Refer to appendix as to 74's losses.

CHAPTER VI

91 Squadron, 'Jim Crows' and MSFU 'Catafighters'

No 91 was an unusual squadron. It was based at Hawkinge right on the Channel coast, up in a shallow depression just above Folkestone. At this time I'd completed 121 operational trips and had a fair amount of experience. But 91 didn't operate as a squadron, rather as a group of specialists flying as individuals. Sometimes, such as on air-sea rescue missions, we flew in flights of two or four. Our job included acting as spotters to check on stragglers returning from sweeps, to go on lone shipping and weather reconnaissances along the French coast and to escort Defiants and Lysanders dropping inflatable rafts to pilots downed in the cold Channel waters. We were often scrambled to protect minesweepers and other small coastal craft.

I didn't care much for the shipping recces. They were hairy affairs. Every hour, on the hour, two machines were airborne and our pilots had complete freedom as to how they did their reconnaissance. Height, direction, every decision was the pilot's own. The idea was to keep radio silence, so as not to alert the Hun, and, as one pilot covered the Dutch coast from Flushing in the Netherlands to Cap Gris Nez, the other flew along the Fécamp to Gris Nez strip. This was the longest hop but sometimes we only had to cover between Ostende and Dieppe.

If we were attacked we were obliged to fight our way home and not scream for help. There were many lonely, desperate scraps for 91 pilots.

Our problem was in counting shipping movements along the enemy coast without getting caught. Sometimes we flew high, and, by diving fast, screamed over docks and wharves 'counting' barges and shipping in the heavily defended harbours. Sometimes we sneaked at sea level along the coasts, heaving up and over the harbours in heart-stopping sorties, dodging streams of flak and

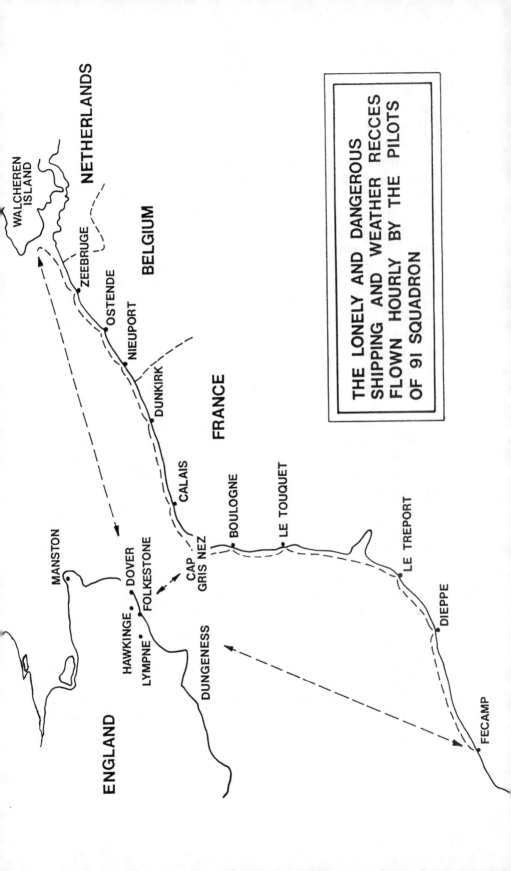

THE LONELY AND DANGEROUS
SHIPPING AND WEATHER RECCES
FLOWN HOURLY BY THE PILOTS
OF 91 SQUADRON

NETHERLANDS

WALCHEREN
ISLAND

BELGIUM

ZEEBRUGE

OSTENDE

NIEUPORT

DUNKIRK

FRANCE

CALAIS

CAP
GRIS NEZ

BOULOGNE

LE TOUQUET

LE TREPORT

DIEPPE

FECAMP

ENGLAND

MANSTON

DOVER

HAWKINGE

FOLKESTONE

LYMPNE

DUNGENESS

running the gauntlet of fighters just as fast if not faster than ourselves.

It was exciting but not funny. To do the job properly you really took your life in your hands. Why the powers-that-be didn't fit us with oblique aiming cameras, I don't know – our guesstimates must have caused some rare old panics in intelligence headquarters. To give us more speed, they 'clipped' our wings by removing the beautiful pointed wing-tips and fitting blunt edges to the wing ends. Some aircraft had four machine guns removed to save weight and increase manoeuverability.

Escorting the Defiants and Lysanders was mostly dull work. We'd be scrambled off to join up with the rescue planes sent out to search for ditched aircrew. On finding the blokes in the water, the Lysander would fly up wind of them and drop self-inflating dinghies and we'd circle about hoping the poor devils could swim to them and not drown in the process. Or we'd hang around while air-sea rescue launches sped out from Channel ports to pick them up. Many times we watched wounded aircrew drown and were helpless to save them.

On one dreadful occasion a Defiant pilot, worn out to the state of complete irrationality, actually took off without rafts and circled a drowning pilot. He hadn't had them loaded as 'they slow the machine down too much'. He was whisked away LMF (lack of moral fibre).

May 7th, Sortie No 151: Out of the corner of my eye I saw sparkles of light and a red flash. Turning towards them I spotted a black shape diving on one of the balloons.

'Tally Ho! Black Leader turning to port! Go!' And off we went, my No 2 and I. It was a 109; its pilot brave, stupid or blind. One minute he was happy as a lark and the next minute he was juddering under the hail of my eight guns. The gun crews on the convoy started pounding away and of course, as usual, were behind target but spot on for me. However, we soon drew away and the 109 dropped down to sea level, fuming with smoke and the motor windmilling lifelessly. A dull red flash in front, a whump! and a cloud of stinking cordite – an AA shell nearly collected me. Furious, I pulled away losing sight of the Jerry. My No 2 had become separated and so I had to return to the Lysander and carry on protecting the sluggish thing. It was hard to settle down again knowing I could only claim a probable – I'd got the bastard all right.

Cannons! At long last, after all manner of rumours, we've got 'em! And now to try them out. They were long and stuck their blued-steel greasy barrels out from the slim wings. They had dirt-excluders like thick French letters rolled down over the 20mm muzzles. We couldn't wait to test-fire them. We went in pairs to the Beachy Head cliffs and banged away at the sheer faces. Most satisfying crumps and flashes as the Hispanos whumped away, making the Spitfires seem to pause a little with each coughing burst.

May 13th, Sortie 160:   'It's not my bloody fault! I asked Ops and they said, Yes!'

'The thing was free and floating along trailing wires and ropes – it was drifting towards France!'

'Well, it was a special device of the Navy's – it was designed to reach the French coast at night and drag over and short-out electric power cables.'

'That's the most stupid idea! And in any case, why weren't we advised about it? Bugger the Navy bigheads.'

I was furious – I had found this strange balloon sailing along at about 500 feet, and had got permission from Ops to hack it down. Now I was on the mat. There was unthinking lack of co-operation between the Services in some matters, but this was ludicrous. I'd have liked to know the type of gas in it. Incendiary bullets, De Wildes, tracer, all had failed to ignite it and eventually after over 1500 rounds expended, the thing had slowly sagged down into the sea and flopped about like a huge jellyfish.

May 18th, Sortie 168:   Engaged my first E/A with cannons! Tony Lee Knight and I caught a couple of 109's off Gris Nez and blew large hunks off them but they escaped in low cloud.

'You've completed over 180 hours, Spud, 173 sorties. You are getting stale so I'm sending you off. What would you like to do?'

The idea of being an instructor at some God-forsaken OTU appalled me. Group had been canvassing squadrons for experienced pilots to join a new unit now being formed and it sounded like fun.

even if it meant flying Hurricanes. The Merchant Ship Fighter Unit was being assembled at Speke, near Liverpool. The idea was supported by Churchill and entailed merchant ships being fitted with catapults on which obsolete MK1 Hurricanes were mounted. When a Hun reconnaissance bomber approached a convoy, the Hurribird would be shot off to fight it. The Jerries would shadow convoys radioing the position, so submarines could converge and attack.

Hundreds of thousands of tons of vital shipping was being sunk – and the position was desperate. For the Hurricane pilot the position was pretty desperate too – he had three choices after being launched – having dealt with the Hun he could (1) fly to the nearest land if within his range, (2) crash land on the sea, or (3) bale out into the sea. But the rewards! I couldn't imagine a more fantastic experience – fancy getting a huge four-engined bomber in front of you! And of course, there were the trips to the States! What I hadn't thought of were the hours of deadly monotony once beyond the German plane's range, and the fact one would be standing still in so far as squadron seniority and promotion was concerned.

Speke was a pretty barren sort of place and Liverpool dour with bomb damage. The MSFU pilots turned out to be a motley crowd of characters, mostly RAF bolstered with Fleet Air Arm types. Those pilots who had not flown Hurricanes were sent off to familiarise themselves with the type and returned in two dramatically different frames of mind. The Fleet Air Arm blokes, used to outdated, sluggish naval machines, were ecstatic; excited, happy, The Spitfire boys dismayed at the 'tired birds'.

Next, we were all sent off to Farnborough to do a familiarisation flight in Fulmars preparatory to being catapulted. The Fulmar was like a midget Fairey Battle – another old gentleman's plane, heavy and underpowered. I did 35 minutes droning around, felt I had it taped and landed. The mechanics wheeled it to the catapult which was set on a concrete pad on the edge of the 'drome.

This catapult was something new – it wasn't steam-powered – it had over a dozen rockets mounted under a sled on which the plane was poised. Behind the unit was a blast shield, protection from the rocket discharge. On a merchant ship, protection was by concrete pads bolted to the bridge.

'It's a great feeling! Bit of a shock at first – there's this helluva bang! You'll see a glare out of the corner of your eyes and next thing, you've browned out. Can't see a thing! But you can think OK, and in a few seconds, you can see again and you're staggering off and flying.'

Sounded quite cheerful.

'Whatever you do, don't pull the stick back. Just hold it loosely and it's OK.'

I sat in dread while clankings and fiddlings went on behind and under the Fulmar.

'OK – set your flaps, run up to full revs, lock your throttle open, check your magnetos. All OK, then raise your hand. Soon as you're ready drop your hand onto the stick and lean back against the head rest. Three seconds later we shoot you off.'

Dumbly I nodded. Bloody fool, I thought, what in hell did I take this on for? It could only get worse!

The instructor scuttled away to hide behind the blast wall as I started the motor and followed instructions. The plane shook and roared away. No rev drop so, with trepidation at the unknown, I raised my hand, leaned back and stared fixedly along the engine cowling through the blurring propeller disc and lowered my arm.

One – two – three – BLAM! A great reflection of orange flame; pressure forcing me back, back – three and a half g's, a roaring and huge sensation of movement.

Vision faded in a brown mist. Too late I remembered not to grip the stick hard and as we cleared the catapult the nose climbed and the aircraft waffled. Quickly pushing the stick forward, I braced myself for the coming prang. WHUMP! The wheels hit the grass and we bounced into the air like a stag and staggered off! On landing the instructor drew me aside.

'Not bad – not good. Tell the others to go off for half an hour while we get the undercart checked out.'

Feeling pretty self-conscious and foolish, I tottered over to the others waiting initiation.

'Cor blimey!' was all I could say to cheer them.

While waiting for the Fulmar's check-out we wandered over to where Boffins sat in the sun. There were deck chairs and civilian waiters, tea and biscuits. There didn't seem to be any sense of urgency – just a leisurely life-style. I had foolishly imagined frantic activity – everything in top gear, slide-rules and formulae. After all this *was* Farnborough, one of Britain's most prestigious development facilities.

Sadly disillusioned, perhaps without real justification, we wandered back to the catapult and the now ready fighter.

Wing Commander Louis Strange, the OC Training Flight, was an amazing chap. As a young fighter pilot in WWI he had tried to replace an empty Lewis gun magazine in a dog-fight. While wrestling with the jammed drum his Martinsyde scout rolled over, his harness broke and he fell out of the cockpit to be left dangling clutching the drum and praying it would stay stuck.

By struggling and kicking at the joystick, he managed to right the plane and slide back into his cockpit!

Years later, after the fall of France in the present conflict, Strange flew an abandoned unarmed Hurricane back from France to the UK. He had never flown an advanced high-speed fighter before and, driving off attacking Messerschmitts with feint attacks, reached home safely.

Two months short of his fiftieth birthday, in the first launching from Speke, Strange rocketed off in a Hurricane. And now he addressed us as a combined group of Naval and Air Force personnel on a very secret and important matter.

'You chaps have to form yourselves into teams of two, or, if you include the servicing airmen, teams of six. I suggest you don't rush into pairing up. Take your time and pick someone with whom you can be friends. You'll be a long time in close contact – even up to three months on some of the longer-hauls. You Navy deck officer types have been posted to this unit – perhaps not what you wanted but I know you'll fit in with your pilots who are all volunteers. This is an important job – air attacks on our convoys by long-range bombers and the shadowing by Focke Wulf Condors are causing heavy losses. This is one method by which we can drive off or discourage the Huns.'

Going further, the silver-haired Wing Commander, laid down the training schedules, the do's and don'ts for the MSFU and outlined what we could expect in the days ahead.

Some strange and exciting things began to happen – we were fitted out with civilian clothing for wearing ashore in neutral countries.

Passports were issued with our description as merchant seamen, assistant pursers and the like. Binoculars for the fighter director Officers and wrist watches for the pilots. Odd people came and went and rumours ran riot.

Speke mess was based at the old Liverpool Civil Airport. Comfortable, with good dining facilities and a well-stocked bar, the mess was home for a continuously changing mixture of Fleet Air Arm and Air Force pilots and Naval deck officers. We were allowed the unusual privilege of entertaining civilian guests providing they surrendered food coupons.

The 'drome's perimeter and gates were guarded by airmen carrying pikes. Pikes! It was unbelievable that small arms were in such short supply that men had to be equipped with spears of wood with sharp metal tips.

It was 6th June, a grey, foggy day and all flying was cancelled. We sat around the mess yarning, reading or just snoozing in comfort. Playing snooker, my new FDO and I had a few pre-lunch pink gins. He had been pestering me to take him up – he had never been flying before.

At about two o'clock the sun came out and, feeling very cheerful, I 'requisitioned' the CFI's Tiger Moth. He jealously monopolised the thing almost as if it were his own. On seeing it careering around the 'drome doing hairy low-level aerobatics, he rang the duty pilot. Enraged, he ordered the DP to ground me on my return. Landing, to get rid of my FDO, now green and puking, I was about to taxi to the dispersal when the DP rushed over and shouted, 'Take me up, Spud!'

Happy as larks we trundled away.

I don't remember much of the rest of the day – just some startling impressions of a great mansion, lawns, a great tree and running figures. I remember the tearing and rending of the smashed starboard wing folding back. And, later, coming to in an ambulance with a still figure on the adjacent stretcher.

The next two weeks were spent in hospital with minor concussion and chemical burns to my left shoulder. Benzine had drenched it. It was a miracle we hadn't been incinerated. I was taken back to Speke under armed guard. Court martial tentatively set for 25th July. One of my friends was detailed off to be my escort and we took it in turns to wear his revolver. At first, I was not unduly perturbed –

19th, July, 1941.

TO:- The President of the Court

FROM:- Wing Commander Malan, D S O., D.F.C.,
R A F Station Biggin Hill.

This is to state that Pilot Officer R.
Spurdle was under my command as a Pilot in 74 (F) Squadron
for Six Months during which time he completed over two hundred
hours operational Flying.

He proved himself to be an exceptionally
keen pilot, full of fighting spirit and was involved in only
one accident which was due to a faulty undercarriage
necessitating landing with undercarriage retracted.

During this time he was credited with eight
Victories - Four confirmed and four probables - and
several damaged.

I am of the firm opinion that a lenient
attitude in his case would benefit the Service as a whole
and would serve as a valuable lesson to the Pilot
concerned.

A. G. Malan

A copy of the testimonial to the court written by Sailor Malan with (opposite) his
covering letter to me, and a testimonial from Squadron Leader Green.

R A F Station,

BIGGIN HILL KENT.

20th. July, 1941.

Dear *Spurdle*,

I enclose herewith a testimonial to hand
to the President of the Court when your case comes up for
trial, I deeply regret that I was unable to send it to you
before but the delay has been occasioned by my having been
absent from this Station on leave.

I enclose herewith also a copy of the
original testimonial for your information.

Sincerely,

Aismaler

PS. *Good luck.*

From:- Squadron Leader C.P. Green.

To:- Officer Commanding R.A.F. Station, Speke.

Date:- 22nd July, 1941.

Ref:- Tactics/10/41

General Court Marshal of Pilot Officer
R.L. Spurdle

Pilot Officer Spurdle was under my command in 91
Squadron immediately prior to his posting to M.S.F.U. having
come to me from 74 Squadron. I found him to be an efficient
and capable pilot and he was well disciplined both in the air
and on the ground. He appeared to have had above the average
experience as a pilot in a fighter squadron during which he had
destroyed four enemy aircraft and probably two others.

G. Green.

Squadron Leader

court-martialled pilots were two-a-penny – almost a club. But the
DP's injury made me feel sick inside; it was my fault and it was a
canker constantly in my thoughts.

'Come on, Spud! It was his own fault! He was ordered to ground
you by the CFI – not get you to take him up!' The Air Force was not
going to punish him – the loss of his left foot deemed punishment
enough.

I wrote to Sailor for a testimonial; I'd need all the help I could get.
He responded magnificently. Wing Commander Strange was
marvellous, personally burning our bar-chit books so no suggestion
of drink would come up.

It's happened! The rumours are true. Hitler has invaded Russia!
The idiot corporal has started a second front; the cardinal error that
has been the downfall of so many would-be conquerors in the past.
Now it is not just the British Empire against Germany and her allies,
but another huge and potentially powerful nation.

The only doubts we have about our new allies is their ability to
withstand the onslaught of such an efficient war-machine as the
Wehrmacht. Russia's performance against the little Finnish Army
had been pathetic and their invasion of Poland, a callous
stab-in-the-back, made us distrust the Communists as allies. But at
least these campaigns showed they had no false illusions about
Germany's ultimate objectives and had fought them as pre-emptive
strikes to establish buffer zones against the Huns.

The Russian Bear proved a strange and secretive ally. There were
so many simple and practical ways they could have speeded up the
destruction of Hitler's Germany – such as providing aerodromes for
use by RAF fighter and bomber squadrons. It was a practical
concept to fly bombing missions to targets beyond our normal range,
land in Russia, refuel and rearm and on the return flight to the UK
do another bombing sortie. After endless negotiations the Russians
reluctantly agreed and three 'dromes in poor condition were made
available for a period.

Merchant and Royal Navy seamen, exhausted from the dreadful
Murmansk convoy runs, were not allowed ashore to recuperate or be
billeted out of danger from Hun bombers attacking their ships in
harbour.

Continuous carping by Stalin for a second front was hopelessly premature. But the Russians' only concern was for themselves and this was horribly demonstrated later in the war when Polish patriots rose in Warsaw in a coordinated uprising when the Red Army drew close. The Russians then deliberately hung back until the unfortunate Poles were decimated and destroyed before continuing with their advance. This effectively killed off Huns at no expense to themselves but the real bonus was that Polish leaders and future possible thorns in Communist flesh were thus disposed of neatly.

July 25th, 1941: The day of my court martial arrived. It was a solemn and, for me, a frightening affair. I heard of some antics which surprised me, my memory completely blank over much of the episode. One of the witnesses was a gardener from Speke Hall where we'd crashed.

'Sor, he wor very unlucky! He hit the tallest tree in the park!'

'Yes,' rejoined the prosecuting officer, 'but at the lowest branch!'

Verdict! The Court found him (Spurdle) guilty of the charge and sentenced him to take rank and precedence as if his appointment as pilot officer was dated 20th October 1940, and to be severely reprimanded.'

'Clot!' my CO said. And so, chastened, I was marched out and back to my interrupted duties.

My FDO had gone, part of another's crew, and he was replaced by Sub-Lieutenant Charles Moreby. He was a good bloke and we became friends.

I ferried my Hurricane to Abbotsinch in Scotland to supervise its loading onto our CAM ship – a frightening experience as I had to sit in the cockpit and retract the undercarriage before the machine was lowered onto the catapult. The lifting wire looked as slender as a spider's thread and, as we slowly rose, twisting sixty feet up, some fool dropped a heavy pulley-sheave which hit the tailplane jerking the joystick forward to smash instrument panel glass giving me a fearful fright!

However, my fitters and riggers repaired the damage OK and I entrained back to Speke with my crew. We embarked on the *Eastern City* when it joined the gathering convoy off Merseyside – destination America!

The next couple of days were spent checking and storing the pile of aircraft spares; tools and ammunition and supervising the arming of the rocket sled as we ploughed along in convoy.

Escort vessels took up their constant circling and land-based fighters flew on patrol for the days we were within range of their aerodromes. Soon as we were beyond their aid and from just before dawn to dusk we stood to. Every few hours the aircraft had its engine run and warmed up – poised and ready for instant take-off. I had to 'stand to' in full flying kit as on this ship I was the only pilot. Some had a 'spare' in case of fatigue or sickness.

After a few days the anticipation of a fantastic duel became dulled. Discouraged and bored, Chas and I stalked around the bridge and stared out at the long lines of merchant ships churning along. Each ship followed a splashing, leaping marker towed by the preceding ship. This way, in darkness or driving rain, formation was maintained.

Each convoy was limited to speed by that of the slowest ship. We ploughed along hour after miserable hour searching grey skies for the dreaded Condors. Nothing – and after a few days we were beyond their range and were 'stood down'. Having been signed on as ship's crew to comply with International Law (we were, after all, serving members of HM forces and therefore liable for internment in neutral countries) we now were required to stand regular ships' watches. This hadn't been explained to me and for a time there was a clash with the ship's master.

Halifax was cold! We went ashore by ship's launch which pushed aside thin crunching sea-ice. Our cold-weather gear helped little to keep out the freezing wind. 'Halifax is the World's arse-hole!' said Captain 'Black' Meak as we stepped ashore onto a jetty slippery with hoar frost. Actually we found it quite fun but then we were just passing through.

Chas and I discovered the Green Parrot and found we could 'buy a Drunk, not a drink' as a local aptly put it. The crazy liquor law barred solitary drinks – one bought a full bottle and mixers. We settled down to a heavy session of Canadian Club and coke and got legless. We visited the cemetery where some of the victims of the *Titanic* disaster shared a mass grave. Also that of hundreds killed when an ammunition ship had blown up in the harbour in WWI.

I got in an hour and a half's flying from the local RCAF station

Dartmouth in an MSFU Hurricane just to keep my hand in. On landing, wandering about, I entered a hangar. In a dark corner, covered with dust, stood a Hurricane cannibalised for spare parts. On the sides of the fuselage were emblazoned the gallant and brave words 'MacRobert's Reply'. For a long time I stood there in angry disbelief. Lady MacRobert had lost several sons in the RAF. For each one she had donated money for a new fighter.

And here was one of them! What unthinking insensitive, dull clod had chosen one of these? The least the god-damned engineer officer responsible could have done was to spray it over and advise the Air Ministry to choose another to bear such magnificent defiance.

Rejoining the ship we set off in the reformed convoy for New York some 600 miles south-east.

New York! What a fantastic sight after a year of blacked-out Britain! We steamed past the Statue of Liberty and Manhattan's fantastic sky-line.

The Hurricane's guns and ammo had long been cleaned, greased and stowed away – now was the time for civvies and passports to be brought out. Uniforms were folded carefully and tucked away in suitcases for smuggling ashore.

In New York we had a ball! While our ship was loaded, re-provisioned and a new convoy organised, Chas and I gathered up our airmen and taxied into a form of earthly paradise. Leaving the others to do their own thing, Chas and I found ourselves in the Harvard Club drinking Cuba-Libras and being commissioned as 'Honorary Colonels' in the 'Confederate Army'. We were taken to live stage shows and to my huge delight met in person Fay Wray – gorgeous! And even kissed Betty Grable–!

The General Manager of the New York Office of the Royal Exchange Insurance Co took me flying over New York in a Piper Cub. He insisted on demonstrating how slow the runty little thing could fly. As we sagged down and wandered among the jagged spires of Manhattan, I got the twitch properly – he'd only just got his licence!

I bought a little Bell and Howell 8/mm movie camera and lots of film – I could envisage all manner of exciting subjects.

Too soon we were recalled to the ship and the long slow slog over the Atlantic began again. This time we had over 250 tons of explosives (stored directly beneath my cabin!), a couple of great greasy tanks as deck cargo, plus crated aircraft. Once again, the long eye-watering watches day and night, once again the nagging fear of a torpedo's blast. There were four CAM ships in the convoy this trip.

The Hurricane was re-armed with its machine guns and the ammunition replaced; the rocket sled with its critical wiring checked out. We struck a horrid storm and driving spray sheeted across the plane. The wind was so fierce it forced the propeller around against the Merlin's compression and screwed the strong canvas covers into shreds! We looked at the sodden thing with distrust. Days of work by the airmen got it cleaned down and once again, on entering the danger zone, I donned Sidcot suit, Mae West and lucky scarf.

We had a few sinkings and the metallic crumpings of depth charges did little to cheer us up. Wreckage and a bloated body floated past. I became very conscious of the fortitude of these Merchant Seamen. Poor conditions – days, weeks of constant danger, and a horrid lingering death if the worst happened.

At last! We were stood down when shore-based fighters flew over to protect us. I had the armourer strip all the ammo from their panniers into which Chas and I stuffed our bottles of vodka and gin, bourbon and scotch, well wrapped with nylons. As we were to be shot off in Liverpool Bay, I decided there was not much sense in taking along the parachute so discarded it and filled the seat-well with more liquor cushioned with lingerie. Cartons of fags were tucked in odd corners. Captain Meak turned the ship into wind and after shaking hands with the ship's company, I climbed into the cockpit. With a huge roaring, a bang and flaring comet-tail, I shot off to turn and give the Eastern City a wizard beat-up. The day was grey with rain squalls and visibility down to about half a mile. I saw the flash of one of the other Hurricats take-off. Soon all four of us were nattering to each other and to Speke's tower.

At Speke airfield customs officers would be waiting and no way was I going to pay duty or have my goodies confiscated. Flying in the heavy mist at sea-level I made my way up what I thought was the Dee Channel but on nearly collecting a balloon cable anchored to a barge, I realised I was in Mersey water. After half an hour's dicing in the balloon barrage I threaded my way out crossing the low land to the Dee and into the Hawarden circuit.

Wing Commander Hallings-Pott DSO shook my hand warmly and I asked if I could leave my bulging parachute bag in his office for a few days. As I made the request, I stood a bottle of bourbon on his desk. We eyed each other in perfect understanding. He was a great sport and asked no questions.

A few days later I flew over from Speke and collected my loot.

Alec Lumsden, in one of the other machines landed at Sealand and so got his stuff ashore unmolested. The other two pilots, unfamiliar with the area, got themselves lost in the thick fog. Gerry North force-landed out of fuel in a field near Bangor and Norman Lee put down on a beach near Wallasey. By pure chance he had landed near an Ack-Ack battery. He asked the soldiers to drag his plane above high tide mark while he rang Speke for a recovery team. Alas! When he returned the tide had got his airplane – he'd forgotten to release the brakes and, grunt and heave as they might, the soldiers couldn't shift it.

This all caused a big stink and the unfortunate Lee was posted off leaving a thousand sodden fags for the soldiers to mourn over. No doubt his grog was confiscated!

Back at Speke things were much the same with the crews returning and departing, some new, some old faces. Training launches with the newly installed catapult caused deep rumbling booms and glares which never failed to get the adrenalin going. Ashore, the MSFU was pretty dynamic -- afloat boring, boring, boring. Already it was getting hard to entice pilots into the job. By the time I left the unit, the reward offered was a pilot officer's rings for a Sergeant pilot's chevrons. Chas and I practised our RT procedure and he vectored me around the local training area.

Most of August and all September had been wasted for me in some ways. Certainly, there had been wonderful moments and experience but I was losing squadron seniority and flying hours on this job. It was time to face facts, but I felt I owed the MSFU at least one more trip.

Chas and I embarked on the SS *Novelist* bound for Galveston and Houston in Texas. It was going to be a long haul. Once again standing-to from dawn to dusk, once again disappointment at no action.

Right in the middle of our convoy we had the Free French

submarine *Surcouf*. It was the world's largest, carrying a floatplane in a watertight 'hangar' and armed with two eight-inch guns. Its presence was cunning – should we be attacked by a surface-raider the convoy would scatter and the *Surcouf* submerge to engage the pocket-battleship by stealth. What worried me was the question of our Hurricane's role – no doubt a determined attack on the bridge would knock off a few Huns and break glasswork. But, providing we survived this adventure, there would be little chance of being picked up when fuel was exhausted.

At Galveston, with the *Novelist* moored alongside a dusty, gritty wharf, the entire crew was lined up for a 'short-arm' inspection. Not having experienced one before, this infuriated we land-lubbers. And to have to present our gear in full view of passing dock-workers was a pretty poor show. Well, it may have been a good show, but certainly in poor taste.

I think the port doctor must have been rabidly anti-British; he was also a sadistic bastard. I had a horrid boil throbbing away on my right index finger. To treat it he stood me behind the chief steward who clamped my arm under his. Held out firmly, my finger was lanced forthwith. Lucky the steward was a big man – I nearly took off!

Once more we smuggled our uniforms ashore and made our base the Jean Lafitte Hotel where I latched onto a stunning lift operator. When she rummaged around in her handbag for a card, I noticed a little chrome-plated automatic.

'What's that for?' I asked.

'It's a pretty rough town. Muggings and rape – you know – that kinda stuff!'

Dubiously I asked for a date and later, after her shift was over, we took a taxi to her flat.

'Have you got any rubbers?' she asked.

'No, I don't like them.'

'Well, you'll have to get some.'

This was a poser which I put to the driver. He considered it a while and said.

'I guess I can help out, buddy.'

We drove a few blocks out of our way, stopping outside his home.

Muttering something about not awakening his wife, he sneaked inside and, coming back a few minutes later, he remarked.

'If the old bat had caught me, it would have been curtains! She'd never have believed it!'

Considering the risk he'd run, he must have been a staunch Anglophile and I was indebted!

In our best blues we went exploring the old town and were taken in tow by a well dressed chap to a Rotary Club dinner. Fantastic. The local GM dealer stood up and offered us the use of the latest model Chevrolet sedan for our stay in Galveston.

'How about a licence? I've never driven on the right hand side before.'

'That's OK, fella! If you get stopped, just give me a call. I'm the Chief of Police!' This from another Rotarian.

'What if I kill someone?' I was a bit concerned.

'Just make sure he's coloured!' and everyone laughed.

Next day there it was – long, low and beautiful and full of gas. We ran the driver back to his huge showroom. It was a very generous gesture and when we left Galveston to go up to Houston our benefactor said;

'Call on my brother! He's the dealer in Houston!'

Once again, we had a shiny monster to tool around in.

The Galveston-Houston ship canal was surprisingly narrow and passing cargo ships seemed to be kept apart by the pressure from their bow-waves. Slowly we cruised for miles past farm lands, great industrial sites and the giant refineries of Texas city.

Our airmen, proud of their Hurricane, kept starting it up and running the motor. Eventually they flattened the battery and they had to be content to sit on the wings in the brilliant sunshine and wave to gaping bystanders on the canal banks.

In Houston, several USAAF officers came down to see the novel unit. They were very impressed with the legendary Hurricane and the strange rocket sled. Chas and I were invited to Ellington Field where we went for a flight in a Beechcraft AT7. On board were a group of embryo navigators fooling around and goofing off. Little did they realise the grave shortcomings of this branch of the American

Airforce. Poor navigational skills were to cost untold lives, lost gliders, lost bombers and on one notable occasion, a whole squadron of fighters wandered around and ran out of fuel and crashlanded in France or the Channel.

The pilot let me fly the machine for an hour and insisted I landed it although twins weren't my cup of tea and my landing a hairy thing.

It was 7th December and odd reports came over the radio newscasts. In between toothpaste ads etc, fragmentary bizarre references were made to Pearl Harbour, Hawaii and bombs being dropped. No one seemed to know what the hell was going on – it was hours before coherent statements were made by US Government officials and the full import of Japan's sneak raid was realised. The streets became largely deserted while people clustered around their radios. Bars were crowded; rumours rife.

Fantastic! Brilliant! Churchill declared war on Japan before the US! Unbelievable but true – he was a clever politician and with one bold stroke, anticipated the inevitable and tied in America as a full ally in Europe as well as the Far East.

Someone invited me to give a pep-talk to the soldiers at Fort Crockett. Addressing over a thousand excited men, all suddenly faced with the certainty of combat, was quite an experience. More than just a Limey flier, I represented, in the flesh, someone who had already clashed with the enemy. Full of rum and coke, teetering, I hope my exhortations were not too confusing. Shopping, I bought myself a gold Bulova watch, also some baby terrapins which I kept in the handbasin, much to Chas's disgust.

Novelist, full to the Plimsoll mark with a load of sulphur and ammunition and with dissembled Hudson bombers and General Grant tanks as deck cargo, cast off its mooring ropes and set off to New York and home. Christmas Eve: Chas and I stood at the ship's rail gazing out at Miami's glittering lights and the headlights of cars streaming along the freeways. We were pretty drunk and seriously considered jumping ship. We were so close, we could have swum ashore.

Again no joy! Not a sight of a Jerry bomber. Back in Speke I requested a posting back to 11 Group. While awaiting confirmation and travel warrants, I took up a Hurricane and beat up a friend's house, bringing out neighbours who may have been shaking fists at me or cheerily waving.

After a particularly steep pull-out, there was a loud bang! Something hit the kite on the tail plane. The machine started to shake and control became sluggish. Bloody Hell! What had happened? Throttling back, I limped slowly back to Speke, landed and taxied over to a maintenance hangar. The starboard side panel couldn't have been properly locked and had come off damaging the tail-unit. A complaint came through from the residents of Sandy Lane, the Liverpool suburb I'd visited, and under a small cloud, I was returned to Biggin Hill.

CHAPTER VII

'Black Section'

After much negotiation with a new-found friend in postings, I got myself back to 91 Squadron at Hawkinge. I was put in 'A' Flight commanded by another New Zealander, Flight Lieutenant Geoff Pannell with Squadron Leader Bob Oxspring as CO and Flight Lieutenant Frank Silk as 'B' Flight Commander. They were an excellent, happy team and under Oxspring, 91, the 'Jim Crow' Squadron, was tops.

Back to the scary shipping reconnaissance jobs and weather recces for daylight-bombing Balbos (named after Italian General Balbo who led some large peacetime formations). 91 had changed a lot as far as personnel were concerned. We were a cheerful bunch of characters; a mixture of British, Free French, Belgian, Canadian, Aussie, Irish, Kiwis and even a Yank. Our formation flying as a squadron was a joke but operating as sections there was not a squadron to touch us for all-round experience. In 91, I met Johnny Heap who was to become my best friend. Debonair, dashing and completely without fear, Heapo was to me the ideal fighter pilot. Together we flew in perfect accord, each anticipating the other's intentions.

On the ground the smooth Heapo could charm birds in a way which seemed incredibly easy. I started to copy his casual drawl and polished my manners. Our squadron doctor was another smoothie; an Irishman. Poor Heapo was having problems and had to be circumcised. He called for the Doc to take his bird out on his behalf.

'Don't you touch her, you bastard! She's mine! But I promised to take her to this show and you can stand in for me. Remember! No funny business!'

The next day Doc said to me with a wink, 'You know what she said to me, Spud? Platonic! Your play and my tonic!'

Poor Heapo.

We spent a few hilarious times during his convalescence telling him risqué stories trying to get him to pull his stitches. In pain the unfortunate sufferer would throw things at us to desist.

It was exhilarating to be back on ops! I had forgotten the strange mélange of dull moments or hours of boredom suddenly interlaced with hectic mayhem. Of frenetic activity, adrenalin pumping, things going bang! Or just fooling around with the chaps playing cards and snooker or getting ready for a night on the tiles.

91's role hadn't changed much in my absence – it was still sending out hourly shipping and weather recces. We still had no cameras. With air/sea rescue work and scrambles for aerodrome defence our lives were never dull. Fighter sweeps were continually being sent across France using small groups of bombers as bait to lure up German fighters. In this way pressure was taken off the Russians – as many of the best GAF squadrons had to be kept in the Pas de Calais and surrounding areas.

These sweeps were a nuisance to us entailing many tiresome hours patrolling over the channel identifying straggling aircraft or escorting damaged machines back home. But we were a very flexible squadron and if we got too bored with all this, and things were quiet, we could get Group's permission to swan off in pairs just to plague the Hun.

On 18th March (sortie 182) I had an extraordinary experience when on a shipping recce from Gris Nez to Zeebrugge. I'd just completed a dicey shipping count over the heavily defended port of Ostend and, still twitching, continued up the coast to Blankenberge on the Belgian coast. There was supposed to be a flak training school there and, remembering this, I turned away out to sea before setting course for home. Idiot! I should have been weaving because I heard a loud Zap! and for the blink of an eyelid saw a black disc shrink before me. Then there was the red flash and black smoke of an air burst.

I'd actually seen the shell as it passed within inches of my canopy, through the propeller's arc and, being on the same trajectory as my aircraft, momentarily visible before bursting dead ahead.

'Bullshit!' cried the boys back at base.

'Bullshit yourselves! I've seen something like it before! You fire a .22 at a white cloud and you can see the slug!' But they didn't believe it. Lady Luck had once again looked after me and to prove it I was promoted 'A' Flight Commander when Geoff got posted away on rest on 11th April 1942. It was for me a marvellous moment and feeling of fulfilment until I faced the board.

I'd forgotten the bloody board and the heavy responsibilities that it represented. As I sewed on my second broad rings, all that the position entailed came into focus. I was very conscious of the power invested in me – I would decide who flew and when. I would decide if the pilot concerned was fully capable of a particular job or when he should be sent out on his own at risk in the interest of his training and furthering of experience.

As a flight commander I could recommend (through the CO of course) that a chap needed rest, deserved a gong, should be posted as unsuitable and so forth. But the hardest part was to stand before the board, chalk in hand, and allot the days flying with its terrible risks to friends.

Let's not beat about the bush – the position could be grossly abused. I knew of flight commanders who enhanced the chances of ridding themselves of unwanted aircrew by giving them extra dangerous missions or an unfair share of them.

There and then I swore to myself that if I didn't care for a chap or if his flying was not to my liking and so a probable risk to others, then I'd have him posted elsewhere. My pilots could trust me and I them – with our lives.

My 'A' Flight was detached at Lympne aerodrome, a small satellite field just three miles from Hawkinge, our nominal base. It had been an aero-club before the war and to our huge glee we found that the underground fuel tanks had been locked and forgotten. We broke the locks, dipped the tanks and found them full of low-octane fuel, useless to our Service aircraft but perfect for our vehicles. Being untinted* it couldn't be detected by stains around our car's carburettors.

The best kept secret of the war, in my opinion, was the drawing off of this juice which, to my certain knowledge, was still going on in April 1944.

---

* Aircraft fuel was tinted green to aid in the detection of 'misappropriated' petrol. There was a continual struggle for petrol for our cars. Random checks were a serious hazard!

At Lympne we were quartered in the great mansion of the late Sir Phillip Sassoon, Under Secretary of State for Air. It was magnificent – a swimming pool, crushed brick tennis courts and even one extra special loo built like an armchair with a padded velvet seat! There were two old gardeners who pottered about trimming hedges and lawns.

As our operational hours crept up and we slowly grew tired, our sense of propriety blurred and our excesses became bizarre. We drank far too much and any excuse for fun would start a party or madcap escapade. Heapo and I developed a dangerous sport.

Donning our heavy sheep-wool goon-skins and steel hats, we'd position ourselves one at each end of a 50 yard lawn lined with high clipped hedges. As the sun set tiny bats would flit along from one end to the other catching moths. We'd try to shoot them. It called for a lot of skill as they jinked about and at the flash of a gun you'd duck your head. Pellets would hiss past or ping off harmlessly. But you couldn't afford to blink in case you missed that red flash!

One of our most popular pilots was 'Sammy' Hall, later to win the DFC and write a moving book, *Clouds of Fear*. He was a big chap and one hot day got well and truly plastered. He locked himself in an upstairs loo with a skeet gun and blasted a tray of drinks off the patio balustrade scaring a batman (who'd just put it down) and the rest of us almost rigid. Naked as Adam, Sammy climbed out the window and down the ivy which tore off in a great dusty mess. We grabbed the giggling monster and tossed him in the pool to sober up.

I encouraged a 'standing patrol' of off-duty pilots to scour the fields and woods for game. We needed to augment our miserable meat rations with rabbits and hares, pheasants, quail, pigeons. Sometimes a duck, hen or goose got clobbered and local farmers got a trifle tetchy.

One memorable night we took two of the cars out onto a gentle hillside overlooking Dymchurch. Using full headlights to chase rabbits, we were pretty merry when, pausing to drink up, we heard the clankings and creakings of tank tracks. There were shouted orders and the sound of jeep engines. Taking fright, we zoomed back to Port Lympne and hopped into bed, boots and all! How were we to know a large rubber inflatable had been found on Dymchurch beach that morning and the wire defences cut?

For aerodrome defence, the RAF regiment had some curious little Daimler armoured cars. They had dual controls so the vehicle could be driven from either end forward or backward. On really pouring wet nights when there was no chance of airborne enemy landings, the cars' crews were stood down. We found a way of jumping the ignition and used to take one pub crawling. We'd bait Army officers because as a breed, they were jealous of our war role and the fulsome newspaper coverage given air crew. They called us 'Blue Orchids' and we dubbed them 'Pongos.' Apart from the rare Commando raids and the thrashing our brown jobs were getting in the Middle East, they had nothing much to talk about. Just years of hard training to look forward to. We gave them hell until enraged they'd fall on us and, outnumbered, we'd retreat to the car, pull down the hatches and roar away laughing our heads off.

Just for fun, I insisted on forming 'Black' section which threw the controllers into a tizz. Sections were 'Red' or 'Blue' etc. As we were always 'putting up blacks' (misdeeds), I thought it appropriate.

It was a glorious spring and with the warmer weather the garden of Kent came to life. I loved this part of England. We were very busy and between 5th April and 26th May, I flew seventy-four sorties, covering the whole gamut of our duties. On the last day we had a panic scramble to search for and find Group Captain 'Batchy' Atcherley who'd got himself shot down into the channel. Unkind rumour had it he'd gone up alone and by radio challenged a Jerry to combat and been obliged. On 3rd June our new VB Spits arrived – these had slightly heavier armour but this was not what we wanted. We wanted cameras! It was ridiculous to expect us to count and identify ships in heavily defended harbours at over 300 miles per hour.

15th June: Sergeant Bill Sykes went missing on a recce to Dieppe. Damned shame – he was a very nice guy. Only bright thing about it was that I had his 'Ray Ban' sun-glasses on 'appro' and now inherited them.

The Jerries were sending over lone weather recce fighters in increasing numbers and it became a mania to catch them. Heapo and I would scramble and be vectored around by GCI (Ground Controlled Interception). We spent hours at it.

'A' Flight was recalled to Hawkinge and Port Lympne given to a Yank squadron! Sadly we packed our gear and flew off and away from our lovely, idyllic, carefree home. We settled into Reindene mess.

They sent us two Spitfire VI's – they had pressure cabins and could stagger around at over 42,000 feet. What earthly use were they to us? The hoods couldn't slide back but were clamped down over us on rubber seals; again no cameras so we didn't use them. Eventually they were replaced with standard V's.

At last! After nine scrambles hunting Hun recce machines, I got within 700 yards of one but it left me standing! Two more tries and no luck. The next time one found me, an FW 190, the first I'd seen – and in the ensuing dog fight an American from Tangmere horned in and jumped me and had a squirt which I answered, but missed. I really must go on a gunnery course!

July 15th, 1942:   A bad day. Flight Sergeant Campbell and Sergeant Clayton were shot down while spotting. Clayton was found and picked up but Cam was gone.

Damn! Bob Oxspring's leaving us to take over 72 Squadron from Brian Kingcome who is being promoted to Wing Co, Kenley. This is a real blow as Bob was a super CO and leader. It looks as if a fiery odd Frenchman who had been seconded to us will take his place. 'Moses' Demozay sported a 'Pancho Villa' black moustache, rarely smiled and left us much to ourselves. Billy Orr, who had replaced Silko as 'B' Flight Commander, and I really ran the squadron and Moses came and went alone on his mysterious way. One day on coming in to land at Hawkinge he was obstructed by a gang-mower and, erupting into a gallic rage, he fired a burst into the airfield near the tractor. The driver took off like a hare and the tractor wandered over to stall against some earthworks. We were all a little scared of Moses.

He wasn't our only problem – the Station Commander had gone around the bend and should have been invalided out of the Service. He'd jog around the perimeter at dusk for exercise. If the guards didn't challenge him, they'd be put on a 'fizzer' and if they did, they'd be verbally abused as fools for not recognising him. The unfortunate erks just couldn't win. Bob Oxspring had tried to protect his men but it was hopeless. It was some time before a 'trick cyclist' (psychiatrist) was called in and had the Wing Co repatriated back to Australia where he shot himself on Bondi Beach.

War's stresses and tensions affected everyone to a greater or lesser extent. One day we read of an aged gentleman who went down to a beach, wrapped himself in a Union Jack and blew his brains out. His farewell note explained it all. In effect he said, 'I am old, I'm useless, I'm another mouth to feed and brave men are dying on the Atlantic bringing food to such as me. This is the only way I can help my country.'

To us pilots, this extraordinary selfless act deserved something better than the Coroner's 'died by his own hand while the balance of his mind was disturbed.'

If this gallant old chap had received a posthumous award the beaches of England could have looked like another Dunkirk so perhaps the Coroner had something after all. His name was Corbett-Smith, an ex-Director of the BBC – like Captain Oates he deserved remembering and a place in our country's folk-lore.

July 22nd: Billy Orr's gone. Shot down by flak over Boulogne. This was a bitter pill – Billy was a great chap, close friend and an able flight commander.

July 25th: Got one! An Me 109 off Calais. I needed this – he seemed green or lost or stupid. No real fun – just flew up to him and zapped him down into the sea. He baled out too late, his chute not opening fully.

July 26th, Sortie No 347 – 30 minutes duration: 'Knobby' Clarkson had 1500 hours of flying experience as an instructor and I felt rather foolish leading him. Still, he was new to the game and there is only one way to learn air-fighting – the hard way. For days now we had flown as a team and tried to trap the Hun weather-recces which came across the Channel every evening. The Huns were keeping a close eye on the build-up of the Dieppe invasion fleet. On three occasions we had caught them; twice lone 190's and once a 109F. We called ourselves Black Section and the Jerries seemed to know us, because every time we were up and being vectored, the Hun radio warned their recce machines: '*Achtung!* British fighters near you!'

It was hot and hazy and Knobby and I were patrolling off Dungeness, waiting for the sweep squadrons to come back from Dieppe. Our duty was to scout for E/A's hanging around trying to pick off stragglers. We were at 3,000 feet and the haze thick and brown beneath us. Way off we could see the white wash from two high-speed rescue launches as they came to take up their positions off Dungeness point. The radio was silent and we settled ourselves down to the boring job. Up and down, from Hythe to Rye in a great arc, with Dungeness's sandy point as a pivot, just riding the haze screen and never above 5,000 feet – up above sudden death could strike, many of our boys had been jumped in the especially dangerous layer between 10,000 and 15,000 feet.

Back and forth, necks craning and eyes watering, continually searching the blue above and around us, the blazing heat of the midday sun beat down in great waves through our perspex hoods and we cursed the sweep and cursed the Huns. The deep purr of the Merlins was almost soporific. The high-speed launches drifted to a stop, their yellow decks lying flat against the cool green of the Channel. By now the beggars were fishing and sunbathing; it must have been rather a pleasant war for them, I imagined.

Hullo – there were four planes way up against the opaque sky – about 8,000 feet, I guessed. They passed overhead and away to starboard. We were heading east in line abreast, and they west in line astern – only our planes hadn't flown that formation for a year!

'Hey, Black Two, do you see those aircraft above at five o'clock? What are they?' It was curious.

'Dunno – they're not Spits,' came the reply, clear and smooth.

'OK. We'll have a look; turning to starboard.'

We turned in a gentle climb. Knobby got busy in his office as I advanced the throttle and had a quick glance around the taps. opening the radiator and putting on fine pitch. Away above, the four aircraft circled round and came back, dropping slightly. They had seen us and were interested.

I called up Ops. 'Black Leader, Angels Four Dungeness. Are there any Bandits near us?'

Ops didn't even bother to answer. We were just stooges and the sweep boys were having all the fun; probably Ops were very busy with the dozen or so squadrons away to our south.

The four strange kites circled above us in the same starboard turn. I couldn't make out what they were and we reached about 5,000 feet before I got a clear view.

Christ! 190's! 'Tally Ho!'

Knobby slid into line astern without being told and I got in a hell of a flap. Gun sight on – lower the seat down a notch. For a shameful second, I weighed the chances but kept on climbing, turning with them and calling Ops.

'Tally Ho! Tally Ho! Black Leader calling, Black Leader calling. We are engaging four 190's three miles south Dungeness. Angels Five. Over.' No answer. I was hoping for support.

The Huns were now only a few hundred feet above. Still no answer. I pushed the throttle through the gate and the Merlin snarled and belched brown smoke.

I could see their squat radials and stiff wings – their shiny perspex hoods and neat rudders. Clean and fierce-looking, their camouflage bluey-grey with black spinners – Knobby's first real fight – I began to sweat and then suddenly felt strangely detached and calm. It was like a fanciful dance – we had our moves.

The Hun leader peeled off – over and over he tilted his plane; now he was clearly visible as he hurtled down from above, his No 2 following close on his tail.

'Turning port!' I shouted and heaved 'K' around. The Hun leader flashed past and I got a snap shot at his No 2. Knobby broke to starboard and I saw the second Hun leader with his No 2 pass above and away.

It was easy to see Jerry's game; we were each to be attacked by a Rotte of two and it was just too bad if we made a mistake. I worried for Knobby but he seemed to be doing OK and was already on the tail of his Hun's No 2. My two playmates zoomed up half a mile away in a climbing turn; it is going to be a head-on attack and I laughed to myself. Jerry No 2's aren't supposed to fire, they are merely stooges to watch their leader's tails and tricks and to pick up the idea of the game. A head-on attack! I laughed again. Malan had been my teacher.

Down they came – two black specks streaming thin brown trails to stain the blue behind. I throttled back, drew a bead on the leader and gave a short burst at some 400 yards. I jinked and gave the second 190 a squirt. The guy's a clot, following his leader much too closely. He jinked violently as my guns flamed, but his leader was made of sterner stuff and never wavered as he flashed beneath me.

Before the second Hun began to break to port, I whipped K over on her side and heaved back the stick. 'K' shuddered – it was just above stalling point and, opening up, I roared after the last Hun.

The leader didn't seem in a hurry to turn but his No 2 was in a flap and weaved violently. Below me Knobby raked the second leader with a shrewd burst. I saw a cannon shell explode on the 190's shiny armoured nose and another blow a cloud of fragments from a wing.

'Did you see that!' Knobby shouted.

Wavy grey patterns from the tracers hung lifeless in the air and far below two white feathers ruffled the channel. The launch boys had stopped their fishing.

My Hun section was turning fast and to avoid over-shooting I chopped the throttle and went into full fine pitch. I could just get a shot at the second Hun. I followed him round, the dot fair on his cockpit, then I tightened the turn. For an instant his black spinner hung steady against 'Ks' nose. I pressed the gun-button and the machine guns spluttered way out on the wings while the cannons thumped and coughed.

Not enough deflection. 'K' heaved around tighter and tighter. My vision browned with partial blackout and my hands grew heavy on the stick. The 190 was somewhere below me but I held the button down for a half-second then eased up. The second Hun whipped from under my nose and, chasing his leader, was off and away. They were going much too fast and slid up above, stall-turning for another attack. I couldn't overtake them – so far I had been trying to gain height and face them head-on.

Here they came again. I pressed the button and the cannon's thudding drowned the machine gun's splutter. The leading Hun dipped, lifted. Suddenly a white cloud burst down its fuselage; his tail tore off and, dragging, whipped at the end of a tangle of cables. God! Hit his oxygen bottles! Blown his bloody tail off!

He flashed by, tumbling, falling nose over, and my heart pounded madly.

'Christ! I've blown the bastard to pieces!'

His No 2 turned out to one side and we circled, watching the flaming wreck hurtling down. Red flames in long streamers trailed back, then a white saucer appeared – the pilot was out. Both his No 2 and I circled around the slowly descending chute, then simultaneously pulled ourselves together.

I opened up 'K's' Merlin and whipped the pitch to full fine. 'K' roared into full life and the second Hun saw me coming and took off in a long power dive to the deck. I couldn't close on him, so gave him quick squirts of machine gun fire to make him weave; to slow him up. The tracers' white smoke unnerved him and he twisted first one way then the other. Now and again I gave him a squirt of cannon and saw some strikes, but suddenly the port gun stopped and 'K' slewed as the starboard's cannon recoil heaved off her target. Out of ammo. I looked around for Knobby – no sign of him. The high-speed launches creamed madly out to sea. My Hun would be picked up. I throttled back; no use tearing 'K's' guts out for a miserable stooge already out of machine gun range.

God! Four more 190's – away up above me – about 15,000 feet! I half rolled and dived for the deck. The brown haze closed around me like a cloak and, flattening 'K', I skimmed the wave-tops. Soon Folkestone's cliffs loomed out of the murk and, lifting up and over the sunny town, I dropped down on Hawkinge. I circled the drome and tested flaps and undercarriage. Everything okay. I couldn't see any holes and didn't think I'd been hit. Sometimes you don't hear a machine gun hit if you're excited or if your cannons are banging away.

Thank Heavens! Knobby's down before me, safe, his kite with a swarm of the boys around it. The bowser was there, pumping away, and the armourer's truck was being unloaded. I did a victory roll, then felt ashamed, just a horrible line-shooter.

Wheels down, flaps down, change pitch and a crude bumpy landing; of course, that *would* spoil it!

'K' coughed to a stop, the cooling exhaust stacks creaked, then the quiet English air flooded soft and warm over us. For a wonderful moment, 'K' and I breathed together, relaxing before the laughing boys surrounded her. The Spy arrived, excited – had already got the gen from Group.

'They've picked up your Hun, Spud! They're taking him to Dover Hospital!'

'Do you think we could see him?' I wanted to savour in full measure this victory. Our Spit V's were vastly inferior to the Focke Wulf 190's and we'd been outnumbered 2 to 1.

'I'll try. See you in the mess,' and Spy was off to the nearest phone.

Knobby and I checked our kites for holes and armament stoppages. Our ground crews were very bucked. The erks had little real excitement other than that vicariously generated by their pilots' efforts.

The Spy returned in triumph with a car. It was hard to winkle transport from MT officers; they were obstinate, uncaring brutes and as a species we pilots detested them.

At the hospital the Section IO, briefed us before we were allowed to meet the Hun pilot. His name was Horst Benno Kruger, holder of the Iron Cross 1st and 2nd class, Goering's bronze medal etc. On him, apart from letters and odds and ends, eleven photographs of himself and three packets of condoms were found. He was a *Schwarme* leader of some experience, in the Richthofen squadron, having shot down seventeen of our aircraft. The Spy had told him his three comrades were dead and that if he wanted his people to know he was OK, he'd have to cooperate or be held incommunicado for some time. He talked!

Kruger was a big fellow, well over six feet, bulky, blond and full of bull. He had only a pricked pride and a broken small toe. As Knobby, tall, goodlooking and in his best blue uniform came into the ward, Kruger heaved up from his pillow, all smiles and with outstretched hand.

'Congratulations!' he cried, embarrassing Knobby, who turned to let me, scruffy, short and balding, come forward. The look on Kruger's face infuriated me. The bumptious oaf! His performance in the air hadn't impressed me and I got malicious pleasure at his obvious discomfiture at being bested by such an insignificant-looking opponent.

Bit by bit more information was gleaned by the IO's shrewd conversation. The unfortunate Hun, being a big-head, had all manner of papers on him which, when dried out, were invaluable Even his Mae West, borrowed for this flight, had its owner's name on it, which proved of use in future trick interrogations. Knobby and I were very impressed by the information gleaned, and on return to Hawkinge we reiterated to the assembled pilots the importance of not carrying any sort of papers whatsoever and giving only name, rank and number, if caught.

That night at Biggin Hill, there was a momentous thrash, for on this day the 900th Hun aircraft had been destroyed by pilots from Biggin and its satellite 'dromes.

One of three pilots could have been responsible; Flight Lieutenant H. Armstrong, Pilot Officer R. C. Kitchen, or myself.

To my intense disgust, no advice of this party was passed on to 91 at Hawkinge which hurt as there is nothing so good as free grog and, after all, at least we had a real live Hun to prove our claim.

*

'Spud. I have some news – prepare for a shock. I don't know how you'll take it.' Spy speaking.

'Shoot,' I said.

'That Kruger fellow claims he shot down two Spitfires on the 15th. They could have been Cam and Curly.'

'Jesus! Did he say anything about the fight?'

'Yes, He said they both jumped OK!'

'Shit! I knew that air-sea search was half-hearted! Cam could have been OK! God damn it! I wish I'd killed the fat prick!'

But it was long over now and shaking my head in distress, I felt the bitter helplessness of irreversible fate.

*

The 28th July was pretty busy for me even by 91's standards. Firstly out spotting for an hour and ten minutes, then a recce to Dieppe of forty minutes, then a scramble with lots of haring around but no contact with E/A – that took over an hour. In the evening Knobby and I went on patrol and caught the weather recce machine – a FW 190 which we severely damaged. There was intense Hun air-sea rescue radio traffic and so Knobby and I took off again to look for our Hun whom we assumed to be down off Calais. The dusk beat us and we returned home in disgust.

On the 30th, we searched for and found, five of our fighter pilots in the Channel and we had the shit shot out of us by our own ack-ack from Dover to Folkestone! One of our air-sea rescue launches was attacked by two cheeky 109's just off Dover and there were eight of our Spits plus two Defiants circling in protection!

August 3rd. Operational Sortie 363: Knobby and I caught two Hun weather recce 109 F's. We damaged both of them. Pilot Officer Wildish of 'B' Flight went missing.

There's something being cooked up! Why all these Hun recce machines? I've tried nineteen times to date and only managed to damage two for all my efforts. They are just too fast for our old VB's. The 190's leave us for dead.

August 14th. Operational Sortie 372: On recce to Ostende with Sergeant O'Shaughnessy (Shag) we came on two tugs and six barges off Dunkirk. We gave the tugs a fearful pasting by boring in to almost point blank range and ignoring the streams of flak.

On the 18th, I found eleven Hun sailors and one officer huddled on a raft. The officer at one end and the others all facing away. We sent out a minesweeper to within seven miles of Calais to collect them. That night Spy gathered us up and we were all briefed on what was to turn out to be a disaster but a necessary one.

To test the Jerry defences and the practicability of seizing a French port for the inevitable invasion, a huge 'raid' was mounted. Now we knew why the Jerries had sent over so many recces – they'd been observing the build-up of landing craft gathering in our southern ports.

A Wingco from Group came down to brief us. Squadron Leader Demozay had been posted and, as senior flight commander, I was acting CO. Along with the Defiant, Lysander and Walrus flying boat ASR crews our pilots were assembled for our instructions.

'Tomorrow we are launching a big raid on a French port. The plan is to try and seize it and hold it for about twenty-four hours. We then will make an orderly withdrawal. One day the invasion must take place to dislodge the Hun. With this raid we can learn a lot about Hun defences and our tactics for the future.'

So will the Germans, I thought.

'I suggest you all get a very early night – you'll all be up long before dawn. There will be about ten thousand soldiers and sailors involved and we expect a big German reaction both in the air and on the ground. 91's role will be recces to look out for German naval ships – we expect 'E' boats out in force. You will have to cope with lots of ditched aircrew and defensive patrols covering the withdrawal.'

Then the Wingco said an extraordinary thing –

'The Canadian Army have been getting extremely stroppy and impatient for action so they will be providing the bulk of the ground troops.'*

At dawn I took off for the vital Cape Gris Nez to Ostende recce and to my surprise (and theirs) flew right over and through a convoy of two 1,500 ton coasters, a large 5,000 ton cargo-ship supported by ten flak ships. There was only one thing to do – I dropped right down to twenty feet off the sea and flew directly through the flotilla. In firing at me, the Huns splattered each other! I got in some heavy bursts at a couple of flak ships, did a 180° turn and hared back to base to report. Five hairy trips and the day was over. The worst one was to Le Havre in the afternoon with E/A all over the place. Purely by accident I found an airman in the drink who turned out to be one of ours – Chas Evans, who'd had to bale out after his engine packed up.

August 20th: Pilot Officer Eddie Tonge has been shot down and lost in the Somme area.

August 21st: Pilot Officer Le Maire got shot up pretty badly but managed to crash land on Hawkinge OK.

The Dieppe raid was over. An expensive exercise. But it did pave the way for the ultimate invasion and success by the use of artifical harbours instead of the projected taking and using of French ports.

Heapo got a Dornier 24 flying boat near Dieppe and is unbearably chuffed, the lucky sod!

* About 5,000 Canadians were involved, about 1,000 British and approximately 50 US Rangers. These US troops were the first to face the Hun in Europe. About 50% of all our forces were either killed or captured.

August 24th: Today I had a letter from 'Reddy' Riske, one of my Harvard Club cronies in New York. He's with the US Army near Cheltenham, a captain in logistics. I got myself clamped into a Spit VI and flew up for a cheerful reunion. Next day, nursing a throbbing head, I droned back towards Hawkinge. After about twenty minutes I found myself being pushed over towards one side of the cockpit by a big shining rubber tube which ballooned larger and larger until it exploded, scaring me rigid. A lot of my instruments packed up and I looked for an aerodrome – anywhere to put down as dusk was falling. I found a bomber airfield and flopped down in the dark. After much hassling, an erk unclamped my hood and I made my way to the gloomy mess. The bombers were on a mission and the place almost deserted. A WAAF escorted me to a bedroom and, bouncing the mattress, remarked, 'Haven't slept in this one yet!'

Next morning at breakfast the starkness and tension of a bomber outfit appalled me. There had been heavy losses and, consequently, many empty seats at the dining tables. They may have had better fringe benefits but give me fighter messes any time!

Back at base, the engineer officer examined my Spit and muttered something about a blocked relief-valve in the cockpit pressuring system.

Our parties grew more uninhibited as our op hours increased. We slept less through fatigue than from a surfeit of alcohol. We got reckless as if there wasn't going to be a tomorrow, indeed our chances of survival were purely academic – we knew that sooner or later we'd buy it and so we drank and partied the nights away with almost desperate abandon.

One of my pilots turned back complaining of engine problems on two consecutive flights. The mechanics began muttering and the engineer officer reported that the aircraft appeared sound. I had a word with the pilot who assured me he was OK, so I sent him off on another French Coast recce. Back he came after about ten minutes complaining of RT failure. The radio was checked out OK so I got the Squadron Doctor to interview the chap.

'He's had it, Spud. I think his nerve has gone. It's up to you now.'

'No way! Too many others depend on squadron morale. I'll advise the CO he's LMF.'*

So without fuss, he was sent away. I didn't know whether to scorn or be sorry for him. 91 pilots had a particularly hard role in the air war.

One day I had to fly up to Biggin Hill and was horrified at the extraordinary sight of five pranged Spitfires tipped over on their noses. They were machines loaned to the recently arrived USAAF 307th Pursuit Group. Back at Hawkinge I tried to describe the scene.

'It looked like a bloody dart board! There were machines and marker flags all over the place! Guess what a Yank said to me – Spitfires' undercarriages are too weak!'

Sure, Spits' 'undercarts' were light – what use were they once the plane was airborne? They, along with starter motors, were just so much dead weight to be lugged around and decrease performance. What was wrong was that the Americans had been flying P39 Airacobras with the new tricycle undercarriages. And other aircraft built like brick lavatories.

However, the Yanks, on learning how to fly their steeds like jockeys and not like farm hands enthused so much about the Spit's performance that they precipitated a Congressional Hearing in Washington, and US General 'Hap' Arnold was sent to Biggin to 'learn the score'. The Airacobras were relegated to coastal defence work out of range of Hun fighters which would have eaten them for fun.

Shortly after the influx of American troops became a flood, Mr Churchill tried, without success, to get the American GIs' wages on a parity with those of the British Tommy. The idea was to lessen the build-up of resentment and tension engendered between the forces.

The prices of small luxuries became grossly inflated putting our service men and women at a grave disadvantage. Mr Churchill's suggestion was that the GIs' extra pay could be withheld in a lump sum for their return to the USA.

But the Yanks would have none of it and the rift widened until our forces, instead of being comrades, split into two separate camps.

---

* Lack of moral fibre – a serious charge and not taken lightly. I saw only two cases of this in six years which involved British Air Crew.

Even more contentious was the fact that US soldiers, without having heard a shot fired in anger, stepped ashore in the UK already wearing two medal ribbons. This was hard for our old sweats, veterans of battles on the continent and the privations and bombings of two years of war, to take. After months of mutterings, the British issued little gold stripes, each one representing six months of service.

August 27th, 1942: Demo is dead – he baled out off Hastings but received head injuries probably from hitting the tailplane. Count Jules de Molene had been my room-mate for almost six months.

In anger, mourning our friend, Heapo, Knobby and I really got on the plonk and were soon anaesthetized. It was a pouring wet night and we picked up three exceedingly willing WAAF's. When the pubs shut there was nowhere to take them except back to Reindene Mess.

'Let's sneak them in – everyone's in bed and we can get them out early,' I suggested.

About four days later we were in big trouble – Heapo's girl, an absolutely gorgeous creature but completely brainless, had bragged about our escapade and the Queen Bee WAAF got to hear of it. Next thing she'd seen the Station Commander and the two of them flew off to Biggin in the station Magister to report us to the Group Captain. Our Station Commander could have dealt with it himself quietly but, being emotionally disturbed, blew the incident out of all proportion. It was made to sound like a gang rape!

The next thing was a signal for we three pilots to report forthwith to Biggin and myself to appear in my substantive rank of flying officer. As we drove out of Hawkinge in the back of a van, with me busy unpicking my flight lieutenant's extra rings, we passed the three WAAF's on their way to exile in some bleak punishment unit in Cornwall.

We paraded in front of the Station Commander, my old friend Group Captain Hallings-Pott. For a mad moment I thought we'd get away with a severe reprimand, but to my consternation I saw his hands trembling and actual tears in his eyes.

'You have disgraced your uniforms as officers of the RAF! The Air Force has a way of ridding itself of embarrassments such as you! You are being posted to Malta and we don't expect you back!'

This was tantamount to a death sentence and later I was to realise only too well the Group Captain's concern for us. I was terribly ashamed and conscious of the jeopardy into which I'd placed my friends. We were dismissed back to Hawkinge to an uncertain future.

It was discovered Heapo and I were operationally tired. I'd done some 214 sorties with 91 and Heapo about the same, and so the Malta banishment was altered to postings to OTUs in Scotland. Knobby, comparatively fresh, went to Malta and death. Heapo eventually went to Scotland but I went to New Zealand House and pleaded home-sickness and concern over the Japanese threat to my homeland. Having completed three tours of operations this request was granted. I had begun having serious doubts over the ability of our allies to halt the Japanese advance before it reached New Zealand. They had no first line fighters and few experienced air crew. The Japs had polished off the Chinese, Dutch and British air-defence fighters with ease. The American planes in the Philippines had been shot out of the skies.

The RAF refused to issue joint communiqués with the USAAF because of their fantastic claims – on one occasion they shot down more Huns than were in the air. Their bombers turned back in disarray after aborting sorties. There had been a mass meeting of their air crews where their General Commanding had ordered them to 'fly like the RAF'.

The Flying Fortresses were equipped with more and more .5 machine guns and armour plate and consequently smaller and smaller bomb-loads. It was found necessary to have a percentage of the big planes set up purely as gun-ships to protect the bombers. The RAF bomber strategy was to fly under cover of night relying on accurate navigation and later by the use of sophisticated electronic devices and by specialist target locating aircraft.

But the Americans were committed to an entirely different strategy. Their planes were used on mass daylight bombing raids which necessitated huge fighter escorts when the Fortress concept proved no match for Jerry fighter defences. To escape the formidable flak defences, the bombers had to fly higher and higher, and to do so had to reduce their bomb loads even further. Later, when the Huns started to collapse, their fighter defences were overwhelmed and the Germans suffered terribly being attacked by day and night.

But in 1942 it was a very sobering state of affairs for the USAAF.

Their vaunted Fortresses had to be escorted and the only fighters capable of doing this job were Spitfires which were short-range high-performance machines. So the fortress forays were very limited affairs until new US fighters were developed. In the meanwhile, the USAAF Pursuit Groups were issued with Spitfires and were then faced with the realities of other shortcomings in the training and inexperience of their air crews.

On 26th September 1942, twenty-four Flying Fortress bombers, on one of their first raids, were to bomb the Brest docks on the Cherbourg peninsula. They were to be given a fighter escort of three squadrons of Spitfires – 65 and 401 RAF and the 133 American 'Eagle' squadron.

Only fourteen bombers turned up and they wandered about, lost over France. The two British squadrons returned home when simple calculations, made by looking at watches and fuel gauges, made it necessary. 133 Squadron, placing foolish faith in their bombers' navigational skills, stayed with them until, sensing that perhaps the RAF pilots weren't stupid, descended through the cloud to find themselves over the Cherbourg peninsula and not Cornwall! Out of fuel, eleven confused clowns force-landed in France. Only the twelfth managed to reach the UK and he crashed into the cliffs of the Lizard. Twelve Spitfires gone without a shot fired!

More and more I became convinced my place was back at home and I kept up the pestering for a posting to New Zealand.

Heapo and I were posted to 116 Squadron at Heston. This was a 'bad boys' outfit with the soul-destroying job of flying Lysander Army co-operation planes calibrating Radar controlled search lights and ack-ack guns.

The English Station Commander told us to get rid of our dogs (Heapo had an Alsatian). We gave them to some Polish pilots who were not under any such restrictions, having their own commander. And so, for the time, we still had our loved pets.

Our CO was Wing Commander Crundall, a very decent bloke, obviously selected for his diplomacy in handling awkward or emotionally disturbed aircrew. He handed us over to the flight commander Flight Lieutenant D. Woodman, another good sort.

Our duties entailed droning around and around in circles at various heights over Army sites, a dreadful, boring punishment. I liked flying Lysander however – old gentlemen's aircraft. There was the odd Spit and Hornet Moth to fool around in for a change of pace.

One day I was detailed off to take some ATC boys up for air-experience in a Tiger Moth. I'd always hated Tigers, bloody awful fiddling little machines which one had to fly all the time, joy stick and rudder pedals constantly in use. So the Cadets could get an idea of the controls the extra dual joystick was left in.

'Now just put your finger-tips on the stick! Don't grip it!' I admonished each ecstatic boy.

One larger than the others climbed in and off we went. I did a very low-level loop intending to come out about fifty feet off the deck. On pulling out I found the dual stick jammed in some way.

'Let the bloody thing go! Let go! Christ!' I could actually see the daisies coming up towards us and still I couldn't get the stick fully back.

I screamed at the happy oaf in the front seat to 'Get back! Get back!' and cursing and in blind panic I put my knees against the instrument panel and pulled like hell. Part of the framing gave way, glass smashed.

We cleared the deck by about five feet and trembling with fright and reaction, I landed, taxied to a stop and climbed out and walked away. The cadet had somehow trapped the joystick between his Sutton harness and his belly.

Heapo left for Scotland. It was hard to say farewell – I didn't expect to see him again.

Another posting – this time to the gunnery school at Suttonbridge. It seemed that a new camera-gun film assessing procedure had been developed and, along with another New Zealander, we were to be trained as instructors and so be of use on our return to New Zealand. My off-sider turned out to be a Flying Officer David Clouston, ex 485 (NZ) Squadron. He was in a pitiful state! He'd taken to sleep-walking and had 'baled out' from his second storey billet to fall onto hard-packed earth fracturing both arms, his jaw and his skull (three places). Marty Hume, another 485 bod, had luckily heard the thump and David was rushed off to East Grinstead and McIndoe's 'Guinea Pig' club.* He had not eaten solid food for three months.

* Sir Archibald McIndoe became one of the world's most advanced plastic surgeons and expert on the treatment of burns. He created the 'Guinea Pig Club' whose members, in their trials and torment, gave one another support and comfort.

We became firm friends and just as well because David had to rely on me to cut up his food, unbutton his fly, shake the old man and do him up again.

Suttonbridge was a ghastly desolate dump near the Wash. The mess was awful, the food poor and the whole place crawling with air gunners being got ready for cannon-fodder in Bomber Command. We did our course suffering mightily with abstruse mathematical equations and fiddling with the primitive G2 cameras to be taken back to New Zealand along with coloured plastic discs of various sizes to represent the 'cones of fire' of machine guns at various ranges. We learnt that bullets come out, not in neat lines like stitches, but scattered as from a pepper-pot. The juddering vibrations of multiple guns spew out bullets which spray in ever expanding cones.

When we'd passed the course we were sent, of all places, to Speke where I was pounced on by the mess secretary for, he claimed, unpaid mess bills! I fobbed him off by writing 'I deny this' across the account and defied him to produce my old bar book, burnt long back by Wing Commander Strange. After about a week, we left for the Clyde and embarked on a tender, in the dark, to join our troopship. As an 'expert' on ship recognition, I was given hell by David when my *Awatea* turned out to be the *Queen Elizabeth,* all of 82,000 tons!

We sailed on 4th November 1942 after a wisp of white smoke appeared from one of the two funnels. 'Oh yes, they've lit the kindling wood to get the coal burning,' a British diplomat kindly explained to us. He was serious too!

On board were over 17,500 passengers and crew – the largest number the QE ever carried. We officers had to parade every day from 10 a.m. to 1 p.m. on the promenade deck with 'other ranks' in files behind us. This was for life-boat drill about which nothing was actually done because, in fact, there was no flotation gear for us! David muttered, 'We should be practising "Nearer my God to Thee" ' which brought hollow laughs.

The sight of American armourers beating rust from the anti-aircraft .5 machine guns' breeches with hammers didn't make us cheerful nor the fact we slept 21 to a first class stateroom designed for one. Nor that we only got two meals per day after hours of shuffling along in huge queues.

Far too valuable to be risked in slow convoy the huge QE raced across the Atlantic, on her own, doing over 30 knots. The actual

YEAR 19+2		AIRCRAFT		PILOT, OR 1ST PILOT	2ND PILOT, PUPIL OR PASSENGER	DUTY (INCLUDING RESULTS AND REMARKS)
MONTH	DATE	Type	No.			
—	—	—	—	—	—	— TOTALS BROUGHT FORWARD
1.October	18	Spitfire IA		" D	Solo	Tangmere To Heston
"	19	Lysander III		"	"	G.L
"	23	Spitfire VB		"	"	Air Test
"	24	" VA		"	"	To Biggin Hill
"	"	"		"	"	Biggin Hill to Kenley
"	"	"		"	"	Kenley To Heston

				Summary	for October 1942 : Types :Spitfire IA
				Unit :	116 Sqdn. " IB
		Gen aic A		Date :	26th October 1942. Lysander
				Signature :	Hornet Moth
					W/Cdr.

| " | 25 | Tiger Moth | – | Self | ATC Cadets | Air Experience |

[handwritten signatures/inscription]

GRAND TOTAL [Cols. (1) to (10)]

8 1 4 .Hrs. 55 .Mins.   TOTALS CARRIED FORWARD

Reproduction of the page from my logbook with Edward G. Robinson's sketch and signed by Alexander Korda and Douglas Fairbanks Jr.

16 Squadron, RNZAF, pilots at Espiritu Santo, New Hebrides Islands, June 1943. *Back row*: J. Voss, 'Hank' Miller, Sharp, J. Arkwright, A. George, Bill Delves, John Black (admin), Jack Day (B Flight Cdr), J. Nelson (CO), Fred Smith (Spy), self, Max De Denne, A. Laurie, M. Van der Pump, McDonald, D Jones. *Front row*: unidentified, A. Bayly, S. Duncan, K. Milligan, N. Pirie, L. Williams, P. Tilyard.

Dumbo Missions were like regattas! Solomons, 1943.

RNZAF Kittyhawks being guided by a Hudson bomber en route to the Solomon Islands.

With 16 Squadron, RNZAF, the Solomons, 1943. *Left to right*: Flight Lieutenant Jack Day, Squadron Leader Johnny Nelson, self.

Noel Pirie, one of the best potential air aces I ever met, but wasted in the backwater of the Pacific.

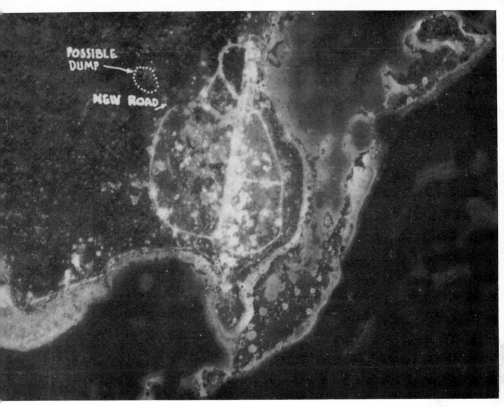

The Japanese-built Munda Airstrip, New Georgia, Solomon Islands, July 1943.

(*Left*) New Zealand tank being unloaded for invasion of Vella La Vella, the Solomon Islands, 15th August 1943. (*Right*) David Clouston.

Kittyhawks over 'Cactus'.

16 Squadron Kittyhawk and ground service party, Segi Airstrip, 1943.

RNZAF Kittyhawks at Kukum Field, Guadalcanal, 1943.

(*right*) 'Hawkeye' —
Wing Commander E. P. Wells,
DSO, DFC.

(*Below*) The 'Bell Boys' of 80
Squadron at West Malling, July
1944. *Front row, left to right:*
Huey Rankin (Austr), Spike
Maloney (Austr), Johnny Weston
(Can), Larry Foubert (Can).
Second row: Gilly Gilhuus
(Nor), W/O Ross, sorry — can't
recall, Lofty Haw, Dobbin
Dorsey, Milne, Andy Anderson
(Austr), Heapo, Jarrold, Slim
Burbridge. *On Wing:* sorry again,
Jerry Bush, the Spy (F/Lt
Nelson), Murray (Austr), Paddy
Bush, self (NZ), Willie Wiltshire.

80 Squadron pilots at Volkel, Holland, October 1944. *Front row*: M. Adams (Austr), A. McLachlan (Austr), R. Anders, J. Weston (Can), D. Price (Can), Jock Findlay. *Middle row*: Bluey Rankin (Austr), Dobbin Horsey, 'Judy' Garland, A. Seager, self, R. McKirchan, Frank Calder (Austr), Frank Lang (Austr), Paddy Irish. *Back row*: Gilly Gilhuus (Nor), Olaf Ullestad (Nor), L. Crook, Ching Friend, R. Verran, Andy Anderson (Austr), the Spy, H. Ross, D. Angier, G. Milne, Jerry Bush, L. Royds.

The magnificent Mk V Tempest Fighter. Powered by the mighty 2,420 hp 24-cylinder Napier Sabre motor and armed with four 20 mm cannon, this aircraft arrived too late to achieve its rightful place in the history of air warfare.

The world's best production fighter, the Tempest Mk V.

'Spud's Speakeasy' — built entirely from scrap material from the wreckage of Volkel, the 80 Squadron pilots laboured to produce a comfortable dispersal hut designed and supervised by Gilly Gilhuus.

Hotspur training glider. Twitch!

Operation Varsity, Wesel, Germany, 24th March 1945.

SINGLE-ENGINE AIRCRAFT				MULTI-ENGINE AIRCRAFT						PASS-ENGER	INSTR/CLOUD FLYING [Incl. in cols. (1) to (10)]	
DAY		NIGHT		DAY			NIGHT					
DUAL	PILOT	DUAL	PILOT	DUAL	1ST PILOT	2ND PILOT	DUAL	1ST PILOT	2ND PILOT		DUAL	PILOT
(1)	(2)	(3)	(4)	(5)	(6)	(7)	(8)	(9)	(10)	(11)	(12)	(13)
65·0	728·35	3·15	9·00	1·00	1·00					16·40		
	·20											
	3·10											
	·45											
	·15											
	·10											
	·25											
	2·10											
	·45											
	12·25											
	7·30											
	2·10											
65·00	735·40	3·15	9·00	1·00	1·00					16·40		
(1)	(2)	(3)	(4)	(5)	(6)	(7)	(8)	(9)	(10)	(11)	(12)	(13)

speed was secret but we believed it to be close to thirty eight miles per hour. Every so often she made changes of course to fox any lurking submarine.

On board were several well known faces and, fetching my log book, I approached the most likely prospect.

'Sir, would you do me the honour of autographing my log book?'

Edward G. Robinson did much more – he quickly made a cartoon sketch of himself, signed it and handed the book on to Sir Alexander Korda. Much emboldened I approached Douglas Fairbanks Jnr, who grudgingly signed. Now completely carried away with this success, I got David to sign which he graciously condescended to do even if volubly protesting against the honour. I think he could envisage possible future complications when the log book would be examined by my next station commander.

By sheer bluff and cheek we talked our way onto the bridge when we made landfall in New York. Keeping a very low profile we were enthralled as Manhattan's mighty towers appeared from the mist. David, a romantic, remarked that it looked 'like fairyland'. A ship's officer, overhearing said, 'More like Hell! You be careful of the fairies, lad!'

When we docked we completed the trio of the world's largest ships, an amazing sight, especially the French liner *Normandie* lying burnt out, sabotaged, on its side in the next berth and the *Queen Mary* with its bows smashed in from a collision with a cruiser.

Customs and Immigration officers descended on us; also an RAF accountancy officer who relieved us of our 'illegal' British currency. He later replaced this with Bank of Scotland five pound notes (valueless out of Scotland). He himself was eventually caught and cashiered for this racket – the bastard. Our New Zealand contingent was billeted at Fort Hamilton down near the Battery. Initially we were refused leave 'because you Limeys carry disease' – quite a wry joke considering that the 'New World's ' gift to the Old was syphilis.

We had ten hectic, happy days in New York, being almost drowned with Cuba Libras by my friend in the Harvard Club. We embarked on the *Akaroa* setting off in convoy to Cuba. Because of the ancient and decrepit US escort vessels the trip was painfully slow. At the big US Naval base in Guantanamo Bay we weren't allowed off the ship by the Americans and the sounds of revelry ashore made us angry. In the morning a passing destroyer displayed washing and bedding put out to air by being draped over its gun barrels. US sailors lounged about smoking. Immediately after its departure a Canadian destroyer arrived with its complement 'dressing ship' in immaculate style. A spontaneous cheer broke out from our whole ship's company – it was easy to be proud to be British.

Soon we had passed through Panama's canal locks and set out for home over the broad Pacific. On board were dozens of non-commisioned Australian and New Zealand airmen being sent back home, having proven unsuitable for aircrew. David and I were put in charge of them – a thankless task.

We called in at Pitcairn Island and dropped off supplies to this lonely outpost. Island men swarmed on board with bananas to trade for 'rubbers'. It seemed things were pretty bleak on the home front at Pitcairn and the last thing needed was a population explosion.

CHAPTER VIII

'We know you RAF types! Trouble-makers!'

Auckland's lovely harbour – we were home. Everyone had been ordered to hand in souvenired *Akaroa* teaspoons, towels, ashtrays etc. or a full-scale Customs search of kit could be expected. A cascade of cutlery etc. poured into the Chief Purser's office and the danger averted.

Down on the wharf friends and relatives gathered to welcome home their failed 'aircrew' LACs. A band played and National Patriotic Workers handed out little packages of goodies and small gifts of spending money. The RTO issued leave passes and free railway travel warrants.

But not to us. We were to report forthwith to Air Headquarters, Wellington. Our small group of operationally expired aircrew, including invalided-back types like David, were perplexed, hurt and angry. A bitter argument ensued and grudgingly the RTO contacted Wellington and in the end we got our way.

The explanation for this unpleasantness was simple enough – returning operational types represented a threat to the cosy club around which the rapidly expanding RNZAF was formed. For in the past, before Japan entered the war, a sizeable proportion of aircrew had been held back as instructors despite their pleas for action. And now battle-experienced men were returning and the home-types felt threatened. We were ordered to remove our New Zealand shoulder flashes so we wouldn't stand out. Being RAF I told them to get stuffed but David and other returned RNZAF personnel were forced to unpick their badges that had been earned and worn with pride. We were being disciplined, conditioned, softened-up – brainwashed if you will.

Very upset and bewildered by our reception. I was caught off-beat in my reunion with Florance. The youth who had gone off to war so cheerfully had got lost somewhere in Europe's skies. I felt unclean and unworthy. I had been doing unspeakable things; had killed and worse, far worse, had got a liking for it.

It was not in any way my fiancée's fault – I was the one who had changed and broken the link.

David and I checked into AHQ Wellington, 8th January 1943. We were told to await posting orders and we went to the officers' mess at Anderson Park where we were flatly refused admission.

'We know you RAF types! Trouble-makers!'

Luckily, David's cousin put us up for the few days before posting to Ohakea, our new base.

Here we were interviewed by the Station Commander, Group Captain Kay. On his desk lay my log-book, opened at the last entry.

'What is the meaning of this, Spurdle?'

My mind had a quick scrabble around.

'Oh yes, sir. I wondered if you'd autograph it for me – there's Sir Alexander Korda's signature. And Douglas Fairbanks Junior's'

'What is this scribble?' the Groupie asked, indicating Edward G's cartoon.

'Sir, Edward G. Robinson did a sketch of himself for me.'

Eyeing me quizzically, Kay signed with the immortals.

*

Ohakea was a large peace-time 'drome with excellent facilities but the stuffy atmosphere was of a dull and rigid administration. We amused ourselves by going our own sweet way and ignoring or circumventing the stupid DRO's pinned on notice boards.

'Reference to the S/East Camp as "Siberia" will not be tolerated. Disciplinary action will be taken against offenders using this term.'

It was promptly dubbed 'Shangri La'.

Our uniforms became wrinkled, shoes dull and dirty, buttons green with verdigris. In the UK, WAAF bat-women would come into our rooms in the mornings, collect our gear for cleaning, and leave us a cup of tea and a biscuit. Here, we were treated as potential rapists or, at the least, hopeless philanderers and the WAAF equally untrustworthy.

Eventually attention was drawn to our scruffy appearance and, feigning ignorance, we bitterly complained about the lax service and made the mess president look a fool.

But we were forced to toe the line and hang our clothes and shoes outside our doors at night and collect cold cups of tea left in the hallways in the mornings.

Working like slaves, David and I got the No 2 Fighter OTU going. The cunning RAF equipment types back in the UK had palmed off on to us outmoded G2 cameras which took over twenty modifications to get working properly.

Some Harvards, Kittyhawks and Vildebeestes were allocated to our school and we were in business. Not having flown either of the first two aircraft, it was an interesting time for us. The Harvard was delightful being a fully aerobatic rugged machine. We had them fitted with .300 machine guns for air to air, and air to ground gunnery.

The Kittyhawks were something else. They had Allison engines which ran very smoothly. They were sturdy, well-made machines with the formidable fire power of six .5 machine guns. They had electric trim tabs and a natty little lock-up compartment to carry personal kit around in.

They had the flying characteristics of a brick.

David and I came up with a bright idea to train pilots in deflection shooting. We'd gathered our pupils, food and drink, ammunition, a .303 Browning machine gun, chain and clamps, a Very-pistol and flares. We'd motor to the beach where we fixed the machine gun by clamping it to a substantial log of driftwood. We were now ready and soon a lumbering Vildebeeste would drone over at about 200 feet. We'd fire off a flare to advise we were ready and the exercise was on.

The ancient torpedo bomber's crew would unreel a drogue to stream 200 yards astern and they would fly up and down the beach past our gun while the pilots banged away. The bullet points had been dipped in red, green and blue paint which marked impact holes on the drogues. Each pilot had his own colour and so scores could be tallied. At the end of each group, the used drogue would be dropped and a fresh one streamed. After the day's exercise, a flare would be shot off and the Vildebeeste returned to Ohakea.

After a few days of this, David and I became bored so we started to pick out the most senior or intelligent looking pupil, put him in charge, then sneak off to the Rangitikei river-mouth where we'd dynamite fish, swim, laze in the sun and drink beer. When the firing stopped and the plane had gone we'd wander back, collect the bods and drive home.

One day, at the end of the exercise, I strolled down to the ocean's edge over which the tow-plane was stooging. Using great judgement, I fired the flare at the big biplane to stir the crew up and enliven their boring day. The magnesium projectile arced up and hit the Vildebeeste fair in the carburettor intake! There was a great banging and burst of flame and brown smoke from pre-ignited fuel as the ancient engine swallowed the flaming mass.

Horrified at the fantastic fluke, yet proud of my feat, I stood there, mouth agape as the airplane tottered around, its engine missing and belching smoke, while the pilot considered a beach landing.

Eventually the thing staggered off and I rejoined the cheering, rolling-on-the-ground pilots. David, laughing like a hyena, clapped me on the back.

'That'll take some explaining!' he chortled.

I got tired of the Gunnery School. Up in the Pacific at Guadalcanal the first of the RNZAF fighter squadrons was in action against the Japanese. It was galling to be on the sidelines training others to go off to the excitement.

By keeping up a barrage of requests and by being a ruddy nuisance, I was replaced as CFI by Roy Bush, who was made an acting squadron leader for the role I had created and held down as a flight lieutenant. My chagrin was cured very quickly by being appointed as 'A' Flight commander 16 (F) Squadron, working up at Woodbourne 'drome in the South Island.

Wizard show! The only regret was that it meant a parting of the ways for David and myself. We'd become firm friends so much so that our nickname on the station was 'Mr and Mrs Spurdle'. I had met a girl with whom I had an understanding and a period apart could be a testing.

Down at Woodbourne, I met my new CO Johnny Nelson, and the other flight commander, Jack Day. The other pilots looked a solid bunch and we got down to serious training. It was at this point I found myself in the invidious position of being the only experienced operational pilot and being looked on as guide and mentor by the 'B' Flight boys as well as my own group. This created an unwelcome tension.

On 19th June 1943 Flight Lieutenant Parry flew us to New Caledonia by DC 3.* After a boring eight and a half hour flight, we landed at Tontouta airfield to re-fuel. Here I saw my first Bell 'Airacobra'. An American 'armourer' was doing the *Queen Elizabeth* stunt of beating rusty machine gun breeches free with a hammer. And this an aerodrome defence fighter! We flew off to Turtle Bay in Espiritu Santo Island, our base in the New Hebrides Islands.

It was as hot as hell and we were told to take Atabrin tablets to prevent malaria. These eventually turned our skin a sickly yellow. Here we lived in the airy comfortable 'Dallas' huts supplied by the Americans. Everything was strange – coconut palms, fruit bats, a million Yanks, jeeps and trucks.

On the 21st, I flew my first operational flight for ten months – No 395 – anti-submarine patrol.

June 23rd: I had the trots. Must have eaten too many green coconuts or perhaps the dreadful food had brought it on and here the CO was putting me down for night flying exercise!

'Sir, I can't fly a Kitty at night! I've never flown anything faster than a Fairey Gordon at night and that was three years ago! Spitfires at dusk yes, but that's the limit of it. Besides, I've diarrhoea – I'll never make it!'

'You'll fly like the rest of them,' said Nelson, and that was that.

Several of the flight roared off and after a last minute trip to the latrine, I took off full of foreboding but empty of confidence and I hoped, everything else.

We droned around and around in the pitch darkness. My kite had its turn and bank indicator u/s and also the gyro-compass. It was not very comforting to know that if the artifical horizon failed I could be in real trouble. There was no moon, just the twinkling stars and all around velvet blackness. On a small islet off Turtle Bay a lone fixed searchlight beamed its vertical spear of light. This acted as a reference point and was left on whenever planes were up in the dark.

One by one the planes taxied out and roared off into the black sky. Just their red, green and white navigation lights gleaming as they orbited in the circuit. While droning around at about 1,000 feet, I saw a Kittyhawk's lights veer off the runway and slide across past the

---

* US C47 or Dakota.

marker beacons. Someone said, 'He's crashed!' and then vehicle headlights started to race around the runway. Bloody Hell! Who was it? Immediately I needed to relieve myself and, cursing the mêleé below, had to concentrate on not making a fool of myself.

After what seemed ages, the ground controller started to recall the kites, the airstrip now cleared. As much as I needed to land quickly, I let the others go first. They'd all done night flying in Kittys and if anyone else was going to crash, it would be me!

Ron Blair had drifted off the flare path and ploughed into coconut palms, ending up crashing into a revetment. The trucks rushing around had been mostly coconut-gatherers. These were the bastards who kept us airborne for so long! I was very angry and remonstrated with the CO at the dangers we'd been exposed to – the lack of ground discipline and the u/s instruments. And in any case, why night flying? We had no GCI and trying to find an enemy aircraft at night would be next to impossible. I knew! Damn it – I had seen it all before!

And on the 25th, it happened.

Despite my protest, one of our most experienced and best pilots was killed. 'Washing Machine Charlie', a Jap recce bomber, came over from the Solomons and Flying Officer Arthur Hyams was scrambled to try and intercept. For some reason, probably Yank panic, the searchlight was extinguished and Arthur crashed into the sea and was killed.

With blood in my eye, I entered the instrument-bashers' work-shop. Here they were, repairing watches, encapsulating coins in plastic and making wrist straps and cigarette lighters for sale to the souvenir-crazy Americans. Enraged I spoke out.

'Last night one of our best pilots was killed. I believe he hadn't enough instruments for night flying and here you bastards are repairing Yanks' watches! You bloody useless parasites!'

In the startled silence I turned and left, shaking with rage. Next day the CO asked me to apologise! That would be the day!

Arthur, my valued deputy flight commander, had been an excellent pilot and a good friend.

*

When Japan brought America into the war, we British were naturally delighted. Now at last, the canny giant was forced into the war. But the fantastic ease with which the Japanese executed their well-planned offensive appalled us. The years of goofing-off, of tennis parties, pink gins and thick-headed lack of foresight by senior career officers were now apparent. Key bastions like Singapore and Corregidor were overrun as the yellow tide engulfed the north-western chain of Pacific Islands.

Now Australia and New Zealand were threatened and with growing horror we Anzacs could see our very homelands in peril. But the Australian Labour Government, true to its Pacifist precepts, buried its political head in the shifting sands of time. Churchill laid it on the line: Britain was completely committed and extended in Malaysia, the Middle and Far East and Europe. Germany was the major threat and was to be destroyed first. Then Japan. The message, brutal and clear, was that we were on our own and for active help we'd have to depend, for the immediate future, on America.

It was ironic that the country that had stood aloof, not in indecision, but by democratic choice, and in financial clover, should now be forced to help us for its own safety. The kind of amphibious warfare now facing us was one which America had always prepared for; at least in theory. What caught them flat-footed was the treacherous surprise attack of which, in fact, they'd been forewarned by British Intelligence several days before it actually occurred. The senior American Army general and his Navy counterpart in Hawaii were quickly removed. The huge effort to provide the men and machines needed to halt and then roll up the Japanese got underway.

On Guadalcanal's beaches, America met head-on the Japanese land forces and it was here, in the Solomons, that the yellow men were stopped. And rolled back to die in their thousands. By 'leap-frogging' islands and groups of islands to establish beachheads and air-strips, the Americans first established air-supremacy and then naval and land control.

It was at this early stage in Japan's ultimate defeat that I was fortunate enough to participate. From the bloody sophistication of European strife we were now embroiled in a completely different kind of warfare. Where I had flown short sorties of perhaps an hour and a half over some three hundred and seventy odd miles across or along the English Channel, I now regularly flew sorties three times as long and against targets 300 miles distant from our bases.

Where in Europe a downed flier would in all probability be picked up, interrogated and be put in the bag, out here your fate was likely to be decapitation by a Japanese officer with a samurai sword. In Europe and the Middle East defeated troops, showing the white flag, were taken prisoner and incarcerated. Here in the steaming jungle the Japanese fought fanatically and had to be virtually exterminated – they didn't quit and surrender even when in a hopeless situation.

There were other nasty hazards – malaria, dengue, yellow jack, yaws, hookworm – a host of diseases. In the jungle spiders and snakes and leeches – in the sea, sharks and stone fish.

But I was back in action and that was all that really counted.

CHAPTER IX

The Solomons

On 28th of June, led by the CO 'B' Flight, plus Stan Duncan and myself from 'A', ferried our Kittys up to Guadalcanal in the Solomons. We were led by an RNZAF Hudson bomber on which we formated loosely in a broad Vic.

The weather was glorious and, as we droned along at about 8,000 feet, we passed islets fringed with white waves curling across the browns and greens of coral shallows. Soon the mountainous peaks of San Cristobal and further off Guadalcanal itself came into view. In a cloud of coral dust the squadron planes landed on the Marsden Matting strips and taxied to their dispersal revetments.

Next day, Stan and I rejoined Flight Lieutenant Bradshaw in his Hudson to fly back to Santos. For the next seventeen days, 'A' Flight practised air drill and dog fighting; even had three scrambles when unidentified aircraft showed up on the primitive Radar screens. I took up a Kittyhawk to see how high it could go and peaked at 28,000 feet where it waffled about and wheezed to its limit. Good Lord! A standard Spitfire could climb almost two miles higher!

On 17th July, 'A' Flight emplaned in a USAAF DC3 and its pilot groped his way to Guadalcanal by following the longer route via the Santa Cruz and Banks group of islands. This way he stayed in sight of land most of the way and we didn't get lost.

Now 16 was whole again and ready for action. That same evening, we were given orders for a B24 (Liberator) bomber escort job the very next day! Whacko! At long last back to the real thing!

Early in the morning Jack and I chalked up our teams and in the blazing heat of another glorious day we trundled out around the perimeter, formed into sections of two, and took off to formate and climb to the rendezvous point 10,000 feet over Cape Esperance on the north-eastern tip of Guadalcanal.

Around and around we circled searching for the bombers. Where were they? We were at the right height and time. No sign of them and twenty minutes later a straggle of planes appeared way below and out to sea heading up the 'Slot'. After a bit of a conference Squadron Leader Nelson led us to them and we took position up-sun and above them in a protective 'umbrella'.

The bomber crews were chattering away and their RT procedure and misuse incredible. This was the first time I'd escorted USAAF planes and I wasn't impressed. The bomber leader was calling for the two American fighter squadrons but for some reason or other they never showed up. I got a bit concerned. Intelligence reports indicated strong fighter concentrations at Kahili, our primary target, and especially on the small island of Ballale nearby.

The Yank bombers' crews were yacking away and, as we neared the target area, their lead bombardier or perhaps the squadron commander cut in and dominated the air.

'For Christ's sake, take it easy! Take it easy! Take it easy!. For Christ's sake, take it easy, take it easy. . .!'

Four miles below, with the Shortland Islands to port and Fauro to starboard, we could see the dust of enemy aircraft taking off from the strip on Ballale. Ahead lay the tiny settlement of Buin and the runways of Kahili. Soon grey bursts of flak appeared, spot on for our height, forming ugly puffs of smoke all around.

The mindless exhortations from the bomber went on and on. It was very hot in our cockpits with the tropic sun pouring through the perspex canopies.

The lead B24's bomb bay doors opened and it started to turn to starboard. Out streamed 500lb bombs and soon all the others were scattering their loads in ragged streams. The next minute we were all committed to a long dive for home. As we turned I saw my first Jap plane about a mile away and below. The radio went quiet at long last. Someone (one of ours, I think) said an ironic 'Thank Christ!'

The Solomon Islands are a large group of quite big islands running south-east to north-west in two roughly parallel lines. The water-way thus formed was called the Slot and was the track up and down which we usually flew. The scenery was marvellous – each green island lay in clear deep blue water. Fringing reefs surrounded most of the shorelines and coconut palms covered a lot of the flatter coastal ground. Up the mountain sides giant trees reached for the sky

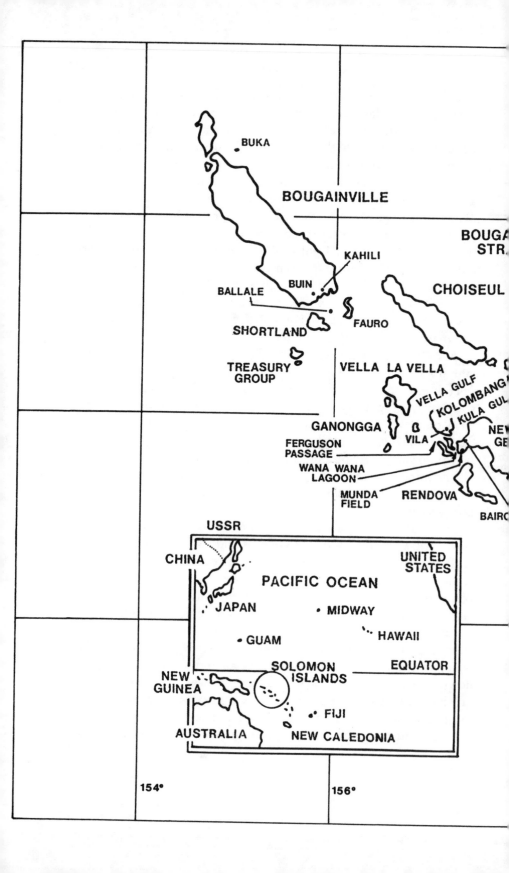

BUKA

BOUGAINVILLE

BOUGA
STR.

KAHILI

CHOISEUL

BUIN
BALLALE

FAURO

SHORTLAND

TREASURY
GROUP

VELLA LA VELLA

VELLA GULF

KOLOMBANG

KULA GUL

GANONGGA

VILA

NE
GE

FERGUSON
PASSAGE

WANA WANA
LAGOON

MUNDA
FIELD

RENDOVA

BAIRC

USSR

CHINA

PACIFIC OCEAN

UNITED
STATES

JAPAN

MIDWAY

GUAM

HAWAII

NEW
GUINEA

SOLOMON
ISLANDS

EQUATOR

FIJI

AUSTRALIA

NEW CALEDONIA

154°

156°

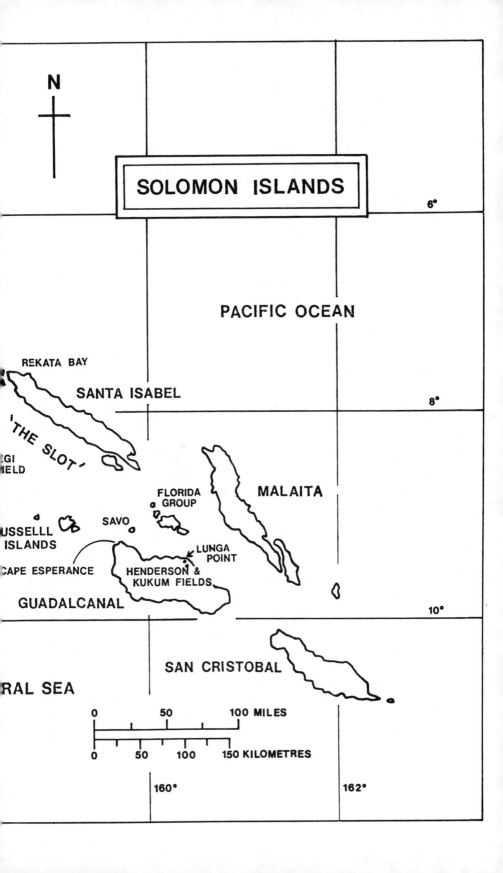

and fields of tall Kunai grass showed in great sage-green patches.

On the 300 odd miles return there was plenty to think about. Surely it wouldn't all be like this! Back at base our chaps were excited at their first great adventure. Flak! Some Jap planes seen! The incredibly beautiful and dramatic flight up the Slot past island after island with myriad reefs and coral shallows. And the big bombers dropping their bombs!

The fact that the whole thing was a farce and a monumental cock-up was not truly appreciated by our squadron of 'new boys'. To all intents and purposes the bombs had been jettisoned, in a diving turn, to fall and explode harmlessly in the sea after a round flight of over 600 miles and against no real opposition.

Something new! The Americans have fitted some of their light bombers with a 75mm. cannon for ground or ship strafing. We've been detailed to escort these B25's (Mitchells) which are reported to be fast. The only catch is that we are to keep clear of their rears when they are attacking. We gather a sort of double charge is fired from a tube – the shell goes out the front and a type of 'counterweight' is shot out backwards which cuts out all recoil. Seeing these bombers have two 1700 hp motors I doubt whether we'll be able to keep up let alone have any margin over them!

Great! With Flight Sergeant Pirie as my No 2, I discovered one small steamer and three motor launches at Gannonnga Island. They were cunningly camouflaged with nets and quite large trees all over. We gave them a good doing over but didn't observe any real results. Just leaves and bits and pieces blown away. Moving on I spotted a Jap barge hidden under mangroves in the Fergusson Passage. We gave it a thorough pasting using up the remainder of our ammo. Returning to Munda we reported in and Jack Day and his flight were scrambled to attack these ships.

For light relaxation and to augment our rations, I turned to dynamiting fish. By cutting out a sort of cockpit in a 90 gallon drop-tank and by lining the sharp edges with self-sealing rubber from a crashed aircraft's tank, I created quite a satisfactory boat. To give stability I welded a hunk of armour-plate to the bottom thus forming a keel. I used to paddle out and ground-bait the coral bombies with chopped-up Spam and kitchen refuse. All went well until one sunny day – I'd scattered the fish-bait and lazed on the calm blue waters. Suddenly a large splash opened my eyes and to my horror there were two large sharks circling the tin 'boat'. Quickly lighting one of my charges I counted down before throwing the 'bomb'. In my haste I dropped it between my legs and only just scrabbled it up and dropped it over the side before – Boom! The bellytank rolled over and sank. Kicking myself free, I reached the beach in a blind panic. That put paid to this form of fishing. There was another way – two of us, each armed with a US hand-grenade, would wait for one of the large landing-craft to nose ashore. Just before it touched we'd lob a grenade, one on each side, to stun the shoals of fish driven ahead of it. We got lots of fish but the howls of fright and rage from the LST's crews got too much, and after being threatened by an armed guard, we quit.

One day the big ammunition dump on Lunga Point blew up. More explosives were expended in the next two days than it took to take Guadalcanal from the Japanese. The Americans had made the old Jap dump into their own. There were tons of all manner of Japanese gear around and souvenir hunters haunted the place.

There were some colossal bangs as big stuff went off and a continuous crackling roar as small-arms ammunition exploded. Soon a great billowing cloud of acrid smoke hung over the revetments and blast-walls.

I was called to the CO's hut.

'What the hell have you done? The Yanks say you were responsible, you and these bloody bombs of yours!'

'Me? I'm not that mad! That's stupid – their own people are knocking Jap shellcases free of their projectiles for souvenirs! I've seen them pour the propellant granules out on the ground while smoking their goddam cigars! You know I don't smoke and anyhow I haven't been near the dump for over a week!'

It was obvious I'd have to get my spare time amusements in some harmless way and several of us took up insect collecting. Doug Greig was busy looking for a crashed Zero fighter reported down in the hills back of Henderson and I had heard of a downed Jap bomber as well. We spent hours both in the air and ground searches for them, working independently.

It was deathly quiet in the dark shadows of the jungle. Just the mournful calling of the bush-doves and the rustle of palm-fronds.

Butterflies, iridescent blue, shimmered as they flitted across patches and shafts of sunlight streaming from the green canopy above.

Then I found the reason for my search. Over and entangled in a huge clump of giant bamboo lay the twisted wreckage of a Betty bomber. And to one side, snagged, crucified into a ghastly scarecrow, one of its crew. Just the skeletal remains, dried skin and ligaments held together by a rotting and torn flying suit. The urge for further exploration died in me and I backed off and left the horrible scene. While slipping and sliding back down the jungle trail, grabbing at dirty roots and avoiding the sawtoothed grasses, I had time to mull over the past and probable future. Not a happy or reassuring day and shortly to be even less so.

Back at Kukum Field, Doug Greig was busy setting up a Japanese 20mm cannon recovered from the wreck of the Zero which he'd at long last located. Having got the gun securely bolted down, the next step was to fire it. There was an old wing from a crashed Kittyhawk and, using this as a target, Doug let fly a few rounds. Too many, I thought, and with the wrong audience. Our pilots were a pretty subdued mob when they saw the havoc this potent weapon could wreak – and a Zero had two – plus two machine guns.

July 21st, Sortie 407: Patrol to Bairoko Harbour. Lots of action strafing Jap gun positions and watching with disbelief US Navy dive bombers plastering their own troops' positions. Helpless to intervene we could only circle and wonder. Pat Tilyard crash-landed at Segi 'drome out of gas. Some sort of leak as the others had plenty left.

July 22nd: Escort for B24's attacking two transports and escorting destroyers in Bougainville Straits.

Again the whole thing was a silly waste of time. The flak was fairly thick and accurate and my machine sustained a shrapnel strike near the radiator. An RAF squadron would have forged on but these big babies started their usual turn and bomb technique which scattered their eggs harmlessly in the sea.

Later, after we had returned to base, SBDs (Dauntless dive bombers) and TBFs (Avenger dive and torpedo bombers) were sent up the Slot to successfully bomb the transports but now empty of troops.

That evening, when showering, I found a little piece of shrapnel in the flesh under my arm near my left elbow. It was the only time I would have liked to be a Yank! This nick would have qualified me for a 'Purple Heart' and a huge source of amusement.

On 24th July we were detailed to escort B24's again and once more they were late, 4,000 feet below and heading in the wrong direction.

Something strange and horrible happened. As we droned along up the Slot at about 20,000 feet there was a sudden howling. It went on and on without pause. Away out to our starboard, I saw a US fighter in a vertical dive. The continuous screaming yell went on and on and when the plane splashed in, the cry cut off instantaneously.

'Thank Christ!' someone remarked and we droned on wondering, what the hell?

July 25th, Sortie 410: This time we were supposed to escort the very fast B25's but they'd left twenty minutes too soon! Stooging around trying to locate them we came on masses of dive bombers, about sixty, giving Munda hell. Back at base we refuelled and took off again to escort the B24's for another Munda strike. They didn't show up so we did a patrol over Rendova to see if anything was doing.

I was getting fed up by all this nonsense. The CO, not having any operational experience whatsoever, thought it par for the course and considered my bitter criticism as just plain carping.

July 26th, Sortie 412, 4 hours and 40 minutes duration: Hey! They've got their act together at last! They turned up more or less on time, more or less at the right height and on course, for Kahili. Flak again, moderate and accurate and this time the bombing was in the general target area. There were a few Zeros but they didn't come in close to our formation. We did however, watch with interest an American buy it when he was shot down in his Corsair fighter off Rendova. Doug, Mac and Pirie dropped in at Segi 'short of fuel' but in fact just to look at the new 'drome.

July 28th: Off to Segi! Nothing to see along the coastline but that afternoon we were scrambled to seek Zeros reported coming down the Slot. These had been spotted by one of the coast watchers who radioed in the warning. No contact was made and the weather closed in forcing me to divert to the Russell Islands where we landed very short of fuel. I had eight gallons left, Doug and Pirie five each, but Mac was OK. It was a near thing. With very indifferent ground control and poor-to-nil weather forecasting sudden tropical downpours were a very real hazard.

July 31st, Sortie No 415: Escort to dive bombers bombing Munda. The Japs were busy building the Munda airfield. They'd been at it for weeks; coast watchers had reported it was nearly operational. The cunning Japs had strung whole coconut palm-heads on wires over the work going on below while the ground was levelled and rolled hard. The symmetrical copra plantation looked normal from the air but after a while the vegetation started to dry out and the long airstrip was clearly outlined and plain to see. Now the dive bombers went in to attack and they were good – huge explosions of 1,000 lb 'daisy cutters' bowled over serried ranks of coconut palms. The Jap flak gunners had extraordinary guts and kept up a steady barrage through which the SBDs and the TBFs dived to lay their eggs. When finished, we escorted the bombers away and, nearing Segi and about to land, we were ordered by Vega control to climb as quickly as possible back to Munda as Jap fighters, attracted by the battle, were on their way.

The coast-watchers were brave men, formed into a network of observers by the Royal Australian Navy after World War I. The service was designed to keep an eye on the long unguarded coastlines and was comprised of volunteer local Government workers, planters, traders and missionaries. The coast-watchers were organised by Lieutenant Commander Eric Feldt who looked on the islands as a 'fence' around Australia. He organised a radio-linked group of over 100 stations stretching in a 2,500 mile arc from the western border of Papua New Guinea to Vila in the New Hebrides. They advised of shipping and aircraft movements, troop concentrations etc. Some coast-watchers actually formed private armies of loyal natives and killed Japs by the hundreds in small, bitter forays.

We had lost contact with the CO and his flight who, with Flight Lieutenant Day and 'B' Flight, had got separated during the milling around at Munda. It was stupid and impractical to attempt to escort sixty dive bombers wheeling all over the sky by flying at their level and I had detached my flight to act as high cover. Being at 7,000 feet and hearing the scramble order we were in a much better position for gaining height than the other eight aircraft already in Segi's circuit asking permission to land. When over Enogi inlet at 16,000 feet, I heard the other sections ordered to patrol Rendova, twenty-five miles to the south of us.

We climbed as hard as we could to gain even more height and so be between the Nips and their bases, if possible. At about 23,000 feet, I saw twenty to thirty Zeros on my port, some two miles away, and 500 feet above.

Keeping radio silence in case Jap control picked up a 'Tally Ho', I began to stalk them. 'Drop tanks!' and the three others jettisoned their now unwanted auxiliary fuel tanks. My bloody engine cut. This was a common fault with Kittys. After losing some 500 feet the Allison motor caught and once more with power I started the pursuit. The Japs disappeared down into thin cloud and we lost them.

Far below, north-east of Munda, the other eight machines of our squadron, who were supposed to be heading south and miles away, were jumped by the Zeros who shot down two of our kites. Sergeant Williams went missing and Sergeant Sharp bailed out and was luckily picked up almost straight away by a US patrol boat.

Back at base, I was in for some severe criticism for not 'Tally Ho'ing' and so alerting the others. But they knew there were Japs about and they were supposed to be flying south some twenty miles away. In the European theatre one used one's brains. The Germans had sophisticated listening posts and on hearing our planes' transmissions, would alert their formations. Sometimes they even used English-speaking controllers to vector our kites out of the way or into an ambush or even order them to 'pancake' (return to base and land). One didn't blather on the RT like a CB addict.

Whatever the various pilots in this action did, one thing was sure, as their combat reports state, several saw the E/A in plenty of time to take action. Indeed Sergeant Laurie did give warning.

'I saw Bandits at six o'clock about 1,000 feet above and called to my No 1' (Squadron Leader Nelson).

Flight Lieutenant J. Day – 'I saw fifteen to twenty Zeros at approximately eleven o'clock, quarter to half a mile away, about 1,000 feet above. They appeared to be dog-fighting amongst themselves and there were other Zeros all around them over a radius of three miles.' He said nothing over the RT.

Flying Officer S. Duncan – 'I heard Sergeant Laurie give "Bogies at seven o'clock" '.

The cruel facts were these – it was the first real fighter versus fighter action these green pilots were in and they tried to mix it with vastly superior numbers flying vastly superior aircraft.

Major Alexander Seversky, one of the world's foremost aircraft designers, stated, 'Our P40 (Kittyhawk) pursuits are dismally inferior to the British fighter planes. Hundreds of these aircraft sent to England were not even uncrated. They were considered obsolete and "placed on ice" for possible auxiliary use.' A lot ended up as ground attack aircraft in the Desert.

Major Seversky was the first foreigner to fly the Spitfire. He went on:

'I urged United States authorities to come to some sort of agree-

"HEY! LE ROY – AREN'T THESE SUPPOSED TO BE BOMBERS?"

ment with Britain to pool the Spitfire as a joint British-American plane and was accused of being unpatriotic. The blunt truth is that America hasn't a fighter plane in combat that's worth a nickel compared with Britain and Germany's best.'

US General Chennault, commander of the famous 'Flying Tigers', said:

'Never attack alone! One P40 against one Jap is outnumbered three to one!'

These were the aircraft bought by the New Zealand Government for our men to fly, while in the UK American squadrons were being converted to, and given Spitfires for Europe and the North African campaign. Later the Kittys were withdrawn and the Americans kindly let us have Corsairs, unwieldy monsters, really only suitable for ground attack roles.

After a pretty heavy session with Nelson, Day and the Spy, we requested an interview with the US Air Force General, Brigadier-General William Matherny. He was very good about it and kept his cool while I lost mine. I'm sure he had no knowledge of the number of aborted flights and even those of whole missions which never reached their primary targets due to turning away in favour of less dangerous alternatives.

'Sir, I've checked out the names of the pilots who press on – the Schmidts, Wilsons, MacGregors and such like, but the Napolinskis and Finklebergers chicken out! And another thing. The bigger the nude* painted on the aircraft, the sooner it turns back!'

By now I threw all caution away and blurted out, 'It would never be countenanced in the RAF – these pilots are bloody cowards!'

Dismissed in chilly silence, we marched back to our Jeep and so back to dispersal.

But things improved dramatically from then on – some king-sized rockets must have been delivered and now the bombers mostly completed their missions and fighter squadrons tended to stay at least in sight.

I think another factor in the turning back of US aircraft was that they didn't seem to do thorough DI's – the ground crew waited until

---

* The Americans allowed their aircrews to paint mascots or symbols on their machines. Giant nudes were much in favour.

the pilot actually complained of a specific mechanical fault before making adjustments or repairs.

Last night 'Washing Machine' Charlie came over and dropped a few bombs in the bay, completely missing Henderson and the fighter 'dromes.

Next day there was a parade and the pinning on of thirteen 'Purple Hearts'. The recipients had been injured in the raid. They'd fallen over things, had jumped in broken bottle-filled slit trenches etc.

We Kiwis watched in wonder. One night a bunch of us went to one of the many open-air film shows put on by the Americans. When it was over, and we were sauntering back to camp, we saw a group of fellows around a Jeep staring down into the empty space where the engine and transmission had been.

'Bloody thieving Kiwis!' one of the Yanks muttered. Sure enough, some of our mechanics had made good use of the movie's distraction and whipped the whole unit out for parts.

There was something seriously wrong with our purchasing commissions, or supply system for spare parts. Our engineering officers were in a continual state of frustration. Often our ground staff made forays (as above) or finagled bits and pieces from their counterparts in the American Forces who were very generous.

August 2nd.   Escort for B17's and in clear weather with no flak and no fighter opposition, they bombed near Rice Harbour. It was an absolutely model display and somewhat heartened, I felt we might at last be getting somewhere.

August 3rd: 'Dumbo' patrol to Ringana village to pick up three Europeans. There were at least sixty native canoes surrounding the Catalina flying boat – it was like a regatta! Around and around we went gritting our teeth and sweating in our hot cockpits. A four hour and twenty-five minute flight!

On 13th August, we did a squadron patrol around Rendova and the Blanche Channel coast-line landing at Segi. We were to operate from this new strip only just completed and now fully operational. Two escort jobs for B24's over Vella La Vella and another to Rekata Bay. One shipping patrol covering seven large troopers and five destroyers.

The same day and another scramble! This time over the Wana Wana Lagoon leading Flight Sergeant Pirie as my No 2, and Flight Lieutenant Max De Denne with Flight Sergeant Laurie as his. It was 1450 hours, the fourth flight of the day and feeling a bit blasé, I didn't really expect action. At 1530 hours, and at 21,000 feet, I spotted a gaggle of Zeros and Haps at our height about three miles away. They were looping and rolling around the sky – no formation at all! They looked as if they were on holiday. I saw something which made me blink – a Zero went into a loop from level flight, rolled off the top, went into another loop, rolled off the top and flew along 1,000 feet higher than when he had started! And with no preparatory dive!

Pulling myself together, I 'Tally Hoed' and gave Vega the position, number, height and course of the enemy aircraft. It was useless to climb; we had Zeros a thousand feet higher and after the aerobatic display, I just bored straight into the bastards and a dogfight ensued. A Zeke flew directly in front across from port to starboard at about 300 yards range, but I must have missed him not seeing any hits. Turning to port, I attacked another Zeke closing to less than fifty yards and blowing fragments from its starboard wing. Then I saw a Hap slightly below which was boring in to attack. It half-rolled and I closed diving after it in quick aileron turns. Kittys could dive like falling bricks and I got in about a four second steady burst. Four or five Zeros latched on to me and as their Radial motors loomed a little too large for comfort, it was time to leave. I chased the Hap down to 6,000 feet in a vertical dive throttled back in fine pitch so as not to overshoot. My cockpit misted over, and, pulling out to one side and levelling off, I saw the E/A bury itself in Wana Wana Lagoon.

Another plane crashed about a mile further out. I dived again and at sea level, levelled out and stalked the E/A's still fooling around above as if nothing had happened. I kept informing Vega of their course and numbers and several American P39's made contact.

I couldn't see my No 2 and hoped like hell his wasn't the other plane that crashed. It was obvious our scrap was over, so I flew to Rendova Island climbing to 4,000 feet where I was joined by Max. Vega reported dive bombers were coming in so, with Max as my No 2, headed again upstairs.

'Spud, I'm out of oxygen.'

'OK – we'll hang about for a while.' And for twenty minutes we droned around climbing slowly to 15,000 feet over which height it could be dangerous for Max. Gas was running low and so we advised Vega and slanted down to land excited and happy on Segi. Noel Pirie was there chirpy as a cricket despite a bullet hit in a propeller blade.

'Got one! Did you see it? Fantastic. Sorry I lost you – saw you going down in a gaggle of kites! Have any luck?'

'Yes. That was fun! Saw your Jap hit the water near mine! Good Show!'

Sergeant Laurie had joined up with Noel at about 10,000 feet and the pair had swanned off up to 17,000 feet hoping to have another go. Madness! However, all ended well and we got pretty merry that night on US Navy brandy.

August 14th: Gave cover to four American PT boats evacuating 135 Jap prisoners from Vella La Vella.

August 15th, Sortie 431: Top fighter cover for the main landings and the 'invasion' of Vella La Vella. We were very keen for this to be a great success as New Zealand troops were going into action. 'B' Flight got three Vals and one Zero but to our chagrin we couldn't make contact and didn't even see a sausage at our end of the Island. More supply drops to the Army struggling along in thick steamy jungle – we didn't envy them their hard and dangerous job.

Great news from the Army – two aircraft seen to crash Wana Wana area so Noel Pirie's is now confirmed along with mine.

The next day we went on a Dumbo escort job to Rendova. Dumbos were Catalina flying boats normally used for long range open-ocean shipping recces and patrols. Downed air crew paddling around in their dinghies, or rescued by natives and hidden ashore from the Japs would be picked up and flown back. We found that sometimes the collecting of the 'bods' would be a social event and we'd stooge around and around while dozens of canoes gathered about the big flying boats. If Jap fighters arrived we'd be in real trouble. I don't think the Catalina crews realised how terribly vulnerable they (and we) were. We'd curse their lack of urgency.

Somewhere near our living area, hidden in the jungle, was a liquor still run by enterprising ground-staff. They were fermenting mash in a 'rain-barrel' from treacle, tinned fruit, sugar and raisins – anything they could lay their hands on.

The CO instructed me to locate it for destruction. No way was I going to spoil the men's racket. I knew where the still operated, deeply hidden among the great forest of roots of a huge Banyan tree. If anyone was to put the operation out of action, let it be the Yanks – they were the ones buying the stuff.

CHAPTER X

'You take the port one!'

August 25th 1943: Sortie 442. It was a brilliant blue day and selecting Flight Sergeant N. Pirie as my No 2, I took off to search for shipping along the northern half of Kolombangara Island, Vella Lavella and the southern coast of Choiseul. However, things didn't turn out as planned. We took off from Guadalcanal, did a quick recce along the Marovo Lagoon and refuelled at Segi strip. At 1530 hours, we took off again and about one mile east of Kurduramban-gara (!) point I spotted a bomber type rubber dinghy hidden under mangrove trees. At approximately 1640 hours, we made a landfall at Bambatana Mission on Choiseul where a Jap barge was drawn up against the beach.

On with the gun sight! A quick climb out to sea, a 180 degree turn in and down we went in line astern. Pirie saw flames start after his attack and so we left it to burn itself out. We were only a few miles from Balale Island and Kahili, the big Jap bases and didn't want to hang about! We then headed south-east down the coast and near Sumbi Head, I saw something.

Two small islands to our left were curiously uniform in size and I banked the Kittyhawk in a gentle turn towards them. A hundred yards to the right and slightly astern Sergeant Pirie slid across behind me and over to port. At 200 feet I tightened the turn and, banking steeply, we stared down at the green islets.

They were elongated, and covered in thick foliage. They had no fringing coral shallows but lay in the dark blue of deep water. It was awkward to fly close to them in the narrow bay because of steep hillsides and I kept an eye out for steel cables. Sometimes the wily Japanese slung them between high points to snare the unwary.

There was something wrong and when up-sun of the two islands, I saw it. Saw the flash of sun from glass hidden beneath the leaves. Then I spotted a third boat nosed in against the shore.

'Drop tanks! Line astern – go!'

The 90 gallon belly tanks fell tumbling end over end to burst open on the sea. Pirie dropped behind me as I turned away and flew up-sun to position for attack. A wide turn and –

'Ninety-degrees to port – go!'

We dived almost line abreast towards the mystery boats.

'You take the port one.'

'Roger!'

And in we went in a shallow dive. The .50 calibre machine guns chattered out their deadly hail and tracers spiralled away trailing white smoke to lash the sea to foam or be absorbed in the green foliage. Ricochets could be seen caroming away to skitter across the water in leaping splashes. Leaves and branches were smashed and blown away to reveal the motor torpedo boats beneath.

Three of them, and each about 70 feet long! Gyoraitaeis! The grey devils that plagued the Yank navy in the close in-fighting of night actions among the reefs and islands of New Georgia.

With steep climbing turns to avoid the jungle slopes of Choiseul, we flew back down again and again, diving within feet of the sea's surface to flatten out and spray the boats. The sun shone hot into our cockpits and the saliva dried in our mouths with the excitement of the kill. No need for instructions; no need for words. We flew as one.

The damn things must sink or burn soon, I thought, and then decided to fly away for a spell and try to trap any Japs that might attempt salvage. The boats must be riddled and sinking!

For some twenty minutes we scouted the coastline for more game and then returned to the attack. Fuel covered the sea in iridescent swirls but there was no sign of life. Japanese gunners were probably shooting at us from shelter of trees along the shoreline but we couldn't care less in the thrill of the moment. At the first burst of our fire, the tracers ignited the fuel and the 'islands' burst into flames which ran down and spread across the water. Oily smoke roiled and billowed into the blue sky.

It was time to leave – the black column and raging fires would be visible for miles and we were much too near Jap fighter bases for comfort. We turned towards Kolombangara Island and fled the scene like naughty schoolboys, fearful of punishment.

Thirty miles away, looking back over my shoulder and by slewing the tail of the Kittyhawk to one side, I could see the smoke like a huge exclamation mark. Kolombangara's high peaks were dead ahead and in the shallows of the eastern coast Japanese flak gunners liked to bathe. We caught a few in bursts of fire before climbing for the sky and on back towards our base at Guadalcanal. The Kittyhawk might have been a poor fighter but as a ground strafer it was magnificent with its six .5's, lots of ammo and long range.

More and more the RNZAF were relied on to give close support. US bomber squadrons made a point of asking for us to be detailed to this onerous chore. Their own fighters had the much more pleasant (and safe) job swanning around free-ranging the target area. We were used as close front lower cover – the most difficult, exacting and dangerous position.

The Jap's method of attacking the B24's was a quick dive for speed and to climb up, firing continually, in a head-on approach. Then a half-roll diving away out to one side to climb, head off the bomber stream and repeat the performance. Each attack, made usually in threes and fours, meant that we defending escort-fighters had to dip our noses to meet them and so lost height. Then we'd climb as fast as we could back into position.

At over 20,000 feet, a B24, having dropped its bombs, could actually climb away from a Kittyhawk and on this next occasion this is exactly what happened.

August 28th, Sortie No 445:   Close escort for 27 B24 bombers attacking Kahili air-field with 40 USAAF supporting fighters. Kiwis – three.

'Ma port outer generator's gone blooey – am returning to Cactus,' and a bomber peeled off.

'Having trouble with waist gunner's oxygen' and another went. Some just turned away without even an excuse. As we neared Bougainville, more and more chickened out until, out of twenty-seven big four-engined bombers, only fifteen remained. In excellent close formation these stalwarts forged on. Of the forty US fighters, only eleven remained.

You could feel the tension mounting as we droned up the Slot climbing to 21,000 feet. To my surprise the bomber leader kept on until about five miles inland when we wheeled around in a great curve and began the bombing run. The big boys were going fast and we could not weave. The bomb doors opened. Flight Sergeant Pirie took the starboard side and I the port with Flight Sergeant Laurie as my No 2.

Flak started to burst amongst us and then I saw Jap fighters coming up in a quarter attack from four o'clock at Pirie. I warned him and at the same time saw a mix of eight or nine Zekes and Haps at ten o'clock at our level. These machines bored in, in a semi head-on attack on the bombers behind us. I fired on the leader seeing a few strikes. At 400 yards, he started to fire and, rolling on his back, continued to fire but at nothing – he was stuffed. Black smoke from both wing-roots poured out and, looking back and below, I saw the thing falling in a ball of flames.

Up above us the B24 gunners were hosing away, their white tracer smoke streaming out in great arcs. Away over to starboard I saw Pirie get a Jap which burst into flames and hurtle down. Sergeant Laurie had somehow gone over to him and now he came back to drive a Zero off my tail. The fight got very confused, the only focal point being the great bombers which released their eggs in long streams to plaster the airfield below. With bombs away, the squadron commander gave his turbo-charged Pratt and Whitney's the gas. His whole squadron began to climb! We couldn't stay with them; our Allison motors wheezing away in the thin air. Steadily the gap between us widened and now the three of us were left to the Jap hornet swarm. Soon we three became separated in the mêlée. There was only one thing to do and that was put our noses down in screaming dives for the deck.

Ahead of me, I saw a lone Kitty and drew up to it – Noel Pirie. My No 3 Flight Sergeant Laurie had got lost somewhere (he proceeded on his own and landed OK).

Formating together, Noel and I flew along at fifteen thousand feet below the B24's. Above them several Japs were milling about and suddenly there was a huge white bomb-burst near the bombers. Great streaming tentacles of white smoke hung down from the central cloud. The buggers were trying to bomb the big planes with some new sort of weapon! And again but not so close! There was nothing we could do about it and heading towards a patch of smoke on the NE tip of Ganongga Island, we found two small ships on fire. We tickled them up a bit with the last of our ammo. These boats were the craft Jack Day and his boys had attacked shortly beforehand on shipping recce to Buri Village.

Back at base more criticism for 'having left the bombers.'

'Left them? Left them? The bastards left us!!'

What a bloody lovely situation.

I was having a miserable time at night with pain from the injuries received on my bale-out from the crippled Spitfire in England. The heat and sweat were making my life hell and the continual frustrations of these pitiful bomber escort jobs became more than I could bear.

August 30th 1943   Four of us escorted a Dumbo Catalina to the north-east side of Choiseul, dropping off urgent supplies and picking up several white men. Four and three quarter hours of prickly heat, while they frigged around below having a bloody convention! Back at Kukum things weren't so good either. Flying Officer Stan Duncan was lost while escorting bombers.

Evidently top fighter cover was given by an inexperienced squadron of P39 (Airacobra) mid-engined fighters. These chaps were plucky and gave it all they had. But they, or more likely the top brass, had been reading advertising blurbs on the P39 instead of studying performance reports on the Zero. With their hopelessly outclassed aircraft (for this kind of air warfare) and abandoned by their own supporting P40 and F4U fighters these brave innocents battled on as best they could to protect their mates in the big bombers.

I read the other's reports and felt like weeping with frustration. And how did Stan die? Some of the others claimed he collected a jettisoned bomb on his nose cowling. The CO's report is plain enough. Apart from losing a good pilot and friend, Stan took with him most of the squadron's poker money, which was another reason why air crew should not carry papers with them on operations.

It's a terrible thing to be left with a few stalwarts to battle on against superior odds knowing full well that the bulk of your 'allies' have chickened out and left you to it.

The battle area was clearly defined – marked out, in fact, by flak bursts – 20,000 feet over Kahili with American bombers being attacked by Japanese fighters.

I know there were brave and splendid men among the Americans but it was only here, in the Solomons, that I experienced whole squadrons of fighters deliberately avoiding combat. The following combat form tells of just one of the many incidents which destroyed in me, forever, of any confidence in these allies.

1. SUMMARY OF OPERATION   *RNZAF FORM*
   Aircraft Scrambled : Four P40's
   Pilots: S/Ldr J. S. Nelson, F/Lt G. A. Delves,
            F/O M. T. Vanderpump, F/O S. L. Duncan.
   Enemy Aircraft Destroyed: Nil
   Own losses: F/O S. L. Duncan missing
2. PILOT'S REPORT
   Squadron Leader J.S. Nelson

'I was leading a section of aircraft which were detailed to go to the Russells and land and refuel. Together with 8 Army P40's, we were to R.V. with 27 B24's at PLEASANT POINT south RENDOVA IS. at 1420 hours. We were detailed to act as bottom cover to the bombing mission to KAHILI. The four New Zealand P40's were instructed to take the left hand squadron. Upon meeting the B24's we set a course, with the whole formation, of approximately 270 degrees. At about 1530 hours we altered course to 000 deg. and came around BOUGAINVILLE ISLAND, north-west of KAHILI strip, at 21,000 feet 30 miles from the target 6 Army P40's left the formation in pairs and this left six P40's to carry on as bottom cover. Our four and two of theirs.

'Just prior to commencing the bombing run, ZEROS appeared in the vicinity and commenced to attack the top cover aircraft. They were at about 25,000 ft. and had been obviously well warned of the approach of the Allied formation out of the sun.

'When the bomb doors opened, the four New Zealand P40's moved out to the sides and continued weaving. P39's acting as top close cover remained above the bombers and also continued weaving. *The top flight of F4U's top cover broke away* from the formation to the south-west. Prior to and during the release of the bombs, heavy intense and accurate A/A fire was experienced and some of the bombers were hit. No hits on the strip were observed and all bombs appeared to go down to the north of KAHILI. At this stage ZEROS were manoeuvering to port and starboard of the formation out of range, and they did not attack. When the bomb doors closed, the six P40's resumed station under the bombers. About four miles from the target, on the way home, a B24 in the leading formation made it interesting for us by opening his bomb doors and dropping a load of bombs whilst we were underneath. The bombs fell well out to sea. At this stage I saw a P39 go down in flames, but did not see any sign of the pilot. The ZEROS continued to follow us on either side of the formation above and below. They made repeated attacks on the P39's above, and P40's below, but did not come within range of the bombers. From my position I had a very good view of all activity in the air over the target area, and on the way home to Vella Lavella I saw one ZERO dive into the sea east of KAHILI and I am positive no other ZEROS were shot down, by Allied aircraft, in our vicinity. Whilst weaving I noticed four B24's were flying on three engines and one B24 was flying with four engines; the starboard inboard motor was streaming smoke. About 12 miles north-west of PAKOI BAY I saw a P39 go down in flames into the water. A few minutes later I heard a call from another pilot obviously going down. I did not see him hit the water. About 10 miles off PAKOI BAY I saw the smoking engine of the B24 previously mentioned burst into flames. The engine flew out, the aileron and wing broke away and the plane spun down in flames to the water 10,000 feet below and disappeared. At about 4,000 feet, I saw four parachutes open. ZEROS were still hanging around the outskirts of the formation, making passes at us. In GIZO STRAIT I saw a P39 smoking badly and it crashed into the cliffs north-east of GANONGGA ISLAND, the pilot baled out and landed a little distance from the shore. At this stage I noticed that there were only five P40's with the B24's. On conducting a radio check I found that F/O S.L. Duncan was missing.

'We continued with the bombers to south RENDOVA. The three New Zealand P40's then left the formation and proceeded to SEGI to refuel. We landed there at 1730 hours. Upon landing it was found that F/Lt. Delves' port tyre had apparently been punctured by flak. F/Lt. Delves remained at SEGI overnight whilst repairs were effected. I returned with P/O Vanderpump from SEGI at 1750 hours, landing at Guadalcanal at 1905 hours. All the ZEROS I saw were ZEKES and were painted black. East of KAHILI a ZEKE fired at

F/Lt Delves, my No 2, from above so I broke across but did not fire
and the ZEKE went straight down. I did not see F/O Duncan after the
formation was over KAHILI strip and I presume that he was hit by a
heavy A/A present and went down in the vicinity of KAHILI. Over the
target area I saw two large puffs directly in the path of the bombers.
They looked like aerial bomb bursts, or a special form of A/A fire.
The P39's on their first trip to KAHILI made an excellent job of work
as top cover. They took a punishing which should not have been
taken had the F4U's stayed in position.'

September 3rd, Operational Sortie No 448: A hairy do with confused and
difficult fighting. Four hours of tension best described by Flight
Sergeant Pirie my No 2. Here is his report:

No. 16 (F) Squadron R.N.Z.A.F.   *RNZAF FORM*
Intelligence: Combat report
Operation: Bomber Escort over Kahili
Place, date and time: East of Kahili strip. About 1300 hours on 3rd
                   September 1943
Weather Conditions: 1/10th cloud at 23,500 ft.
1.   SUMMARY OF OPERATION
    Aircraft Scrambled: Eight
    Pilots: S/Ldr. J. E. Nelson, F/Lt G. A. Delves, F/O
          Vanderpump, F/Sgt J. E. Miller, F/Lt R. L. Spurdle,
          F/Sgt N. A. Pirie, F/Lt T. M. De Denne, W/O J. C.
          Voss
    Enemy Aircraft Destroyed: Nil
    Own Losses: F/Sgt N. A. Pirie crash landed on a reef.
2.   PILOT'S REPORT
    Flight Sergeant N. A. Pirie:
'On September 3, I was flying No 2 to F/Lt R. L. Spurdle on a
bomber escort to KAHILI. Just as we were making the run over the
target I noticed about 12 enemy aircraft flying in three sets of four,
spaced out about 700 yards apart in line astern. They were at 7
o'clock and 4,000 feet above us. After leaving the target I was
weaving on the port side of the bombers, dodging the flak. I noticed a
ZEKE coming in on my tail and I turned in towards the bombers,
passing behind and below my No 1. Just then I felt a thump on my
left wing, shrapnel entered the cockpit and I saw a cannon shell hole

on the trailing edge of the fairing. I noticed a lot of tracer entering my starboard wing and going past. On looking down I saw what appeared to be a Kittyhawk coming up from the starboard quarter astern. I felt my engine give a jolt then settle down again. I now realised that the aircraft must have been a TONY. But this time I had passed underneath the bombers and I started weaving under them. I called to my No 1 that I had been hit, but received no reply. The ZEROS were now hanging on about a mile behind the bombers and they left the formation about the North tip of VELLA LAVELLA. Shortly after my engine gave a violent jolt and quietened down. White smoke was coming from the exhaust stacks. All my temperatures were normal, except my coolant gauge which was U/S, the needle going to 0. My engine then stopped altogether and I glided away from the formation towards the coast of VELLA LAVELLA. I jettisoned my hood and switched off my magnetos and closed the throttle. While gliding down I pressed the two detonator buttons for the I.F.F. and the radio. I then picked out a coral reef offshore from VELLA LAVELLA, and as I could not get my flaps down and was losing height rapidly, I ran down wind on the reef, then turned into wind, flicked as I turned, but recovered quickly. I straightened out, eased the stick back, and I don't remember what happened after that.'

F/Lt SPURDLE'S Report:

'When I saw Pirie's engine go dead I kept weaving near him to give him moral support. I guessed his RT must have been U/S and, as Vella LaVella was still Jap held, I started to be concerned. A few miles away I saw the wake from a small high-speed craft but couldn't ascertain its nationality.

'The crippled machine was heading for the pale green and browns of a shallow off-shore reef. There was a terrific cloud of spray as it hit and skidded to a halt. Cutting my speed to about 120 m.p.h., I crabbed by and saw movement in the cockpit and then the pilot climbed out and started to inflate his dinghy. I opened up and flew to the main shoreline for a quick recce up and down the coast. There was a Jap barge hidden under mangroves; close by a small native settlement appeared quite deserted – lifeless. This was a sure sign of enemy occupation so I straffed the barge out of commission, gave the village a squirt for good measure and flew back to Pirie.

'I gave him the 'Stay Put' sign and, such was his training, he paddled back to his kite and hung on to it. Then I flew out to find the launch which turned out to be an American Higgins boat. I flew around and around it waggling my wings violently and then heading towards the crashed Kittyhawk. The crew wouldn't respond so there was only one thing to do – I fired a burst across their bows and shepherded it by force and by signs towards Pirie. Twice it tried to turn away and twice a short burst made them re-think and get back on course.'

Flight Sergeant Pirie's report goes on:

'The next thing I knew I was getting out of the cockpit and saw my rubber dinghy inflated and floating alongside the fuselage. I saw the P40's circling around me. I then had a look at the cockpit and found the gunsight smashed, the wooden seat was smashed in, and one of the straps was broken. The propeller had come off and was lying a few yards behind the tail. I saw another rubber dinghy on a sandbank with something alongside it. This dinghy was a black one, probably an old Carley float. I got in my dinghy and paddled towards it, but did not get very far as one of the pilots in a circling P40 waved me back. I pulled up alongside the wing and tied the dinghy to the harness strap which was unbroken. I saw a boat coming round the corner towards me a few miles off, so I waited until he got close and then waded towards the boat. I got on the Higgins boat and they took me to a Mission where I got medical treatment for cuts and bruises. The next day a P.T. boat took me to RENDOVA, and from there a Higgins boat took me to MUNDA. I spent the night at the hospital and returned to GUADALCANAL by SCAT the next day.' Finish of report.

Having seen Noel off safely in the Higgins, I headed off. Short of fuel I put down at Munda, refuelled, and did a recce back to Guadalcanal. Next day, on Op Sortie No 450, I completed my Pacific Tour with an escort job to Ballale Island. 16 Squadron's tour was coming to an end but I'd had it and wanted out. The CO criticised Pirie for landing 'down wind' on his crash-landing and that just finished me off.

'A' flight were withdrawn by DC3 to Espiritu Santo and I took the opportunity to see the MO to get myself invalided back to New Zealand along with Noel and some sick airmen. We landed at

Norfolk Island after a five and a half hour flight then took off to Whenuapai base in New Zealand.

After a week's leave, I was admitted into the Wanganui Public Hospital and, in trepidation, waited for the knife.

CHAPTER XI

'How would you like to join my wing?'

Came the day of the operation and a smiling moon-faced character armed with a cut-throat razor. He was dressed in white longs and a US Marine Corps 'T' shirt.

'Off with the pants, Limey,' he drawled.

'What for?' I asked.

'I'm going to shave you.'

'No way! I'll do it myself!'

'No can do – this gotta be done right – Doc's orders.'

I suddenly realised what this character was – one of the Marine Corpsmen found psychologically unsuited for warfare and relegated to useful work in safe areas.

I bared myself and flinched as the wanker waved his shining blade in one hand while he grasped and pulled the old man like a chicken's neck with the other.

The blade was blunt and soon a necklace of nicks made me wonder if I'd have to be rechristened Roberta.

'Take it easy! Take it easy!' Memories of the mad B24 leader flashed through my mind.

'Hey, Nurse! Come and look at this guy's toes curl! And he's got a medal!'

A day later, the job done, Shirly came to visit giggling and teasing me. Now I knew how Heapo had felt!

I was released and posted to Ohakea on communication duties ferrying odd bods about New Zealand. I was ordered to report to the Air Member for Personnel at AHQ Wellington. Dressed in my best blues, I turned up curious to hear the reason for the summons.

As I sat in the waiting room, Nelson came out, gave me no greeting but an enigmatic look. Curious!

I was 'wheeled' in, came to attention, and saluted.

'Ah, Spurdle.'

'Sir.'

'We are sending you back to the United Kingdom.'

'Good! Thank you, sir!'

'Not good – you are going back with an adverse report!'

I was absolutely flabbergasted. My mind raced madly – the thought of Nelson's glance gave me an inkling. I decided to attack.

'I don't understand, sir! I set up the Gunnery school at Ohakea successfully and in 16 Squadron my No 2 and I accomplished as much as the rest of the squadron combined.'

'You are accused of having undermined your Commanding Officer's authority and this we cannot tolerate.'

'Sir, I respectfully submit that I was put in a most invidious position. As the only pilot with experience of air-combat the men naturally turned to me. I couldn't deny them the benefits of my knowledge.'

'Be that as it may, you also, according to combat reports, abandoned bombers under attack in the face of the enemy.'

This was bloody unfair and I asked permission to explain what had happened. Now the bitter facts came out to the AVM's surprise. That our obsolete machines when under attack from ahead and below couldn't maintain station with empty B24's climbing at height. That RNZAF aircrew were being made use of by the Americans in the more dangerous situations and that a number of our squadron pilots were unsuited for combat duties. I was asked to name them which I did most reluctantly but in the firm conviction it was for the good of the service.

'Sir, I have a request – can Flight Sergeant Pirie accompany me to the UK – he's one of the best potential aces I've met. He's wasted out here.' But in a sense, this was illogical, as was pointed out to me. If he was that good, the RNZAF needed him. It was useless to expound my theories based on personal hard experience that continuous and comprehensive fighter recces could completely cripple Japanese shipping movements in the islands, as they were hopelessly vulnerable to air attack. Being a veteran of some eighty-nine shipping recces off the French Coast, I could speak with authority. I was also firmly convinced that the Americans didn't really want us with them – we were like a bad conscience to them, visible examples of what reliable and dependable pilots in the execution of duty should be.

Air Vice Marshal Bannerman had been a fighter pilot in the Great War, credited with fifteen victories and winning a DFC and bar. He knew only too well the hazards of an operational pilot's life and was sympathetic towards me, listening with respect to my report. The upshot being that I was posted back to England with a clean sheet, Nelson was replaced in 16 Squadron by the experienced Johnny Arkwright and several ho-hum pilots relegated to non-operational roles.

As the war in the Pacific developed my predictions came true. The American forces moved on leaving the Aussies and New Zealanders behind to contain and harass the abandoned Japanese garrisons dotted about in no longer strategic enclaves. The Americans went on to fight and win the great battles up north while we, poor country cousins, were soon forgotten in the grand scheme of things.

Now that I was being sent back to England, I persuaded Shirly to marry me – I wasn't going to have another soul-destroying separation as before. Being RAF I could take my wife to England but unfortunately we couldn't travel on the same boat.

Along with several other RAF 'trouble-makers' and a large contingent of RNZAF ground staff and aircrew, I joined the *Umgeni* for the long haul back. We had European officers and a Lascar crew who ate curry so hot it was almost inedible to whites.

We went via Melbourne and for the first time, I saw signs of the war's most travelled and elusive character. Written on a pub's loo door –

> Here I sit full of joy –
> I got here before Kilroy.*

and in another hand below it –

> A dirty lie she has been spoke –
> Kilroy was here but his pencil broke.

Two days in Aussie, then off in a great arc to Colombo in Ceylon,

* Nobody has ever established who 'Kilroy' was or if he actually existed. But this slogan 'Kilroy was here' appeared all over English speaking war zones. It became a kind of cult.

where we had a couple of days shopping, sightseeing and whooping it up.

Near us, moored alongside a Dutch supply ship, was a Royal Navy submarine. Never having been on one before, a friend and I walked along the dockside, up a gangway and over the Dutchman's deck to climb down onto the sub's casing. We were surprised to find a New Zealand rating in the crew. He was a pretty hard shot and evidently delighted to brag how tough kiwis were.

Down in the oily confines, surrounded by strange tubing and wiring looms, we were entertained by the cheerful sailors enjoying a spot of port leave.

'Hey! Your kiwi cousin reckons all you blokes are tough! Try this for size!' and a laughing matelot handed us each a glass, brimful with neat Navy Rum. Manfully we struggled our way through the dreadful pungent stuff. Feeling queer with the diesel and rum fumes we made our exit as gracefully as possible. We had not shamed our countryman!

On the Dutchman's deck we were invited to join a merry group enjoying the evening sun and bottles of Bols. 'Haf dis vun!' and we were faced with large glasses of colourless, stinking fire. Again the stoics!

By the finish of this exercise in public relations we were heaving and gagging and only made it down onto the dockside and behind some rolling stock before the inevitable happened. However, we were unobserved and so New Zealand was not disgraced. I've never faced square gin again!

Then on to Aden where we were re-coaled by unending streams of filthy natives, men and women, unfortunates who struggled up the steep gangplanks to empty their heavy sacks into holds. Every now and again a carrier would 'stumble' and drop his or her load into the sea. Down below, operating from small dhows, natives were busy salvaging the lost coal with grabs – a kind of continuous rip-off being engineered.

Up through the long channel of the Red Sea and through the Suez Canal we steamed stopping at Suez to take on a canal pilot. Dropping the pilot off at Port Said we cruised on under an umbrella of fighters to Alexandria.

It was a gorgeous day and we were at long last granted shore leave.

Large barges came alongside and our chaps filed down in a chattering holiday throng. I arranged to go ashore by the RAF high-speed launch used to take mail to and from the troopers in port.

'Hey Spud! You're making a mistake! That thing will be doing a dozen ships before going ashore!' someone shouted but, by now committed, I carried on. The launch master kindly ran me straight to a pier where a Greek Naval officer gave me a lift through the dock gates and so into town.

My big ambition was to buy bottles of hard liquor to take to England and with this in mind, I stopped in one wine shop after another. By sampling a bit here and a bit there, I not only collected two large crates of mixed liqueurs, but got a real buzz on. Leaving the boxes with an obliging storekeeper, I wandered out into the heat, flies and dust to look around the ancient city. And had an amazing piece of luck. A rather handsome woman, complete with some kind of housekeeper-companion, made friends with me and took me sight-seeing. She had a big car and seemingly unlimited fuel. We visited the ancient Catacombs and in one of Alexandria's fantastic museums saw ancient relics collected from over 2,000 years of civilisation.

Back at her flat, cooled by slowly rotating fans, we drank Turkish coffee and sipped anisette and ouzo until, almost legless, I was delivered to the store, collected my cases and was deposited on the wharf. Her companion whispered, 'Her son was killed by the Germans – this pleases her.'

A chartered bum-boat took me out to the *Umgeni* and I teetered up the gangway with willing hands (on which I carefully checked) heaving up my loot. But the cat-calls from hundreds of perspiring brassed-off blokes perplexed me.

'Where the hell have you been?' Master-at-Arms enquiring.

'Ashore.'

'I can see that! How the hell did you do it?'

'Went in the mail launch, why?'

And then it came out – the shore-leave parties had been cancelled and the crowded barges recalled. Of all the hundreds on board, I was the only one who got ashore! But what was worse was that ten days out of Alexandria, crew and passengers started complaining of mechanised dandruff-crabs.

'Not me! Bloody Hell, I'm just married; I didn't fool around ashore!'

But they were not convinced – I think somehow the ship's laundry, done ashore, had been salted (if that is the word); certainly I was not the culprit.

The *Umgeni* was marshalled into a convoy and once again, under an umbrella of land-based fighters, when available, we made the run through the Mediterranean to Gibraltar.

Gibraltar was an unhappy place with no shore-leave and sleep almost impossible. All night small craft patrolled the anchored ships. As they idled along, 4lb charges of Amatol were dropped to explode under-water, the idea being to stun or discourage frogmen operating from Spanish bases. The continual metallic crashes now near, now far, kept us in sleepless tension all night.

Leaving Gibraltar's sheltered harbour in the black of night, we made off for England keeping well out to sea to avoid the searching Condors.

England! Back to austerity and the black-out but also, to my huge surprise, Shirly! She'd gone via the Panama Canal – a shorter route. Full of her great adventure and with a new-found friend, my wife was safe and happily set up for the moment sharing a flat in London. We had a few happy days before I had to report in for a posting. Shirly begged me to keep off ops, but heck! The invasion was looming up, and selfish or not, *no* way was I going to miss this!

Another battle with Group.

'You've done four tours! We've hundreds of aircrew who haven't had the chance of even one; the Empire Air Training Scheme's turning them out like sausages!'

'Well, you won't want a bunch of sausages for the Invasion! You know you'll need every experienced man you can get!' and on it went back and forth. Then all of a sudden my mysterious friend was on the line and the hiccup was cured.

'How does 130 Squadron at Horne sound?'

'What are they flying? No! Forget that! I don't care if they are flying Tiger Moths!'

'They're on 5B's.'

'Great! Thanks again – you've been a real pal to me!'

'Cheerio, Spud. Look after yourself and good luck!'

Oh hell! I'd been on 5A's which were much the same thing, when with 91 Squadron eighteen months before. 130 was a good bunch and, flying as a section-leader, I did six ops before being summoned by Wing Commander 'Hawkeye' Wells to Hornchurch for an interview.

'Hawkeye' had been a prominent New Zealand clay-bird shooting champion before joining the RAF with a short-service commission. He flew in the Battle of Britain and was the first British-based fighter pilot to engage Italian fighters sent to help escort GAF bombers raiding England. The Italians, for largely political reasons, wanted to share in the conquest of Britain and sent their obsolete Fiat CR42 biplanes over the Channel. After a few disastrous flurries against our Spitfires, the survivors were quickly withdrawn.

'How did you get on with the RNZAF? How did the Japs perform?' Hawkeye had had a rough time when on loan to the RNZAF in October 1942 and had been advised that, 'You might be an acting wing commander in the RAF, but here (in New Zealand) you are considered a flight lieutenant!'

'Well, I was returned as a nuisance – you know the score! The Jap planes are good, but they're an odd bunch – they seem to fly in huge aerobatic swarms. No real formation – just a mass of planes, heading generally in the same direction. Very hard to attack and hopeless to mix with. The Liberators keep breaking down – they don't seem to do proper DIs. They don't press home attacks over the target but bomb while turning. Jettisoning their loads in fact. All sorts of Mickey Mouse stuff like that. The Yank dive bombers are good – plenty of guts but often as not do their own positions over.'

'Yes – I can well imagine it. We'll have a real session later. Now, how would you like to join my wing? You'd come in as a flight commander and in line for your own squadron.'

'Wizard! What's the squadron and what are we flying?'

'80 – they're just back from Italy with an excellent record and are being re-equipped with Spitfire 9A's. You'll join them at Sawbridgeworth. The present CO is a Norwegian, Major Björn Björnstad – his English is pretty horrible but he'll be moving on soon, I think.'

And so it was settled. I said goodbye to 130 and tore up to London to tell Shirly the good news. We decided to defer looking for more permanent lodgings until things got settled, and she stayed on with Flight Lieutenant Wally Raymond and his wife, another Shirley. Wally had passed out in the same course at Wigram with me at the beginning of the war. Fortunately, he was to survive the war. The four of us drove in Wally's car to Sawbridgeworth where I was greeted by the CO and introduced to the squadron pilots.

From Sawbridgeworth, 80 went to Hornchurch and Detling and Merston and Gatwick, West Malling and Manston and lastly to Coltishall in the space of just four months! A lot of this time was spent under canvas, the idea being to harden us up to the rigours of living rough on the Continent when the invasion came off.

I settled in with 80 very happily – they were a good tough bunch – a mixture of Commonwealth pilots forming just the sort of squadron I'd always considered the best. National type squadrons like the all-Canadian or all-Australian or all-New Zealander units were too parochial in their outlook and, in my opinion, tended to be back-scratchers. Eighty squadron had originally been formed at Montrose in Scotland on 10th August 1917, and its first CO, a Major V. D. Bell. The squadron's logo was a bell and its motto was 'Strike True'. This was not as macho as we would have liked especially as our nickname with the other squadrons became 'The Bell Boys'.

I could see how the Air Force was changing – as war's attrition thinned out the original air crews, and as survivors were withdrawn from operations, or promoted to higher ranks, the RAF became for the much greater part an air force of duration only personnel. It was the sheer numbers and fresh innovative outlook of these volunteers, leavened by tradition and the guidance of switched-on Regulars, that created the mightiest Air Force ever. Air crew or ground staff, men or women, machine for machine, the RAF was incomparable. Weeded out wallies and wankers disappeared into the woodwork – relegated to jobs where they could potter about and do little harm. Unfortunately internecine scufflings amongst some top brass sometimes overflowed and affected the fighting men with stupid directives or priorities. I suppose this was to be expected as the only thing history teaches us is that history doesn't teach us.

My first flight with 80 was for familiarisation with the Spit IX to 39,000 feet. At about 18,000 feet, the second stage of the supercharger cut in with a bang and the plane was rejuvenated. This was more like it!

May passed quietly enough with only seven operational sorties escorting bombers over France. All manner of rumours were afoot – certainly something really big was about to happen. Several times the squadron was alerted to be ready for an early morning scramble; leave was curtailed and we were sent on more and more shipping cover patrols over the Thames estuary where hundreds of large barges, tank landing craft and coastal boats were tied in serried ranks. We had to be careful not to fly near the AA towers erected in the Estuary as they were very trigger happy. Our aircraft had great alternating black and white bands painted under their wings and around the rear fuselage for easy identification by our ground troops. It made little difference, Pongos being trigger happy and the Navy always blasted at any planes foolish enough to fly near them.

Late one night, the CO drew me aside and, in his mangled English, told me to organise a strong team for the morning and to see that they got to bed early. Getting hold of 'Slim' Burbridge, our 'A' flight commander, we tossed as to who would stand down so the CO could lead the squadron. I won and, not knowing all the pilots' abilities thoroughly, got Slim to help me sort out a good bunch.

I chose 'Willy' Wiltshire as my No 2. He was tough and reliable. Flying Officer Louis Graham Smith (from Trinidad) was to lead Warrant Officer Ross, and Jerry Bush would have 'Bluey' Rankin. The CO selected Flying Officer F. Lang as his No 2.

All night heavy planes droned overhead – we'd never heard anything like it before. It was *ON*! Invasion! The great gamble planned for years and prepared for at such a huge cost. Thousands of planes and boats of all types and tens of thousands of men and machines in a huge armada on and above the Channel. We were awakened well before dawn by excited batmen, scoffed a hurried breakfast and tore off to dispersal.

We waited and waited. The CO was almost beside himself with frustration and pestered Ops for a job for our squadron. But everything had been planned and planned again. Our job was to stand by and be ready for any special job which might crop up. We were being held in reserve!

Björn wasn't a patient man and it was amusing to hear his pleas, threats and cajolings in fractured English. As the day wore on we got more and more brassed off. History was being made! The Huns were bound to react in what could be a giant air battle! Bits and pieces of news filtered in from the Radio section and the BBC squeezed out some obviously heavily censored gen. Noon came and went – nothing!

Then all of a sudden everything changed and we were running to our kites. Glider close escort! As soon as we strapped our Spitfires on, we took off to join a glider 'train' of Albemarles* towing Horsa gliders at 6,000 feet. Then a group of giant Stirling night-bombers black and menacing hove in sight lugging huge Hamilcar gliders to join our group.

Below, stretching as far as one could see, were rows of ships of all sizes. Some towed silver barrage balloons which floated along in the air like kids' toys. We weaved back and forth riding 'shotgun' for the otherwise almost defenceless 'train'.

Loaded ships heading for the beach-heads kept in huge lanes while emptied craft streamed back to England for reloading in separate channels. We could see towering clouds of smoke from fires on sea and land. Destroyers laid more screens of smoke as myriad tank and infantry landing barges shuttled back and forth from the transports lying off shore.

Naval units were duelling with German shore batteries and Typhoon fighter bombers dived to blast gun positions with their rockets. Over and around this fantastic mêlée Allied fighter squadrons patrolled. Out of sight more and yet more fighters acted as a screen to hold off any GAF units trying to break through to attack the giant armada.

Our glider tugs weaved slightly aligning themselves for the run-in over the coast. Two of the wooden Albemarle tugs were hit by flak to fall in flames.

One of the Horsas couldn't release; perhaps its pilot's dead, or its mechanism jammed, and, as its tug pulled it down it shed its wings and fell in a cloud of bits and pieces. A few of the tug's crew baled out

---

* Designed as light twin-engined bombers and constructed of wood like the 'Mosquitos' these aircraft were relegated to this more prosaic task.

and their parachutes blossomed but the others died with their machines in dreadful crashes.

Released gliders stooped, curving down to plough along the grassy banks of a small river near a bridge. By this time our squadron had descended to some 2,000 feet and I spotted a tracked vehicle pushing through a hedgerow towards the landing zone. It was indicated quite clearly by tell-tale marks across a field.

'Railroad leader! This is Blue leader. Am attacking ground target to port. Blue section line astern go! Spread out!' and down we went to strafe the Jerry machine. It was probably a tank and our bullets and 20mm shells would bounce off it but at least it would scare the shit out of the bastards. We gave it a thorough pasting but there was no obvious damage and it remorselessly ploughed on. It would take bombs or rockets to pierce the heavy armour.

'Blue section – reform angels four' and up we rose to rejoin the others and head off for home.

Nearing the English coast I didn't think we could make base safely and so, advising our shortage of fuel, we landed at Hawkinge. It was deep dusk before our kites were rearmed and refuelled so I opted to stay the night and contacted Detling.

Our squadron Spy promised to ring Shirly and let her know I was safe – all our civilian lines being sealed off. That night turned into a wizard thrash – pilots from a dozen different squadrons had been forced to land for refuelling or with their machines shot up by ground fire.

Early next day, with aching heads, we buzzed back to Detling and were de-briefed.

June 8th.   A busy day with a shipping patrol and two sweeps over France. The first was a long one of over two hours but the second cut short by the weather closing in. No flying next day – everyone worried as winds lashed the Normandy coast and our beach-heads threatened by the Huns' growing resistance.

June 10th. Sortie No. 471.

Off to Beachy Head to cover the invasion fleet – the water crawling with hundreds of boats of all types and sizes. One stood out – the new cruiser *Black Prince* and, circling above, Gerry Bush called out that his engine was packing up. Pulling out of formation, with black smoke and white glycol vapour streaming, Gerry prepared to bale out. He was too far out and too low to attempt gliding to shore.

We could see Gerry shed his helmet to free himself of its oxygen tube and RT connections. Then over he rolled but instead of falling clear he was held backwards by the slipstream, forced against the head rest and canopy rim.

'Bale out! Bale out!'

In mounting horror we watched his machine dive vertically and then slowly, as its speed built up, start to pull out and level off. Diving alongside I could see Gerry kicking and struggling to free himself. Just when we thought he'd bought it, he scrabbled out in time to pull the rip-cord and float down into the sea where he was picked up OK.

June 12th. We were off on another fighter sweep over the beach-head. The Spy had advised us that an emergency landing strip had been formed at St Croix sur mer. This I must try out! Sure enough four of us managed to burn up enough fuel to make a landing imperative and down we dropped. Bugger this for a lark! The strip was very short! While the kites were being refuelled, after being pushed under trees and covered with camouflaged netting, the four of us stretched our legs into the village. No money, and liqueurs to be bought!

Hey! There was money in our plastic escape-kits and, breaking the seals, we had 100 francs each. Well, it *was* for emergencies! At a little estaminet, we bought a queer meal of tinned foods. A passing Tommy told us of a booby-trapped dead Hun nearby and we viewed the gruesome bloated corpse. Just then in a howling dive came a FW190 chased by three Spitfires. The ruddy local Bofors guns opened up and through streams of flaming shells the fighters tore. Cannon fire thudded out and the Jerry went down in a ball of fire. It was time to get back home to Detling!

June 13th. Escort to bombers south-west of Caen with really horrible flak bringing down two of them.

June 14th. Another beach-head patrol and Red Section, led by the

CO flew right over the city with 40mm self-destroying flak winking all around them. Actually it was a funny sight – but they didn't see it that way, nor do it again!

June 16th   and our job to escort the *Black Prince*. This was a fine and stirring experience for all of us – our King was on board – actually in the firing line along with thousands of ordinary folk.

June 17th.   Another fighter sweep and just before due to return for home, I detached myself and my No 2 with 'engine trouble'. The two of us landed on a new airstrip 'B3' and helped refuel our machines from 4 gallon jerrycans. High octane slopped over our hot exhausts and we were pushed under orchard trees draped with netting. We had a horrible night – no food – shells bursting all around and shrapnel thudding down from our defensive AA-fire while Hun intruders tried to bomb the place. We slept under a plywood table and prayed for dawn. I didn't do this again!

Bloody Hell! Another shift! This time to Gatwick.

June 19th. Sortie No. 480.   Escort to Lancasters dropping 12,000 1b bombs near Calais – fantastic! The huge bombs just seemed to hang in the air before curving down to vanish thousands of feet below. Actually the big four-engined bombers rose as soon as the bombs were released giving this curious illusion. It was all very hush-hush – at the time we didn't know of the giant gun, buried under yards of earth and concrete, aimed to lob shells on London ninety miles away. This was just one of Hitler's secret weapons – the Hochdruckpumpe with a barrel 150 yards long! The 12,000 1b 'Earthquake' bombs tilted the huge concrete cupola-shield and put finish to this bit of German 'frightfulness'.

More and more escort jobs – supply drops by Stirlings with hundreds of containers swinging down on parachutes. On the 29th, our Wing Commander, 'Hawkeye' Wells, got hit by flak but force-landed in France OK. In a magazine I'd seen pictures of our WAAC girls serving anti-aircraft guns, handling the computers etc. I knew that German girls did the same and it seemed particularly beastly and revolting to think of women shooting at men. The thought of killing girls or of them killing my men was, to me, the ultimate perversion in warfare.

Confusion over my ambivalent emotions made me almost paranoid about anti-flak missions and I'd attack with a viciousness I found hard to understand. Our squadron doctor couldn't help me, nor the padre.

One day 'Hawkeye' told me of his experience back home in New Zealand: 'In August 1942, as a rest from operations, I was sent to Canada and the USA to give a series of lectures on our latest fighter tactics against the Germans and our experience of theirs. I was also offered the chance to go on to New Zealand for a few weeks combining some home leave there with whatever lectures the RNZAF might wish to arrange.

'In due course, I arrived in Auckland by B17 bomber, which was en route to Guadalcanal. After the prescribed 7 days home leave, I reported to Air Headquarters in Wellington. Upon reporting there for my instructions, I was told that the Chief of the Air Staff (whose name for the moment escapes me) personally wished to see me. Upon being shown into his office the conversation went something like this:

' "Well, Wells, so you are back in New Zealand at last."

' "Yes, sir."

' "Well, I have been giving some thought to your future employment here. Tell me, what is your substantive rank?"

' "I really don't know sir, but I suppose it would be Flight Lieutenant."

' "Yes, I think that is right, we'll have to find you some post in that rank. I say this, because you should know that your rapid promotion and decorations overseas have caused considerable ill-feeling and resentment here, among those who have not had your opportunities. In my case, for instance, I spent twelve years as a flight lieutenant." (I then began to see where at least some of the resentment lay).

'Absolute astonishment on my part, plus a feeling of anger and outrage at such a chilly welcome home. Then, after a short pause without words, I said sharply:

' "I don't think you are entitled to do that, because my movement orders, which I have with me in my hotel, require me to be back in the UK by the end of January at the latest for future duties with the RAF."

' "Well, we'll soon see about that. I'll signal Air Ministry today."

'I turned and left the room in a fury without further words. I then went to the Royal Oak Hotel to collect my movement orders and returned and showed them to the personal assistant to the CAS. However, he said that in the interval of my absence, the CAS had despatched a signal to Air Ministry, in effect, asking that my movement order be cancelled and that I remain in New Zealand under his command. So I would have to wait until their reply to learn my fate.

'Next day the personal assistant, with a wink, allowed me to see Air Ministry's reply, the text of which, as far as memory serves, went like this: "AMP for CAS RNZAF. Wells is not to be detained beyond the date of his existing movement order. Nor is he to be employed in any rank below that of Wing Commander." How does that grab you?

'Well, now I can see why David Clouston and I got such a reception. And all the others. Makes you feel pretty bitter! Thank God I was RAF.'

*

That's nice! We are now allowed to wear our little gold Caterpillar Club badges but only *under* our right lapels! Sometimes RAF top brass showed a sense of humour! This edict was made after pressure from the thousands who had had to take to their 'brollies'.

CHAPTER XII

The Best Job in the Air Force!

It looked as if Björn was off to the States on a lecture tour! With his English?!! Wing Commander Wells called me to his office.

'Bob, I'm putting you up for 80! You are to go up to Uxbridge for an interview!'

I didn't know what to say at first – felt choked up with deep emotion. To be a squadron leader was the best job in the Air Force.

'I don't know how to thank you, Bill! You can rely on me to give my best! 80 is a great outfit. Thank you!'

'Well, you haven't got it yet. Some old coot at Group will check your manners, so see you use the right forks.'

The wheels of the train clickety clacked saying, 'This is it! this is it! this is it!' and the miles flew past.

Heapo! I'd get him as a flight commander! Slim Burbridge was overdue for a rest and Heapo was still being stultified in the wilds of Scotland.

On arrival at Uxbridge I was interviewed by a charming old group captain who no doubt checked my fingernails, shirt collar and cuffs, could understand my English and noticed I hadn't forgotten how to pass the port.

July 20th.　80 was mine! I had a signal sent off for Heapo and a few days later he arrived as excited as a kid. I introduced him to Shirly and said, 'If we ever have a son, my love, I want to call him John!'

'You said you wanted David for a namesake!'

'I do! I do! We'll incorporate the two and toss which name comes first!'

On 24th July 1944, leading Flying Officer Gerry Bush I did a weather recce in preparation for a special 'No Ball' raid. It was a grim flight with 10/10 low cloud and on landing was refuelled immediately to take off and lead seven others as close escort for six

Lancasters and two special 'Pathfinder' Mosquitos to the Flexicourt area. They must have been using some electronic locating gear because the Mossies put down flares through the cloud and the bombers dropped six monstrous bombs. Back at base, another quick turn around and off to France in the Laval area on armed recce.

Tearing along a country road was an ambulance. We had been briefed that the Huns were suspected of using them to transport ammunition to the front and returning with wounded. I decided to find out and, in any case, I believed it stupid, Geneva Convention or not, to give comfort to the enemy and allow wounded to be patched up to fight again.

'Railroad aircraft! Line astern go!'

'It's got crosses,' someone called.

'I know! I know!' and down we went. As the first flash of my cannon shells exploded on it the ambulance blew up in a series of violent pyrotechnics. The bastards *were* misusing their red crosses!

One day, flying in West Malling's circuit, doing an air-test on a repaired Spit, I spotted a lovely house near the aerodrome – it had a swimming pool! On landing I collected the Adjutant and requisitioned it. There was a bit of a fuss as it was owned by a Naval Officer who was at sea. However, we soon had his wife out and our pilots moved in to Springhill. Not all was perfect however – a Mosquito night fighter and intruder squadron moved to West Malling and we were evicted from our dispersal.

And where did they put us? In converted airmen's lavatories. How quickly our fortunes changed! One moment we were No 1 and next minute the horrible V1 Doodle Bugs stripped us of our importance. Typhoons and the new model Spitfires were being used to chase the evil little robots by day and at night the Mosquitos took over.

There were rumours of a new Hawker fighter – the Tempest. And several of our curious jet fighters had been spotted but we couldn't get any gen on them. Only that they were fast!

One night when my wife was staying at Springhill I heard the curious harsh throbbing of an approaching V1.

'It sounds like an evil motor bike!' exclaimed Shirly. It was a remarkably accurate description. It *did* sound evil. Soon it came into sight heading straight towards us and Shirly got scared.

'Don't worry, love, as long as the motor keeps going we're OK!'

And with that, the thing conked out. We could hear the whistle as it dived towards us.

Grabbing my wife and yelling to the others in warning, I heaved Shirly under the bed just as the V1 hit the earth and exploded in a horrid roar. Glass from the French windows clashed all around. For a confused moment I thought we'd had it, but soon the shouts of our aroused pilots indicated it was a near miss. Bits of wood and debris banged down on the garden and we kept inside under cover until all was still.

Another Doodle Bug flew by at about a thousand feet with its pulsating yellow tail and ugly drumming row. Next day I sent my wife back home to safety in Birchington.

August 15th. Sortie No. 510.   A fantastic operation! Over 2,000 heavies escorted by a thousand fighters clobbering a dozen or so GAF airfields. We were with the group that attacked Eindhoven in Holland and I took movies with my little Bell and Howell camera.

August 23rd. Sortie No. 513.   Leading Flying Officer MacLachlan (Aus) and with Heapo leading Flying Officer Calder (Aus) we found and destroyed a large half-track which burnt well.

I was getting a bit tetchy about our formation flying. It was obvious we'd have to brush our act up especially with new aircraft arriving.

'Heapo, you lead me and we'll put on a real demonstration of how we want formation flying done!'

I got all our pilots out in front of the dispersal hut and said, 'Now you chaps! This is the way I expect you to fly in future!'

Heapo and I roared off down the runway with me tucked in close échelon. We did a perfect circuit and landing, our planes almost touching. My frigging tail wheel got caught in a faulty patch of steel matting and got pulled clean off and so I finished in a screeching of tortured metal and had to walk back to the cheering 'Bell boys'.

August 26th. Sortie No. 516.   My last Spitfire operational trip – a Rodeo in the Lille area.

Hawkeye left the Wing and a Wing Commander Wray took over.

He soon earned the nickname '45 minute Wray' because his forays were somewhat short affairs.

Our Tempests arrived! Brand new; shining in the sun! They seemed huge after our dainty Spitfires. But could they go! We found they cruised at almost 100 m.p.h. faster than the Spits, climbed like rockets and dived at incredible speeds. They were magnificent gun platforms and, apart from a slight tendency to swing on take-off, had no real vices. We were delighted.

Something very sad happened which profoundly affected us all – ground staff and pilots. We were being split apart. Our men were being detached and reposted en masse and from now on our aircraft would be serviced by TAF ground crews.

Several of the 'old sweats' had been with 80 for seven years – from the date of this famous squadron's re-forming at Kenley in 1937. They knew every nut and bolt, every rivet in our aircraft. They had waited in anxious tension until their pilots and machines returned from action in Egypt, Greece, Libya, Palestine and Italy.

I was very upset when I noticed Chiefy and some others actually weeping.

I protested to Group at first but was put in the picture – 80 was to be sent onto the Continent soon and the transporting of 300 odd men from drome to drome was just not logistically possible. How strange – one by one the RAF was adopting procedures long proven and used by the GAF. First the finger formations, cannons, fighters carrying bombs and rockets, and now this.

The fact that we were to take our Tempests overseas was marvellous – we hadn't been able to use them over enemy territory in case one got forced down and evaluated by the Hun. As if it mattered at this stage of the war!

Now we were practising wing and squadron formation flying for our raids across the channel. I could see more of Shirly who was sure a baby was on its way. She was nervous and concerned for me but I was supremely happy and confident that all would be well.

It was a fantastic thrill to have my own squadron – to lead this bunch of fine pilots flying the best fighter in the Allies' stable. Looking first to one side and then the other at my boys flying in perfect formation; all of us so confident in each other and our powerful machines. With over two thousand four hundred horse power, the 24 cylinder Napier Sabre motors let us outperform anything else to about 14,000 feet. Above that height the super-chargers of other aircraft gave them the edge but below this ceiling we were kings!

September 10th. Sortie No 517.   We're to strafe Leeuwarden Airfield in Holland! Now we'll see what the Tempests can do!

We took off, formed up with 274 Squadron Tempests and flew low across the Channel. Nearing Texel we climbed steeply and crossed the island at about fourteen thousand feet. Below, on our starboard, was the long causeway across the Zuider Zee which 'pointed' almost directly at the big airfield.

With the target in sight 80 peeled down in a screaming dive with each flight of four aircraft almost in line abreast.

'Drop tanks!' and the auxiliary fuel tanks tumbled away. Some heavy flak opened up but far too high and, as our altimeters unwound and we neared four thousand feet, we were doing over four hundred and fifty miles an hour. Light flak started to stream up at us from dozens of positions but, excited in action, we ignored it and rapidly scanned the airfield's perimeter and around hangars and tarmac for E/A.

I saw a twin-engined kite by a hangar and opened fire. There was a brilliant flash in my cockpit! The bloody gun-sight light-bulb had fallen out and swung on its wiring scaring me rigid until I identified what it was. I held the gun button down and steered the dancing cannon stream over the Hun machine.

Perspex shattered, exploding shells winked over its wings and a brown haze enveloped its fuselage. Pulling out of the dive I gave two hangars a good pasting before climbing for the sky.

Out of the corner of my eye I saw one of the 274's planes blow up a petrol bowser. I couldn't get the hot bulb back into its socket with my bare hands so had to abort any idea of a further attack. In any case, to attack the same target again could have been suicidal.

'Reform over target Angels Ten!' and one by one 80's boys came together and we set off home. Back at Manston we found four of 274's planes had been holed and one had to force land in the sea. The pilot was picked up OK.

We had a big thrash to farewell 'Hawkeye' – things would not be the same without him. The next day we escorted twelve Invaders to bomb Leeuwarden and the following day, Sortie No 519, Squadron Leader Wigglesworth, CO of No 3 Squadron, and I flew off together hunting V2* rockets south of the Hague.

We flew along about 400 yards apart in line-abreast at about five hundred feet ignoring the odd bursts of light flak. Suddenly I spotted a huge Meillerwagen V2 transporter under some trees and then the fifty foot needle-pointed rocket standing upright ready for launching.

'Target at 2 o'clock under trees! Break starboard!'

Wigglesworth was quite close to it and turning quickly he opened fire while still banking. I saw his shells flashing on the monster and then a colossal explosion as almost eight tons of liquid oxygen and ethyl alcohol blew. The war head of over a ton exploded and my comrade flew directly into the huge ball of flame – and didn't come out.

Absolutely horrified I flew around the scene of desolation – the huge crater and flattened trees. Odd nameless lumps smoked and fumed on the ground; brush burned, but there was nothing to indicate what had been a Tempest.†

The next day we were to look for V2s actually in the environs of the Hague. Intelligence reported that V2s were hidden and being launched from parkland within the city's boundaries. With my leading Pilot Officer Anders, the two of us flew up and down the main street of Hague at 200 feet to Leiden and found some German vehicles which we destroyed right in the middle of the city. Fantastic!

On the 16th, leading six others near Arnhem, I attacked a train of twenty-one flat cars and twenty-six covered vans. Olaf (Captain Ullestad, Norwegian) flew across 'Spike' Maloney's slip stream and was hit by the streams of empty 20m shell cases pouring out as

---

* The 'grandfather' of the modern Intercontinental ballistic rockets.
† He could have saved hundreds of lives. Knowing the risk involved this brave man took the chance and the V2 took his life. There was only one VC awarded to a fighter pilot in W.W.II. Surely this man earned one! Now, after all these years I realise I should have 'put him up' for the ultimate honour. It just didn't occur to me at the time and now it is too late. Or is it?

'Spike' fired. He was wounded in the face. Spike was hit by ground fire and force-landed in a field. He waved to us from his cockpit.*

Returning to Manston we quickly refuelled and four of us flew back to try to locate Spike's machine and destroy it. We couldn't find the blasted thing, but found a loco which we disintegrated plus a truck and trailer. That night we were advised to go to bed early as next day we'd be on a special op. I rang Shirly, a selfish thing to do but it had been a bad day for me. Spike was my first loss and I felt it keenly and needed some loving words to cheer me. Besides, I knew what the morrow entailed, and had the twitch. I couldn't speak of it but wanted to hear my wife's voice again.

September 17th. Operational Sortie 523.   Anti-flak for glider train to Arnhem. I selected my team of eight and briefed them.

'I'll detail someone to fly low over selected spots decided on at the time. Whoever goes down is to act as a decoy and not attack anything unless the target is a flak post. OK? Red Section will act as top cover and Black do the first lot of strafing. On the completion of your first strafe, climb and join top cover. The next time it's Red's turn and so on. If we get separated, act independently and press home your attacks. The gliders and their tugs will be sitting ducks for the Jerry gunners.'

None of us were happy at the job. It was going to be tough.

'Check your kites out carefully – test the gun sights. See your windscreens and mirrors are spotless. Work with your riggers and the armourers. Leave nothing to chance.'

At about 10.25 on this bright Sunday we took off and were soon off the Dutch coast. It wasn't hard to identify the particular area 80 was to dominate. There were four small armed ships in the Hellegat which would have to be destroyed. Their multiple cannons could wreak dreadful carnage with the air armada now approaching the coast dead on course.

'OK Railroad Black section. Target-four boats 11 o'clock below. Line abreast go! Black three and four take the starboard ships. Going

* Later, at the Nuremberg War Trials, a farmer was found guilty and hung for the murder of Spike. He had caught and hung this brave Australian. One of the Hun's slave workers reported the deed to Allied officers.

down,' and down we dived to straddle and pour our shells into the fire-spitting boats. As we broke clear we climbed almost vertically with the excess speed of our dives.

'Red section attack at will' and down Heapo went with his team.

The boats were finished and sinking before we left. We flew on at 4,000 feet and started to get ground fire. There was no need for a decoy to locate the guns.

'OK Railroad aircraft, we'll dive together. Red section take the north bank.' We were flying over the Ooster-schelde waterway.

Again the heart-stopping dives, mouth dry, nerves tingling. My kite took a hit in the fuselage somewhere and I saw my No 2, Warrant Officer 'Blondie' Godfrey, buy it with a direct air-burst. Streams of tracer shells flicked past and around as the flak gun-pits grew larger in front of me. I opened fire at about a thousand yards and kept firing until break-off point. Godfrey's Tempest, or what was left of it, crashed among the gun-pits now silenced.

Heapo called out –

'Red Leader to Railroad Black. Am returning base – sustained damage, Red aircraft carry on.'

'Roger! Red section aircraft join up Angels four over Wemeldinge.'

But we got horribly thick flak and sorted ourselves out over open water.

'Railroad Leader to railroad aircraft. Anyone out of ammo escort Red leader home.'

Three Tempests peeled away. The other two formated with me and we went back and down into the inferno. Up above us the glider 'train' had arrived and flew on in a great stream. There were over 2,500 gliders, 5,000 fighters, bombers and transport aircraft. But we anti-flak aircraft had the lonely task of attacking the very devices designed to destroy us.

When we left, out of ammunition, we could see other squadron fighters diving and firing on the gun positions. Typhoons by the dozen were rocketing the Jerries and their smoking projectiles lanced down trailing smoke to burst and explode in red flashes. Burning aircraft on the flat fields marked the lane the air armada had taken. Our four flak ships had sunk, Blondie had died and with very mixed up feelings, we flew home.

It was the 18th, and again we were detailed for anti-flak – more airborne reinforcement gliders were being flown to Arnhem.

My 'S' had been repaired and, strapping it on, I took off leading seven others. At Zijpe, on the eastern tip of Schouwen Island, 'Lofty' Haw bought it while attacking a multiple flak post. I saw him hit and his Tempest reared up, flattened off into a smoking glide and staggered away across the Grevelingen Channel. He was too low to jump and an extraordinary thing occurred. Still doing about 200 miles per hour, Lofty struggled out of his cockpit and, hanging onto its edge, stood on the port wing root. It was amazing – why was he doing this and, more amazing, why wasn't he blown off?

He'd left his parachute in the machine and as I formated with him I could see his fair hair pressed close against his head. The Tempest hit the sea and Lofty cartwheeled ahead of the spray cloud to burst like a thrown egg on the water.

Feeling sick, retching, I did a climbing turn and re-attacked the flak emplacement. The Huns stopped firing and as I flashed by I saw figures sprawled in the gun pit, now wreathed in grey smoke.

'Railroad Leader, Red Four calling. Am attacking flak ship at Mastgut!'

Jesus! What was MacLachlan doing over there? That was the trouble with Tempests – a broad turn and you could be miles away in no time.

'Red Four to Railroad Leader. Am hit and returning to base!'

Well, that would figure on happening to anyone – uncoordinated lone attacks on flak ships were stupid, but that was the trouble with Aussies – too cocky!

I saw a Tempest go in.

'Bob's been hit!' someone called.

'Bullshit! This is Railroad Leader! I'm OK!'

'No! It was Bob Hanney! He's bought it!'

'Railroad Leader to Railroad aircraft. Escort Red Four if you can find him. Railroad returning to base.'

Two days to lick our wounds while at Arnhem our men battled on in a hopeless situation deprived of air support from the American long range fighters. The two US Radio Control teams hadn't the correct crystals in their sets to call down and direct the very fighters detailed for this job.

Seven days' leave! Shirly and I packed our gear and loaded up Susie, our little 10 hp Ford. When we got to the Raymonds' flat in London, there was a recall – two of my pilots were missing and the squadron ordered to the Continent.

'What happened?'

'Well, we don't know exactly. Willy and Aussie went on an anti-shipping strike and just didn't come back. No one saw what happened except it must have been flak.'*

Led by Wing Commander Wray we set off for 'B82', our new base in Belgium, but the weather got bad right down to the deck and we returned to Manston to refuel and await the clouds clearing. I grabbed a night at our little cottage and gave Shirly all the news. Heapo got pretty merry and slept on the sofa.

September 29th. Another bad day, but we took off, regardless, for Grave. My radio packed up and so I just led my flight of four machines following Wing Commander Wray who was leading the formation.

It started to drizzle and we stooged up and down the French/Belgian coast. It was obvious that the Wing Commander hadn't the faintest clue where he was so, waggling my wings, I flew ahead leading my three companions into the murk. We were supposed to go to a new forward airfield at Grave near the Maas River about ten miles south-west of Nijmegan. Not being as good as I thought I was, but determined not to be bitched around anymore, I headed inland. And got lost. Having no RT I waggled my wings and my No 2 slid alongside. I indicated my earphones and microphone and the happy oaf just kept formating on me. I tore up my map, flung the bits over my head and pointed to him, then dead ahead, indicating he should lead. The clot just looked at me, fat, dumb and happy! I could see I'd have to sort this out myself but no longer having a map and with Jerries within ten minutes flying time in almost every direction I turned the flight around until we came to Antwerp. Doing a wide sweep around it I found the main civilian

* F/O 'Willy Wiltshire was taken POW. He made a second attack and flew into a big barrage from the aroused Hun gunners. I don't know what happened to 'Aussie' (W/O A.S. Williams).

'drome, saw some kites with roundels and landed. What a miserable night! Rain, fog and nowhere to go.

I had a signal sent off to Manston saying all was well and next morning, with a fresh map and the RT usable, we took off on the twenty minute flight to Grave.

'Hey, Boss! They're shooting at us!'

'Who's that?'

'Me, Black Three.'

'Who's shooting?'

'The bloody Jerries in the trenches!'

And then I saw the zig-zag line of trenches and strong points on the north bank of the Maas River. Sweeping my flight low over the grass airstrip I saw waving figures and a parked Auster, then a RAF flag on a short flagstaff.

'Black Leader to Black Section. Line astern and land independently.'

I was pretty hot and teed off about the damned Jerries' cheek so climbed to a couple of thousand feet, put S's nose down and dived on the sods.

The trouble was they saw me coming and probably I only got two or three as all they had to do was duck down in their deep trenches. But the explosive shells would tickle them up a bit!

Landing at Grave, the local Adj said,

'What did you do that for?'

'Because I don't like being shot at!'

'You've only annoyed them. They make life bloody unpleasant for us here!'

'All right. We'll go away back to the UK!'

Eventually, we got on the outside of some grog and all was forgiven. Grave's perimeter was so close to the Huns that immediately on take off we had to do a steep and low turn to avoid flying over their lines.

At Grave the big trouble was the Me262 jet bombers which were so fast and quiet in their diving attacks to scatter anti-personnel bombs that they often caught us out in the open with no cover.

Our tannoy, 'The Golden Voice' announced,

'Personnel are strongly advised to throw dignity to the winds and themselves to the ground immediately on hearing unusual whistling sounds or the firing of the local ack-ack. It is better to be laughed at than mourned over! Warning will be given if time permits the Golden Voice to hang around long enough. The great thing is to fling yourself flat and not attempt a 50 yard sprint to a slit-trench, or even round and round in ever decreasing circles seeking still nearer shelter!'

We were living pretty rough, having found some abandoned Dutch houses with plenty of straw for bedding. Food, cooked in field kitchens, was shared by all, ground and air-crew – a good thing which brought officers and men together. Our mixed nationality squadron was a joy to belong to – so many different life styles and backgrounds – so much to compare and discuss. Not just beer, sex, football, sex and what was happening back in Whakatara.

We were joined by our other flight at last and Wing Commander Wray was pretty tetchy with me. I made it up by explaining my RT had packed up and I got lost etc. etc. We started armed patrols to seek out ground targets and on 5th October I found, near Zwolle, a PZ11 tank.

This was for me!

'Railroad aircraft maintain angels four. Black leader and Black two going down.'

My number two slid behind me and down we dived. Half a mile ahead there was the stationary tank with its turret hatch open and, standing in front of it, hands on hips, one of the crew.

He just stood there, legs apart, arms akimbo, looking up at me. He was blown away with the first few shells. One of the explosive projectiles must have entered the open hatch, setting off the tank's ammunition, because there were violent flashes from inside its turret. To our great surprise and delight a series of perfect smoke rings were ejected from the opening to rise and expand in the still air. A crew member clambered out and my No 2 hacked him down.

Why had the first man just stood there? I think he was either arrogant to the point of idiocy or he deliberately committed suicide. A strange thing. Soon the tank glowed dull red and we flew off seeking other prey. We got a small truck before going home.

On the 5th, we found a loco in the Zwolle marshalling yards and all had a go. As I cruised around waiting for the others to rejoin, I had the amusing (and it was) experience of seeing Andy Anderson (Australian) getting hell from flak.

My No 2 and I got two trucks and a trailer and, on finding another train, I made a hash of my attack and screamed over the railway siding seeing dozens of troops dashing for cover. Something held me back from repositioning and re-attacking. Some sixth sense – maybe I was getting the twitch.

A useless gesture! Op Sortie 528 – attacked five giant Tiger tanks discovered on railway flat-cars. Our 20mm shells winked all over them and damaged paint work. However, we reported them in clear over our RT and a squadron of Typhoons were scrambled and rocketed them to destruction.

Grave, primitive and exposed, was abandoned by us. It was too close to the enemy and not large enough to accommodate our growing wing. I had 'put up' Heapo for squadron leader. I didn't want to as it would mean a parting, but he was too good and experienced a pilot to hold back for selfish reasons. To our huge delight he was given 274, our 'sister' squadron, and so, in a sense, we were still together.

I detailed my two stalwart flight commanders, Flight Lieutenants A. Seager and W. McKichan, to take the squadron to Volkel, a large ex-Hun aerodrome near the village of Uden.

The Doc and I went on a joy ride in one of the jeeps to explore and see if there were any souvenirs or 'loot' to be had. But the flat desolate fields of Holland were pretty barren and we arrived at Volkel to be greeted by Group Captain 'Jamie' Jameson who tore a strip off me.

'Spurdle, when one of my squadrons flies in, I expect it to be led by its Commanding Officer! And I expect him to be freshly shaven and not looking like a scruffy hobo!'

Jamie was quite right and I took heed. Group Captain Jameson DSO was one of thirty-six survivors from 1500 in the *Glorious* disaster when this aircraft carrier and the destroyers *Ardent* and *Acasta* were sunk by shell-fire on being intercepted by the German battle cruisers *Scharnhorst* and *Gneisenau*. He had had a distinguished career as a fighter pilot and had led our 122 Wing, 83 Group, up in the advance from Normandy.

Volkel was a mess. Hangars blown up, buildings blasted. What our bombers hadn't smashed had been destroyed by the retreating Huns. Heapo and I surveyed our dispersals and set about making shelter for personnel and parachutes. 'Gilly' Guilhuis (the other Norwegian in 80) had been an architect in civilian life and designed 'Spud's Speakeasy' which we pilots set about building from salvaged timber and concrete blocks. At one end was the small parachute room which had to be kept warm and dry by Kerosene heaters. Our big crew-room had a very fancy and large brick fireplace built in a corner because, with winter coming, it could be very cold. We worked extremely hard between flights and were proud of the results.

However, 274 decided to dig down to save on materials and time. A dozen pilots dug a large hole and, shoring the sides with timber, covered the whole affair with an iron roof. It was safer from air attack than our place but, as winter set in, the water table rose and rose and rose. The first lot of duck boards had to be covered by a second and a third. Soon there wasn't room for the unfortunates to stand upright and we Bell boys laughed ourselves silly.

CHAPTER XIII

'Not Heapo! It can't be!'

We were billeted in what we dubbed the 'Monk Factory' in the village of Uden. Here we displaced, to the top floor, the Capachuin monks who wore long habits of coarse brown wool and open-thonged leather sandals.

Heapo and I shared a small 'cell' on the second floor with our camp stretchers set up on the bare boards. The little village offered nothing in the way of entertainment and we felt very sorry for the kids who obviously were suffering vitamin deficiency and, due to an almost complete absence of soap and disinfectants, suffered from rashes and sores.

One night the squadron Doc and I were invited by the local medico to an evening meal. It was pitiful and next day Doc Gallagher and I organised a whip-around for sweets for the kids and commandeered extra rations for their parents. I think the Dutch had a much harder time, ration-wise, than the Belgians or French. I suppose it was because they were nearer to the Hun homeland and so subjected to more severe pillaging.

At this time 80 was at full strength – we had two Norwegians, six Australians, one each Rhodesian and South African, twelve British, two Canadians and myself representing New Zealand. Also Flight Lieutenant Louis Graham-Smith from the West Indies for whom I had an especial regard. As a flight commander one became, by the nature of the job, slightly detached from one's fellow pilots and the gap widened vastly on becoming the commanding officer of a squadron. One couldn't play favourites and, in my opinion, it was absolutely essential that complete harmony should exist. Perhaps it developed a 'mother-hen' complex in me but it paid off handsomely. We were a very happy squadron and in action each and every pilot could rely on his comrades.

It was strange how the air war had changed – in 1941 it was mostly high altitude stuff, squadrons trying to get height advantage to 'bounce' their opponents. Now we flew on our strafing missions cruising around at about 4,000 feet. This would have been unthinkable before we gained air supremacy and the Huns forced to conserve flak ammunition, planes, and fuel. Our strafing forays became more and more effective and locos, rolling stock, motor transport and a huge variety of static targets were attacked and destroyed.

The Typhoon squadrons were particularly successful being so much more versatile with their bombs and rockets plus four potent 20mm cannon. But it was the Tempest, faster and more manoeuvreable, that concentrated on targets of opportunity and was detailed more for 'free-ranging' while Typhoons were controlled more for specific targets asked for by the Army.

Every now and then Hun E/A were found by our Tempests and, hopelessly outpaced, we clobbered them. Only the Me262 jet fighter bomber was faster. It was considered such a threat with its lightning bombing attacks on our 'dromes (mostly with anti-personnel bombs) that standing instructions were that when one was sighted, it had to be reported in clear on the RT. Immediately every free-ranging fighter converged on the nearest known 262 base and hung around in case one flew in to refuel. With their short range and special ground-servicing requirements, the jets were vulnerable on coming in to land at their known haunts. The Huns created flak 'corridors' along which the returning 262's would fly at treetop height. It was extremely dangerous to attack them but our chaps, excited by the challenge of bagging a 262, took fearful chances braving the concentrated fire of dozens of multiple flak posts.

In this way one of 80's pilots, a quiet unassuming chap, Warrant Officer H.F. Ross strafed and killed Major Walter Nowotny, one of Germany's leading aces. There have been many versions and claims for this encounter but, as I recall, Ross saw this 262 taxiing near some hangars on the Rheine runway and, ignoring the intense flak, dived to strafe it.* The E/A ran into some trees and the pilot was killed.

'S' had a few holes in it from the last sortie so to start off November properly, I took 'G' out on a weather recce for fun. There were usually railway targets in or near the Utrecht marshalling yards and,

* Ed. Note: This claim was for 6 Nov. 1944 and Nowotny was shot down on 8 Nov. 1944, probably by an American Mustang pilot.

lo and behold! A train puffed away as it lugged thirty or more small freight cars. Down in a screaming dive and with the cannon shells flashing all along the row of rolling stock, I guided them till they reached the loco. It must have had a full head of steam up because the boiler burst in a great cloud of vapour and fiery embers. A great zoom for height before the startled flak crews got into action! It wasn't often they were surprised! Feeling pretty pleased with myself, the next target was a half-track near Deventer which burned fiercely sending a great pillar of smoke into the still, cold air.

We had heard about a winery just over the Maas River at Nijmegan and, on a non-flying wet and miserable day, we took a 3-ton truck and jeep to see what we could get. Nijmegan was a mess and, picking our way through rubbly roads, we approached the big bridge, prime target for so many bombing attacks by both our, and more lately, Hun bombers.

Our drivers, as innocent as the rest of us, parked their vehicles under some huge old plane trees on the river's edge while we gazed in fascinated horror at the green mummified remains of a German corpse. There was a curious tearing whip-like crack! More of them! Branches crashed and shrapnel whacked around. We were in full view of a Jerry 88mm battery on the other side of the river! There was a frantic scurrying to save our truck and we tore around the corner to safety, much shaken.

Determined to get grog, Louis, Mex and I made another approach. Crouched in a slit trench to one side of the bridge's approaches was a Tommy soldier who acted as 'traffic controller'. When he raised his green flag we tore out from shelter behind a building and roared across the huge bridge with our jeep motor screaming and tyres scrabbling on the broken surface. Once across, we drew breath and hunted about for the winery. It was more or less intact and rummaging around, we collected several cases of curious dumpy little bottles of coarse wine. Another Tommy tried to charge us for the grog which was a foolish and hopeless exercise. There was a deserted furniture factory nearby from which we liberated a couple of easy chairs before groaning back across the river praying to make it in safety!

During the next couple of weeks more pilots not down for flying duties braved the dangerous trip but eventually our Groupie called a halt to it. There was too much confused fighting on the other side of the Maas river and we could have been cut off. 80 was detailed for more and more patrols over the invaluable bridge; German frogmen guiding floating mines connected by steel cables, were discovered trying to destroy the big pillars. The army created artificial 'moonlight' by shining searchlights against blank walls. The reflected light bathed the black waters in an eerie glow to reveal any swimmers and their floating charges. As winter's chill and damp weather cut our flying hours, the Jerries, desperate to move men and machines into contested areas, took more and more chances and, sometimes, if the mists and clouds broke we'd be scrambled to search and destroy the many ground targets. Flak got more intense as fresh munitions reached the Hun lines.

*

Four days' leave! A cheerful group of 80 and 274 pilots set off for Antwerp in a 3 ton truck going south for rations.

The Jerries still held some of the docks and were bitterly defending the Scheldt Estuary, effectively barring the use of the great port to the Allies. The British 21st Army Group (Montgomery) entered Antwerp on 4th September and here we were, exploring parts of the excited semi-liberated city while 'White Brigade' (Belgian equivalent to the French Maquis) men and women rounded up collaborators, smashed or confiscated their possessions and generally meted out rough and ready 'justice'.

At the big Municipal Zoo* we saw the extraordinary spectacle of humans held in the animal cages for public ridicule and vilification. One expensively dressed woman, tall and handsome, stood rigidly upright in the centre of what had been a tiger's cage. She looked neither to the left nor right seemingly impervious to the jeers of the crowds eddying in front of her. White Brigade types, brandishing an amazing variety of firearms, maintained a modicum of order. Gobs of spittle splattered the traitors and the scene was so fierce and ugly we left in case worse occurred. The collaborators were handed over to the Belgian Military courts.

---

* In 1940 all the dangerous wild animals were killed off for reasons of security.

That night some of our party, drinking with the jubilant Belgians, went Hun-hunting down in dockland. Their transports were commandeered trucks bolstered with sandbags for protection for the drunken characters waving bottles and guns with equal abandon.

After the survivors' incoherent reports of what had been a ridiculous adventure, this sport was barred to our boys. We confined ourselves to 'liberating' cars confiscated from collaborators. One of our crew obtained a magnificent Buick 'straight eight' coupé. At the first Army checkpoint the Pongos relieved him of it which browned us off as we knew their own officers would keep it.

*

No! It can't be! Not Heapo! A chill silence fell around us like a fence; like an icy mantle smothering the outside world. The Spy concentrated on a spot over my shoulder; couldn't look me in the face. He waited for my composure to return, for the impassive mask to reshape as usual.

'What happened?'

'Heapo's motor cut on take-off and he force-landed in a field just over the 'drome's perimeter. The plane slid into an embankment. He couldn't have had his harness locked because he knocked his forehead on the gun-sight. Just a tiny little wound.'

In absolute misery, I wandered off down the echoing, gritty stairs, away from the room we'd shared, the jumble of magazines, the odds and ends. Out into the noisy courtyard and on into the slush and mist of Uden's wasteland. Fields of nothing. Far off on Volkel the roar of aircraft motors. A lone bird call.

Heapo! Oh God, why had I asked for you to join me? You were safe at the OTU in Scotland. This was all my fault.

I rang the Station Commander who, understanding only too well my anguish, granted me 48 hours' leave. The horrid weather precluded going home to Shirly – I was desolated, alone.

To escape the dreadful nightmare I tried running from it. In confusion and sorrow, I drove all night to Brussels and the Jockey Club. Here, in its cheerful atmosphere I could drink to oblivion and be cared for by the one-legged owner and his two mistresses.

Instead a pleasant-looking woman took me to her flat, listened to my maudlin weepings; cooked breakfast. There was no sex – just an understanding soul who had her own cross to bear and gave her time to help me carry mine. She would accept no money, only some rations from the Jeep. Sure, she was a prostitute but for me she was a caring friend and a surrogate mother. I remember her with respect.

*

Back at Volkel a new CO for 274; a new voice to command 'Talbot Leader to Talbot aircraft. . . .' But I didn't want Squadron Leader Fairbanks to share digs with me and I had our squadron Adj move in as room mate. Another pilot would have only been a reminder of the happy days now gone.

There was one more thing I had to do before closing the book on Heapo. There was still the letter to write for his people. Johnnie's folk had brought him into the world, loved and cared for him. Knew all of his youth and young manhood but Mine, Ours, was a world they could never enter or fully understand. I had to recap it so their pain would be eased in the sure knowledge that their son had stood out in the company of the brave. All of us were proud to have flown with him. Of the dozens and dozens of similar letters I had had to write, this one was the hardest. I owed it to Heapo and I hoped, if my time came, that someone would take the same care in writing to my Shirly.

Life went on but the spark had gone and strafing became an ugly obsession with me. Each attack a merciless and vicious act of hatred pressed home to kill.

*

On Sortie No 551 some USAAF Mustangs jumped us. Enraged, I turned on my particular tormentor and scared him fartless by firing bursts first on one side and then on the other while he twisted and turned helpless against the far superior Tempest. Formating alongside I shook my fist at the stupid jerk and then zoomed away. We should have hacked a few down to teach them aircraft recognition. We were sick of their trigger-happy stupidities.

One of the wing's pilots painted a white star on his machine adding it to his string of swastikas. He was told to remove it. The squadron commanders of the wings under Air Vice Marshal Broadhurst's control were assembled at Eindhoven for a general briefing on future operations and on the war's progress. The AVM, in passing, told us that if our aircraft were subjected to any more bouncing by our gallant allies, we could retaliate and no enquiry or disciplinary action would be taken. An extraordinary scene followed – cheering, back-slapping, laughing pilots surrounded our popular commander.

We'd had more than enough of this sort of aggravation.

The next three weeks were a long nightmare. I couldn't shake off the knowledge that by getting Heapo out of the Scottish OTU I had set the stage for his death. Why hadn't I left well enough alone! The Wing doctor reasoned with me – that each one of us can cause a reaction like the ripples from a cast stone that no one can control. But the analogy was flawed – I had cast that stone. I had caused the reaction that led to Heapo's death.

To blank out my deep sense of guilt I drove myself harder by leading every sortie against the foe. In the next thirteen flights we attacked and destroyed – or at least heavily damaged – fourteen locos, ninety plus loaded railway trucks, a three-ton truck and trailer, two searchlights and their barrack buildings, two multiple flak posts, a steam tractor and trailer and several assorted motor vehicles. On 8th December, Sortie 555, along with Pilot Officer G. Dopson, Captain O. Ullestad, Flight Lieutenant Johnny Weston (Mex), Flying Officer W. Long and Flying Officer A. McLachlan we strafed Bielefeld 'drome, catching Ju 188's on the ground, of which I got two. Johnny Weston hacked down a foolish 109 from a timid gaggle, orbiting their base. As we had already shot up two locos, twenty to thirty rolling-stock and a factory, we were low on ammunition and couldn't risk the 109's, so flew away cursing with frustration.

December 16th and lousy weather, fog and snow. The day before we'd done two sweeps, one to the Minden-Hamm area and the other, unproductive, in the Osnabruck-Munster sector. Thick haze and nothing moving.

I collected Frank Lang, Louis, Gilly and Olaf for two nights in Antwerp – we took our two little Opel Kadets (liberated from Belgian collaborators) and, slithering and spinning the cars in the snow for fun, covered the seventy five odd miles to the city putting up at the Century Hotel.*

* Now the 'Keyser' Hotel

Next day, with aching heads, we decided to go to the big Rex Theatre just across the road and see the movies.

'Hey! Hold on! I've forgotten my cap! I won't be a minute' and with that I dashed upstairs. On rejoining the others in the foyer we stepped out into the street. There was a fearful crash, glass flew and we were bowled over against shop fronts in a dusty, panting heap. There was a hot blast of air, a heavy rumble and another boom. Our startled faces looked up at the great white finger lanced down from the stratosphere at us. A V2 rocket! The Rex was just a smoking hole in the ground. Bodies lay all around, some still, some crawling or staggering like broken dolls. Bricks, bits of plaster and broken timber strewed the De Keyserlei Avenue and a huge cloud of stinking smoke enveloped a scene like Dante's Inferno.

Picking ourselves up, appalled at what had happened and marvelling at our fantastic good luck, we ran across to see if we could help the survivors. This one rocket killed 567 people, 296 of them being servicemen. Another 291 were wounded, 194 being servicemen. More than 130 buildings were damaged.

Way up on a blasted wall, where a lavatory was exposed, an old woman stared down into the ghastly pit. She was teetering on a few feet of flooring left jutting out over the carnage. We called to her to stay put and the first fire engine to arrive laddered her down, trembling and totally confused.

We called off the rest of our leave and decided to return to Volkel where it would be safer! On the way back we called in at the Eindhoven Mess but were told to get lost. So we relieved the bastards of a case of champagne from their insecure store and drank most of it driving home. Back at Uden all hell had broken loose and we were ordered to return it. Fat chance!

December 17th. Sortie 560 – scramble over base and my windscreen oiled over so I had to abort but the others went on and the wing shot down eleven Huns but we lost Gilly and Mex. Gilly was seen to take a flak shell in his cockpit. They didn't know what happened to Mex.

December 18th. Sortie 561. An armed recce near Bielefeld and we had a ball knocking off three locos and their wagons, then two tractor and trailer units, an RDF station and barracks, finishing off with blowing holes in a factory roof. Four FW 190's – the new long-nosed jobs in orbit at Bielefeld! I got behind one as it came into land and pressed the gun button again and again in a fury of frustration. Out of ammo! Beside myself with rage, completely irrational, I tried to ram it in the tail unit with my wing tip. Just as we were about to collide, the Hun put his flaps down and the 190 humped up and I passed beneath it, collecting two gashes from his propeller in my starboard wing tip. The Jerry must have had a fearful fright.

We played around with the Huns for a while and then I called:

'Railroad Aircraft return to base! Someone will buy it in a minute!' and so, in disgust, we flew home all out of ammo and only lousy ground targets to show for our outing.

*

New Year's Eve came and went with a big thrash and we staggered off to bed confident it would be our last year of war. Next day, as we drove along the road from Uden to Volkel, I spotted some low-flying planes heading our way. It was about nine o'clock.

'109's! Out!' and we slid to a stop and rolled out and into a snow-filled ditch. The Jerries roared across the airfield in front of us, firing in a sustained crackle of machine-gun and cannon-fire. They didn't turn for another go but continued on towards Eindhoven, some twelve miles away. We dusted ourselves off and, climbing back into the jeep, sped off to dispersal.

'What's up?' I asked the duty airman.

'We've just been strafed! They just made one pass!'

'Right! Have you rung Ops?'

'Yes – the officer just said they were too busy to talk to me. They won't answer our phone!'

This was madness.

'Judy (Flying Officer J.W. Garland) scramble your section for aerodrome defence Angels Four' and the chaps rushed out the door.

We heard some excited nattering on our hut's radio – some other squadrons were out on sorties but this was something else. Eindhoven not answering the phone left us in the dark. I decided to scramble the rest of the squadron but on taking off my wind-shield got covered in oil – someone hadn't cleaned out weepage trapped in the spinner.

'Railroad Black Leader returning to base. Black Section join up with Red Section Angels Four. Red Leader take over.'

I was furious at having to abort and even more so when the others returned after a hectic hour. They had intercepted some 190's at tree-top height and Judy had shot two down in flames. 'Ching' Friend had clobbered a staff car and the others destroyed two locos and damaged a further four.

The Jerries had taken advantage of our known weakness for whooping it up at New Year. They'd mounted a massive fighter strike against the twenty odd airfields in the British sector in Holland and Belgium.

Over a thousand 109's and 190's in three large groups, led in the initial stages by fast bombers set course for their targets. One group came over the Zuider Zee almost to Brussels, another to Eindhoven and the last down past Venlo to American fields.

From prisoner interrogation we learnt that Volkel was to have been hit by a force of ninety machines, but due to a fluke only four or five arrived and they continued on to Eindhoven where almost complete carnage wiped out the Canadian, Polish and 124 Wing's planes. At Brussels/Evere over a hundred aircraft ranging from Flying Fortresses, Typhoons, Spitfires, C47's etc. were destroyed.* Scuttle-butt garnered over the next few months put our losses at over three hundred machines destroyed on the ground in just a few minutes.

Our losses were offset by some thirty or forty successes by our fighters and perhaps another fifty shot down by our ack-ack. A blanket of secrecy hid the true facts but one thing was sure – we'd suffered a mighty blow, the last one the dying Luftwaffe was to deliver. They lost about a hundred pilots, irreplaceable, and we lost machines which were replaced within ten days.

We never discovered the fool at Eindhoven who could have called on five squadrons of the world's most formidable fighters. He should have been shot.

---

* I have never been able to unearth the full facts of this debacle, probably buried by the Official Secrets Act. But it was the greatest air disaster and a major defeat for us brought on by complacency and lack of foresight. We were just too confident of our air supremacy.

CHAPTER XIV

Operation 'Varsity' – The Rhine Crossing

January 4th 1945. Sortie No 564 1 hour 10 minutes. The Dortmund-Ems canal ribboned along, smooth and shining in the afternoon sun. Four thousand feet below, near some lock gates by a large pine forest, a small tug puffed clouds of steam.

'Railroad Black Section, tug below. Attack at will! Re-form Angels five.'

Stick hard over, full throttle, fine pitch, gun sight on, safety off. The Tempest's speed climbed to 400 on the clock and I throttled back, curving down in an attack from astern.

There was something wrong. Something clicked – there was no wake from the boat. It must be anchored. A flak trap!

'Hold it Black Section! Break off and climb!' and with that the Hun gunners opened up. Streams of red, green and orange tracer hosed up in graceful curves, to flick close by from a dozen hidden positions. Pulling out of the dive the G's built up and with face-flesh dragging, almost browning out, I spotted on the edge of the forest, two concrete flak towers like ugly long-stemmed wine glasses. It was too tempting. Dipping the Tempest's nose again, I steadied her and opened fire with two quick bursts, one in each concrete cup. One of the towers got off a short burst before the hail of 20mm shells found them. There would be some bloody GAF fräuleins doing their last dance!

Again the climb for altitude, veering to starboard over open fields away from the forest. Just as well, because a cloud of rockets trailing steel cables leapt skyward from the trees. Quick-firing pom-poms, the four-barrelled Flakvierling, were streaming shells from flashing muzzles. As my machine clawed for altitude, I foolishly called out on the RT.

'Watch it! I'm getting my arse shot off. Flak trap! Flak trap!'

Back at base, the Group Captain, in the control tower, heard my yell and then and there decided to ground me. He knew that sooner or later I must qualify for a synthetic funeral. 'Jamie' Jameson felt his responsibility deeply and the loneliness of command in committing men to risk their lives, day after day. He felt my nine lives had been just about expended. On my return I was ordered to report to him.

'Sorry, Spud, you've had Ops. I wanted you for Wing Leader but HQ says you're operationally expired. Hell! You've done over seven hundred hours Ops. You've done more than your share.'

Group Captain Jameson had been a good friend to me but there was a limit even to his powers, and with Heapo gone things weren't the same. It was good-bye to 80 and my pilots. I put in recommendations for some of the boys to get gongs and said my farewells. It was good-bye to the strongest bond a man can know; the brotherhood of arms.

Squadron Leader 'Rosie' Mackie, a New Zealander, arrived to take over the squadron. I hated to hand over the lives and well-being of my boys to a stranger. But the die was cast. Suddenly everything seemed to fall in on top of me and, shivering and stammering, I was flown back to England and Shirly. I had completed 564 operational sorties and five tours of operations.

Then began a curious interlude which had me wondering. After a few days' leave, a posting came through as 'Briefing Officer', 83 GSU, Westhampnett. Then to Dunsfold Aerodrome. My job was to 'brief' fighter pilots en route to squadrons on the Continent; issue them with new or reconditioned aircraft, give them maps and courses to steer.

There were at least five other squadron leader briefing officers and the job was ridiculously easy. We organised leave rosters and spent half our time swanning around the countryside. There were plenty of fighters of all types to fly and no boss to say when and if we could.

My wife was patiently waiting for our baby to be born. Luckily it was easy for me to spend a lot of time with her at our little home in Birchington, just a mile from Manston.

Without her mother to support her, Shirly spent her anxious hours thinking of names and came up with 'Anne Gaelyn' should baby be a girl.

In the beastliness and ugliness of war, the miracle of life flowered and, looking at our child, I marvelled at my good fortune. After a couple of weeks, we had Anne christened. When 'Gaelyn' came up, the padre asked –

'Is this a Christian name?'

For a hopeful moment I thought Shirly would have to make another choice but quick as a wink 'Yes!' and the deed was done.

Then the war caught up with us again and I had to return to Dunsfold and my boring job.

*

Slowly, day by day, a feeling of unease crept over all of us. It was too good to last. The job was a sinecure if safety and a long life was your goal. The old itch for action began again.

Fighters were scattered all around the 'drome. Gaps had been cut in hedges and drains boarded over for the towing of aircraft to distant dispersals. Every tree had a fighter under it; every field was lined with gleaming aircraft. Pilots came and went, sometimes from 80 and it was galling to be stranded on the edge of things. One day the price of this lazy job would have to be paid and, sure enough, here came the collector. A wing commander who called us into an office and after a brief introductory bit of nonsense, asked for volunteers for a special job. By this time we were all so brassed off with our petty chores, we would have volunteered for anything.

'Anything' turned out to be more than we'd bargained for, and cost (as these jobs always do) several lives. We got the impression we were to be radio controllers of aircraft used in airborne landing behind enemy lines (true). We got the distinct impression we'd be floating around in C47's (Dakotas) detailing off gliders etc. by numbers when to go in and land, etc. etc. (false).

Safe enough with dozens of our fighters milling about and shooting up flak posts for us, etc. etc. The etceteras should have warned us.

Beaming cheerfully, his job well done, the Wingco left. A few days later a signal came through; Squadron Leaders Vincent and Spurdle to report to 83 Group Headquarters.

We took an Oxford to Eindhoven, only to find some fool had transposed 83 for 38. We turned around and flew back to England via Volkel, Helmond, Dunsfold, Netheravon, Dunsfold, Brussels, Volkel, Brussels, Northolt . . . and at the end of this 'odyssey' we had the twitch properly. Now we knew the price – and didn't like it.

We were to be lent to the 1st British Airborne Corps based near Rickmansworth and would be trained by them in Army co-operation as to their ground support, using TAF fighters and fighter bombers. We were told that the reason, the real reason, for the failure at Arnhem, was that the crystals used to align the army radio sets with the US Airforce long-range fighter-bombers had been the wrong ones.* Air-ground support fire had bogged down. Fighters couldn't be directed onto ground targets to break up Jerry tank and infantry formations. We were told that as the next large-scale air-borne crossing was to be in Montgomery's sector, he had insisted that RAF crew and equipment be used for all air liaison.

This was what we were told. This was what was being organised now and 'Varsity' was the code name for the airborne Rhine crossing. We were to be part of the 6th Airborne Glider Group and would be landed immediately after the parachutists were dropped, in the first wave of gliders. Our job would be to set up radio contact as quickly as possible and direct our aircraft against German resistance. We felt very important, but scared. This would 'really be sumpin'. We were to wear Army uniforms, but with Air Force insignia. No one could mistake us for Majors (the equivalent Army rank) so instead of ordering, we had to ask – this was to prove a damn nuisance to everyone except our own little teams.

My team comprised Flight Lieutenant Dowlin, Sergeant Simpson, LAC Holmes and myself as leader. We were issued with khaki battle dress, parachutists' coveralls, camouflage net scarves, gaiters and huge, heavy, horrible boots. We received the coveted Red Berets and wore them with intense pride.

The next few days were a mad mélange of the firing range, lectures on Army/Air co-operation, map reference detail instructions and so forth. Our jeeps, generators and powerful ground/air RT

* In Christopher Hibbert's book, *The Battle of Arnhem*, Batsford, London, 1962, p. 96 dealing specifically with the British at Arnhem and equally critical of British communications, he claims that: 'American air support parties were insufficiently trained . . . the disastrous consequence was that not until the last day of the operation was any effective close air support given to the airborne troops. There appears to be no information on who erred in the allocation of the frequencies, nor are the names of the Americans known. The two teams who found themselves in the middle of the battle with the means of perhaps changing the entire course of history on that vital day, have never been found. Yet these two combat units are the only American ones known to have been in the Arnhem battle.'

sets were being readied for us. There was some delay in the fitting of the generators and radios in the trailers and we looked forward to practical exercises with our new toys. The Army uniforms fitted like sacks, and felt like them; the boots were blistering curses. We looked at one another and tried to laugh.

*

The jeep sagged in the courtyard on tired springs. The windscreen was cracked and there was no wiper. Torn hood, no side screens, and all the dents and bruises of many hard months' usage – obviously a throw-out from the motor pool detailed to provide us with transport for this most important and vital operation. I gave the worn front tyres some bloody good kicks in disgust; mud dropped from under crumpled mudguards. The trailer was no better – only the generator and radio were new and obviously just fitted.

The other two jeep units were in much the same stage of decrepitude, and two days later, on exercises, one clutch burnt out and another started to slip. Absolutely furious, I wrote out a blistering report to the General, 6th Airborne Division. Here we were, picked RAF crews, lent to the Army to control the vital air support for the ground troops in the biggest air drop in history, and issued with cast-off, flogged-out vehicles. Here we were – the key to success or failure – and some bloody MT officer had taken the chance to get shot of his worn out liabilities.

Less than a day later, we had three brand-new jeeps and trailers being fitted out, and a wickedly stupid clot was on his way to Burma. A one-way trip, I hoped.

While the radio operators checked and tuned their gear, we pilots practised at the butts with Sten guns and our favourite toys, the Inglis 9mm Browning automatics. We ran in the jeeps with long 'egging' trips around the countryside, and even managed a flight in a glider, which appalled us and gave us the twitch. Hell! The bloody things came down at a fantastic angle, air spoilers quivering and moaning in torment, and we hardened pilots gazing in horror at the nonchalant manoeuverings of Army sergeants with, to us, the flying experience of newly hatched owls.

We began to look away from one another, and furtively drew up fresh wills. The army types went on marching and drilling and cleaning their weapons, happy as larks. We found out that for a lot of these men their first trip in an airplane was going to be the glider ride over the Rhine. For many, too, it would be their last.

Then one day the camp was closed, and all telephone calls, incoming and outgoing, were stopped, all mail held back. We now knew the time for action was close and I began to worry about my wife not hearing from me regularly. She had been warned this would happen, but it still seemed imperative for me to send her one last note, and I sat down to write a love letter that could be a 'good-bye'. How to post it was another matter.

We were introduced to our big Horsa gliders, and chained our Jeeps and trailers inside their dark rib-lined bellies, swung the tail sections back into place and locked the holding pins solid. Hours of waiting. Days and nights of fretting behind the barbed wire of the camp. More briefings, study of aerial photographs, sand-models, lectures.

Op. Sortie 565 [my last]   'Up! Convoy moves off in thirty minutes. All up! Up!' And we stumbled out of our Nissen hut and into draughty three-tonners. It was 4 a.m., 24th March 1945. Shouted 'good lucks' to the other two teams, and last-minute hunting for gear, now marvellously misplaced, although we'd been checking and counter-checking for days.

The convoy halted in a country lane and my truck was right beside a letter box. In a flash I was over the tailboard and the letter on its way. The countryside for miles around had been alerted for this operation, with the pub's best customers suddenly confined to barracks, huge movements of gliders, glider-tugs, trucks, tanks and guns all milling about. Hell, my letter wouldn't give the show away! Any enemy agent would have to be blind and deaf not to know 'Varsity' was on. And on right now.

At the 'drome we clambered into the big black glider. Glassy smiles and hollow laughs. The glider crew got in, cheerful as crickets. Thank God! RAF types, a flight lieutenant and a sergeant pilot. Our jeep and trailer squatted in the darkness like fat brown toads. I didn't want to see the long towing cable being hooked to the glider's nose; the huge Stirling bombers trundling past with shining discs twirling vapour trails from spinning propeller tips. The whole air, the very ground trembled to the grumbling roar of hundreds upon hundreds of powerful motors. Our glider jerked, rumbled forward, was heaved bodily into the turbulent air. I'd seen enough and sat back behind the pilots' bulkhead and fiddled with my Sten gun, checked spare magazines: and thought.

How in hell had I got mixed up with all these brown jobs? I must have been mad! Outside the flimsy plywood skin of our glider, the huge armada took up formation; squadron after squadron from airfields scattered miles apart lumbered into the dawn sky, to rendezvous en route to the dropping zone. C47's in hundreds appeared, lugging pairs of the small American Waco gliders to join the huge Stirlings pulling the heavier Horsas and even bigger Hamilcars, which carried earthmoving gear, artillery and 'Tetrarch' light tanks. There were over forty thousand men in the air – glider borne infantry, parachutists, anti-tank men, machine gunners, mortar crews, Padres (no weapons), doctors, signallers – the lot. And, warming up on the airfields of England, France, Belgium and Holland were the fighter-bombers and anti-flak fighters to support this mighty air armada. Further back, light, medium and heavy bombers, the night machines of the RAF and the day machines of the US Airforce, took off to interdict and pound ground targets.

Already the Parachute regiments were well on their way – they were to be the first dropped and their job was to secure the landing areas for the glider-borne troops. Every one of the thousands of air-crew and the tens of thousands of soldiers knew his role in the operation. The huge airborne armada was to descend like a cloud of locusts onto the fields now being marked out with coloured smoke canisters placed by Pathfinder aircraft.

The whole thing was fantastic in its size and scope; over 6,000 aircraft were involved. This time it would be no Arnhem – the RAF were providing the radio links with our army and we had RAF fighter-bombers to give instant close support. And, in their trenches and flak posts, the Germans were ready. They may not have known exactly where the blow was to be struck, but every field was planted with heavy poles to wreck gliders, and mortar crews and gunners had every square yard zeroed for accurate defensive fire. And there were the minefields!

It took us two hours and forty minutes to cross the Channel, drone over the flooded Dutch fields and be cast adrift. Two hours and forty minutes of thinking, worrying, nail biting doubts, regrets and promises to be a better man in the future. If there was to be a future!

The whole glider vibrated, occasionally lurching violently when caught in the Stirling's slipstream. Creaks and groans of straining woodwork, the clinking of chain ends. It was bitterly cold: Dowlin and I sagged in our hard seats. It was too tiring to shout above the sound of rushing air. At the rear of the Horsa, behind the jeep and trailer, were Simpson and Holmes. After about an hour I heard crackings and splintering from the back. Good God, the bloody thing's falling apart! But it was only the two airmen hacking peep-holes in the plywood fuselage with their knives, to see what was going on outside.

They tell me some of the men slept quite soundly on the long flight, but for me the experience was too intense, too bizarre.

We were nearing the drop zone; I could see our Stirling tug slowly weaving as if checking its position. Others tended to drift across our path into some sort of approach pattern. Down below, by peering over the two pilots' shoulders, I saw gun flashes; sometimes rocket-firing Typhoons dived past and through the armada stream to engage German flak emplacements. They'd slide down in speeding curves, straighten up and then rockets streaked away, trailing grey gases, to burst in clouds of earth and smoke.

A thin brown haze smothered the whole area below; above, a brilliant blue sky. Hundreds, uncountable aircraft, Stirlings, Dakotas, Horsas, Wacos, Albemarles, Hamilcars, all in a huge multi-tiered unending stream. Fighters weaved above and on either side. We were in the vanguard group of the glider train, following immediately behind the paratroopers and combat infantry gliders.

Just in front of us a Stirling was hit by flak. A flash, a puff of smoke, then it staggered down to port, falling from the sky. Its glider slipped its towing-cable and veered sharply away to starboard; then the huge bomber ponderously reared up, up, up, to fall over backwards as we curved out of its path. A few parachutes and it was gone out of sight behind us. To our left a glider's tail plane broke off and the crippled machine was hastily cast adrift by its tug, the nylon rope whipping back in the slipstream. The fuselage and wings started to turn end over end at an astonishing speed of rotation; pieces broke off. The tail unit went. First soldiers, then a jeep, tumbled from the wreck. The men looked like puppets jerked by a madman – arms flailing – to fall thousands of feet to the waiting earth.

I'd seen enough and, with thoughts in a turmoil, clambered back to my seat. Now the sounds of battle were continuous – above the muted roar of motors and the hissing slipstream I could hear all manner of thuds and bangs. The thin plywood skin of the glider seemed to quiver with the din. Every now and again there would be a sharp whacking sound as the glider was hit by shrapnel or from flak bursting close by; the air was tainted with the smell of high explosives. I took off my tin hat and tried to squat in it. I guess I was trying to protect my genitals – an instinctive male reaction. Again I ventured a look ahead just in time to see our tow rope snake off and be towed away by our tug. I bet they were pleased to get shot of us. The glider crew were nattering away, the co-pilot gesticulating towards some feature below.

'I see it! Yes! That's it!' shouted the glider's captain, who promptly dropped his map and took over the controls. I clambered right forward and, clutching the pilots' seat frame, stared out at the fantastic sight.

Parachutes hung festooned from trees or lay spread across green fields like fallen washing. Already a few gliders were on the ground and more and more were diving steeply at incredible angles to level off and plough across the rough fields. Wreckage, more and more, was scattered by the planes hitting the German poles erected to deny safe landings.

'Hold on!' shouted the co-pilot, and I clutched harder as full flap was applied. The Horsa heaved up, then dropped, nosing over into a heart-stopping stoop towards the deck. The lift spoilers whistled in the slipstream, tracer shells arced overhead. More and more bangs and thuds with the whole scene wreathed in smoke; men running or lying still on the fields.

Mortar bursts, black and ugly with cores of dull red flame, flickered at random across the earth, more running figures, dead animals, trees, ponds, a farmhouse and then – Crash! – and we were down.

Lurching and rumbling the big glider rocketed and heaved noisily over grassy farmland towards a belt of trees. Both pilots were swearing and cursing as they strained on rudder pedals to steer it clear of obstructions. Hanging on grimly I stared, fascinated, as bushes, fences and gates slid past. A loud bang! and the nosewheel burst through the flooring – the glider skidded crazily on, lurching and bucketing in clouds of sods and dust. A last crunch and we were there.

The noise outside was frightening and we didn't want to leave the frail 'safety' of our plywood box. Bits of metal tore through the glider or clanged against the jeep and trailer. We had to get out – get the jeep and radio gear into action – but we didn't want to leave the shadows and face the sunlit exposure outside. Not outside into the noisy battle; the stink of cordite, and yells and cries of fighting men!

'Come on, you chaps! Let's get going and unload the jeep!' I shouted. I had to do it – such is the price of leadership.

The front of the glider was all jammed up. The sub-structure and nose wheel a shambles. We tried the tail unit and struggled to knock out the locking pins which were under stress. Although I shouted for them to stop and help, the two pilots sloped off, cheerful at a job well done, to join whatever unit they were supposed to fight alongside. Cursing and struggling, we toiled to swing the heavy tail unit out of the way, free the restraining chains from jeep and trailer and roll them out of the glider.

American parachutists went loping past – survivors from their group's unintended drop in the British sector. Fortuitous for us as it turned out – their error of judgment cost them dearly as they bore the brunt of German fire. But they were cocky bastards – one stole my binoculars left on a pile of gear waiting to be loaded on the jeep. They ambled off into the smoke and disappeared. Snagged white or camouflaged green-and-khaki parachutes hung down from the row of trees alongside us. And stretching them, the bodies of dead American paratroopers. Some lay in the fringing pond and some dangled, swaying slowly in the warm, still air.

We kept on struggling with our unloading; the ramp off the glider stuck at an awkward angle.

'Grab this bloke – we'll have to use him as a block.' We heaved the corpse under the ramp and backed the jeep out, coupled the trailer up and set off to find the farmhouse designated as Division HQ. The terrible sounds of battle were clearly diminishing – the heavy thudding of shells and mortars, the tearing chatter of machine gun fire, were dying down as German resistance was overcome. Soldiers appeared and disappeared like wraiths in a nightmare as the pall of stinking smoke cut visibility to a few hundred yards. We drove past a large, fat woman lying dead on her back across a little path between farm buildings – she should have stayed under cover. A magnificent draught horse lay frozen in the rictus of death – locked rigid, head back and teeth bared, as when it tried to bite at a horrid wound in its shoulder.

Another wave of gliders swooped down, whistling and thrumming in the calm air. More bursts of multiple cannon fire sprayed up from a copse over to the left and one of the black gliders disintegrated crashing untidily and strewing men and equipment over an acre of ground. Rumbling, crashing into posts, the big aircraft rolled and skidded in all directions. The rending off of wooden wings, shouts, explosions – all a crazy backdrop of noise. Stretcher-bearers ran by followed by a Padre looking haunted and strained.

We located the site of our command post. Already a small glider-borne 'dozer was scooping out two holes to protect our jeep and trailer. Leaving the others to 'plant' the vehicles and get the radio ready for action I ran off to the HQ command post.

'You! Yes, you! Get after that tank – there are snipers in that wood. They're to be cleaned out!' The tall be-ribboned officer had on riding breeches and, for God's sake, carried a ruddy riding crop! He'd doffed his tin hat for the red beret and by his rank badges, was something more than a colonel.

'Sorry, sir, I'm RAF radio team.'

'I don't bloody well care what you are. Get cracking now and I mean *now!*'

Turning from me he rounded up a couple of passing soldiers and off we went at a shambling run after a light tank churning towards the wood. Clutching my Sten in sweaty hands, I had cause to regret the whole affair, and on rounding a hedgerow, kept on along it and around the far end to double back at a nonchalant walk. This was stupid! What if I were bumped off tracking down some lousy Hun and the army deprived of air support? Busily rationalising, I got to HQ and reported in.

HQ was a farmhouse surrounded by apple trees. One of the outhouses was on fire and a dozen Huns were running back and forth with buckets of water trying to douse the flames. They were soldiers without pants or boots. An incredibly funny sight.

'What gives?' I asked a wounded Tommy on a stretcher.

'They caught one of the bastards with a knife in his boot! Now they can't hide anything.'

Soon we were given targets and quickly got the Typhoons, Hurricanes and Spitfires diving onto pockets of Hun resistance.

The hours flew by and then the day was done. The sun sank below the horizon in a red glow from the smoke haze and, as darkness fell, our radio team was stood-down until daybreak. We opened our tins of Spam and brewed up. But it was a grim night – 88's and mortars had the whole area bracketed and their explosions kept us awake. Worst of all was the vicious banging of Nebelwerfers, whose multiple crashes shook the earth. Hot, sweaty and tired to the bone our little crew couldn't sleep so we yarned away until completely exhausted by the day's excitement, we crawled into our bed-rolls and drifted off to sleep huddled on the sweet-smelling earth by our jeep.

My first day in Germany was over.

*

Long before the sun came up, Sergeant Simpson shook me awake.

'Sir, you're wanted at HQ – the cab-rank fighters are due in about half an hour.'

I crawled out of my sleeping bag, rubbed sleep from bleary eyes, put on my coveralls, scarf and red beret. Clutching my Sten gun I stumbled, navigating by braille, through the orchard to the shadowy group of farm buildings. In a dark hall, bumbling around trying to locate the Command post room I came on a soldier asleep in a passage. But after much shaking of him, I found to my horror it was the sleep from which no one awakes.

'Ah – Spurdle, let me know the minute our fighters are overhead – we've got a hundred targets for them. Here are priority jobs that need immediate attention! Sorry about your other teams. I believe they've had it! They haven't checked in.'

I took a sheaf of co-ordinates back to the jeep joining the others in a hasty meal of beans cooked over our little primus. Our field telephone had been connected up to HQ and we were fully operational at last.

Slowly dawn crept over dewy fields, spider webs glistened. All around fire-fights were erupting as pockets of Jerries, re-grouped during the night, got into action. Our little tanks started clanking and snorting around, backed up by small units of soldiers who scuttled from cover to cover. Snipers started taking pot-shots, – picking people off – we kept our heads down – not our role to winkle them out, thank God!

With daylight came salvoes from heavy artillery and mortar bursts. The 88's had pestered us all night but now with daylight's pearly light we could pinpoint their muzzle-flashes and bring down fighters in retaliation.

Our fighter-bombers roared overhead at about 4,000 feet and we made contact by RT direct to the squadron leaders. We watched in huge delight as they dived on objectives – the rockets hammering down with streaming fire and smoke. More and still more targets were sent for us to deal with – dug-in troops, artillery, motor transport, tanks.

Our motor generator became wreathed in blue exhaust fumes and we moved it to the limit of its cable – luckily there was an unused pit nearby.

The sun rose, hot and glaring, and with it two larks climbed, unconcerned by all the noise, to greet the new day with glorious song. During the night someone had removed the fat woman and encaged the Hun prisoners in barbed wire enclosures. They had been given shovels and were well dug in from their comrades' projectiles.

We needed slit trenches to sleep in at night. An interpreter from HQ rounded up some tough looking SS men from the prisoner cage. I don't know exactly what he told them, but they were scared, and wouldn't dig fast enough. Waving my Sten gun around only seemed to slow them and then it struck me – the wit must have told them they were digging their graves! Having got them reassured we soon had good trenches to sleep in and sent the relieved Jerries back to their own holes.

As soon as each squadron had expended its ammunition, bombs or rockets, it was replaced by another. Sometimes we had up to thirty-two aircraft attacking ground targets at a time. We directed dozens of squadrons against hundreds of targets during the long hot day. We were nearly exhausted at the end of each shift. As each Army 'tentacle' sent in requests for air-support it was answered at once. Down would come the Typhoons, the Tempests and Spitfires and the crumps from each bomb, the tearing roar and crash of rockets, the ripping sound of multiple machine gun and cannon fire echoed across the farm lands.

Soon all resistance inside our pocket was overcome and the 6th Airborne perimeter expanded until sounds of battle became muted. Apart from occasional shells we were safe enough in our dugouts. I was keen to look around the battlefield and, leaving Dowlin to handle the air traffic during a lull, wandered off away from our orchard across open ground to a small pine plantation. In the dappled shadows I found the swathe of broken boughs and pieces of plywood scattered by a crashed glider. Lying in the scented grass and meadow flowers, were a dozen or more young soldiers sprawled casually around the wreckage of their Horsa. Ambling across I was struck by the absolute stillness. Nothing stirred; not a sound, except the chirping of small birds. The sleeping men's faces were white as if dusted with flour. Backing off from the lonesome place, now chill and desolate, I returned to HQ and reported in. A padre gathered up a work party and went off to his miserable duty.

After six days of intense effort the 6th Airborne fought their way to the village of Erle digging in at night and pressing on by day. On the 29th we were 'leap-frogged' by ground troops who had crossed the Rhine by boat and pontoon bridges. Clapped-out and suffering from lack of sleep by living rough, the Airborne troops were relieved and withdrawn to the UK for re-grouping.

The survivors of our RAF crews were flown out, their job done. I was ordered to report in person to Air Vice Marshal Sir Harry Broadhurst at Eindhoven. He wanted to hear first hand the details of our part in Varsity. An Auster and a pilot, Flight Lieutenant Irwin, was laid on and at Eindhoven I borrowed the Auster and flew back to Volkel to see the 80 Squadron boys. It was a strange reunion. A lot of the old faces were gone – dead, missing or posted. Their replacements unknown to me and I was just a part of squadron 'lore'. 80 was another commander's baby and my presence an intrusion. With flights taking off and returning from Ops, with instructions being given and de-briefing taking place in the busy dispersal there was little time for reminiscences. Feeling a deep sense of loss I took off for Eindhoven and lunch with the AVM.

Never go back! Nostalgia can overcome commonsense – the past is dead and gone, gone, gone.

In the luxurious (to us) officers' mess at Eindhoven, where desk-fliers ruled with the dead hand of bureaucrats and whose rations of food and grog far exceeded those of the fighting squadron messes, we sat down to a slap-up meal. I made my report to the AOC 2nd TAF.

It was obvious the war would soon be over. The German Army only fighting on because of mad Hitler's dictates from his bunker in Berlin. Our air forces were roaming at will over Germany destroying anything that moved. More and more prisoners were filling the POW cages and more and more of our own men were being released as the Allied armies rolled on. It was obvious too, that if I wanted souvenirs I'd have to get in quickly. I chanced my luck.

'Sir, I have a request to make; the war's practically over. Can I go on with a ground control unit? Please don't send me back to the UK now that the end is in sight!'

Sir Harry, in an expansive mood, agreed; granted me a 48 hour pass, the use of a stripped-down communications Spitfire and I was off!

It was 31st March and making the machine sweat I was soon at Manston ringing up Shirly. Anne was growing into a lovely, plump, happy little charmer. With love and in complete peace our little family treasured the fleeting hours. Too soon I was off again back to the continent and the final adventure.

CHAPTER XV

'Herr Milch Eier von Wasser Spurdle'*

Strapping on the Spit, I flew back to Holland, landing again at Eindhoven where I re-planed by Auster to B100. Here I was jammed into a jeep with an RAF Corporal and an LAC, along with our sleeping gear, small arms and some food. The airmen were to deliver me to the 11th Armoured Division now battling its way through Germany from the Wesel beachhead.

For two days and nights we rolled along, often getting lost and sometimes crossing the tenuous line separating our forces from the Huns. It was a case of babes-in-the-wood and we were well bushed most of the time. At Munster we had to wait for great snorting bulldozers to clear huge mounds of rubble aside. The place was one vast churned-up pile of bricks and concrete, a dreadful sight, but satisfying when we thought of what had been done to British cities. Strangely enough the big cathedral was still standing.

The first night we pulled into a farm just out of Rheine and I ordered the owners out. We slept soundly in their warm kitchen on huge eiderdowns, guns close to hand.

Osnabrück was next; we followed the 11th Armoured màrkers without too much trouble for the first few hours until we pulled into the outskirts of a small town. Lining the cobbled road were bodies, some moving, others quite still. Light self-destroying flak shells sparkled over the roof tops and shrapnel spanged about, striking sparks on the cobbles.

'Hey! Those people aren't dead or wounded! They're drunk!' shouted the corporal as we drew into and under the entrance of a large building to get out of the whizzing ironwork bouncing and clanging off walls and roadway.

---

* A nickname given me by the tank crews because in our 'stand down' periods I'd search the Hun farms for milk, eggs and water supplies.

A group of roaring drunk slave-workers were smashing the tops off wine bottles and drinking straight from the jagged ends. We slowly dismounted. Leaving the corporal in charge of the jeep and with the airman nervously clutching his rifle and me holding my automatic well out in front like an extended finger, we entered a huge cave-like cellar.

Incredible! There must have been a hundred completely drunken men and women reeling about or squirming in frenetic piles against the walls of the dank, dark hall. We slowly climbed down the wide stone stairs and peered into the gloom at the fantastic orgy going on all around us. 'Right old fumble, ain't it!' exclaimed my driver. I had to agree; these people were really hanging one on – probably the first taste of liquor or mixed company they'd had for years – and they weren't fussy what they got in the way of drink or sex.

'Come on, grab some cases of grog and let's get out,' I said. The erk slung his rifle and we heaved out two cases of white Bordeaux wine on the back of the jeep. The corporal's eyes bugged out. 'Cor! Is there any more?'

'Yes! Go down with your cobber and get something else. I'll keep an eye on this lot.'

They were gone over half an hour and I became worried. I didn't dare leave the jeep. What was holding them up? Loud screams and drunken yells erupted from the cellar. Down the street, semi-paralysed bodies twitched in the gutters and odd air-bursts still cracked and barked over roof tops. The two airmen reappeared dragging two more cases of wine, German booty plundered from the French. They were as tight as ticks. It was time to go; frenzied shouting and the sound of a violent crashing fight echoed from the cellar. We pushed the corks out of three bottles before venturing from under the shelter of our verandah and down the street we went, weaving to avoid bodies and often for no reason at all.

'Damned if I know wheresh we are! Lesh jush keep on down this lane – they're tank truck traksh, so it could be the Eleventh Divsh.'

'Aargh!' agreed the corporal.

It was strangely quiet – we'd not seen any soldiers for hours. Nor trucks, or the confusing army sign-posts. Now we were motoring through gently rolling green countryside. The jeep groaned under the added weight of the cases of wine stacked across the back, while we three huddled in the front, passing a bottle around as the corporal weaved along.

A little village came into view; just a group of small houses in the shadow of some huge oak trees. A small child ran across the street, to be grabbed and heaved inside by a woman who glared at us. She slammed her door shut. There was no sign of life – not a hen, not even a dog or a cat. Dust swirled in the hot dry roadway; oak leaves danced high above, shimmering against the blue sky.

'Don't like thish! Turn aroun' quick!'

And just as the corporal headed out of town, a Spandau opened up and with its second burst, bottles crashed and glass flew, splashing us with sticky foam. The jeep fairly flew down a dip and so out of range. We stared at each other and the LAC reached over, rummaging in the mess for a whole bottle.

'Jesus wept!' he said quite clearly. Up till recently it had just been hiccoughs, ughs and arghs!

We pushed on back the way we'd come. Another section of rolling land and this time a scarlet flame screamed across our path, to hit a fence and go howling towards the sky.

'Foot down! Christ Almighty! The bastards a' shelling ush!' and off we tore down another dip and another ball of fire hurtled past us. An anti-tank gun hidden in a copse some hundreds of yards away was taking pot shots at us.

Every dip was the same – three more times they tried to hit us and three more times the flaming tracer shells screamed close by, to crash into earthy banks. Luckily they were APs which didn't explode.

A few miles more and we pulled up and had another couple of bottles. So far so bad. We couldn't go back – what to do?

'Les' hole up inna farm housh,' I suggested. 'There'sh one there showing a sheet.' I was proud to get that out clearly.

We bumped our way over a rutted track and pulled up under a lean-to. Fat hens clucked about, and in a pen, pigs grunted and eyed us with disfavour.

'I'll have one of those tomorrow,' I promised myself.

The farmer's wife and daughter were quite jolly and tended to fawn on us. The farmer, an ugly brute, grunted like his pigs, but brightened up when the corporal lugged in a case of grog. We soon disillusioned him on that score. We were shown a huge bed with the awful smothering feather eiderdowns favoured by the Hun peasants.

'One of us'll guard alla time.' I was having difficulty speaking, and even thinking of staying awake was unpleasant. 'You guys'll go to bed firsh. Corpl, you do second watch, OK?'

They kicked off their boots and, taking two bottles to bed with them, were soon comfortable, getting out only to pee through the open window. The pigs grunted cheerfully enough and the sun set in flaming beauty. The Hun family seemed to have disappeared and their surrender sheet hung ghostly white in the evening air. Strange creaks and bumps kept me clutching my pistol in a sweaty grip, the wine now sour in my mouth and my head thumping painfully.

At about ten, I dug the corporal protesting from his warm nest.

'First time I've shlep' with a sloshin' Leasher,' mumbled the LAC.

'Shut cake-hole,' warned the corporal taking his bottle away. I was too tired to care. Let the farmer cut our throats. I'd shoot a pig in the morning, I thought, quietly passing out.

It was a dreadful hangover, and as we milled about re-loading the jeep in the early morning mists, I remembered the pigs. The automatic made a hell of a bark, hens took off, and all the pigs set up a dreadful squealing. Soon we had the bleeding corpse lashed across the bumper in front of the radiator. The farmer's eyes glittered but he stepped aside quickly enough, as red-eyed and wary we drove off.

About the middle of the day near the Weser River we saw an 11th Armoured Division sign and just on dusk drove into a very large farm courtyard, where the headquarters' tanks and three-ton supply trucks were laagered. Under hedgerows, in small copses and down in the orchard, the fighting tanks were squatting like huge dinosaurs, their guns trained out towards the perimeters.

'About time you came! Had just about given you up! Hey! Where'd you get the grog?' This from the pilot I was replacing.

'It's for the mess – should make me popular! Haven't the faintest clue where we've been. We got lost after leaving Osnabrück. You're to go back with these chaps.' – And with that I introduced him to the two wrecks frantically trying to hide full bottles out of sight under their bed-rolls.

Flight Lieutenant 'Art' Collins of the 39th Canadian Recce. Wing introduced himself. He was to be my off-sider, in the radio tank. He

Operation Varsity: my glider is next to copse above second guard's head. Americans'
parachutes festoon the trees.

One of the giant Hamilcar gliders used to transport light tanks, artillery and other
heavy material for Operation Varsity.

Sergeant Simpson calls up the 'Cab-rank' fighters. Wesel, March 1945.

Flight Lieutenant Dowlin and myself cleaning our carbines next to our dug-in jeep and generator trailer.

Horsa glider at Wesel in Operational Varsity.

6th Airborne machine gunners in Wesel's devastation.

Shirly and little Anne coming home on the RMS *Rangitata*.

was of my build, slight, about 5′ 8″ tall. He spoke with a strong Canadian accent.

The 11th's Mess was delighted with the wine, but their cooks were taken aback at the sight of the pig, now bloated from the sun and radiator heat. It was much easier for them to open Spam or bully beef cans than cook the monster. I don't know what happened to the unfortunate beast but at least the fine wines were gleefully welcomed and I was accepted by my new army comrades with gusto.

Art showed me over our tank, one of the new Comets. We had two machine guns but the big gun had been replaced by a dummy barrel made of wood to make room inside for the mass of radio communication gear.

Here in Germany was the material evidence of a whole nation's looting of occupied territories. We saw first-hand, the beastliness of the foe which for over six years had made life hell for decent peoples. As we over-ran German positions, hordes of forced-labour groups were liberated to trek back cross-country to their homelands and what was left of their families. Poles, Greeks, French, Dutch, Belgians – men and women, thin and gaunt. Many were worn out or wrecked physically or mentally. In their thousands these unfortunates were creeping back past the long Allied convoys, on crowded roads. Empty supply trucks returning to rear echelons for more war material gave lifts to the lucky ones. But, hardening to these sights, what really choked us were our own boys – the POWs who, standing free at last, sometimes openly wept.

Our forward drive was so fast in certain areas that German soldiers were caught, standing open-mouthed, rifles slung on shoulders, as we ground and roared through village streets. To our embarrassed amusement, our long dummy gun developed a great open crack along its wooden 'barrel'. Lord knows what rumours and confusion it caused.

Messages came through continually from army 'tentacles' – the forward reconnaissance vehicles – of enemy concentrations and strong points. These were passed on to Art or myself and we'd call up aircraft from the 'cab rank' above us. In a moment the particular aircraft under our control would be directed onto the target.

'Ground to Railroad aircraft. Four tanks east corner wood, reference B34, repeat.'

And back, quick as a wink, the aircraft's leader would acknowledge. It was fascinating to listen in to pilots' remarks as they dived to attack. And to report back their results. One day I exceeded my target instructions, and to this day remember with deep regret the faces of two old people made homeless by my decision.

'Enemy rocket launchers in cemetery, reference H17,' was the target given me. The cemetery, according to our map, was on a corner of a 'T' junction some miles away. It seemed logical that the Panzerwursts would also be hidden in the house or grounds opposite, so I had these rocketed as well. Hours later, when we rolled past this position, I saw, standing weeping together, an old couple, their home in ruins. No matter that they were the God-damn enemy; no matter that probably their ja's had helped put Hitler in power and that they had heiled with the rest of them. All I see today is the old man's arms around his wife and the smoking rubble of what had been a home.

At night our tanks would laager-up in a strong position. We, as did most units, had a German-speaking officer, usually a Belgian, Dutch or Frenchman, to handle the Huns. One of his jobs was to pick out a suitable farmhouse (usually the finest) for the officers' mess. These interpreters had no love for the enemy, soldier or civilian, and, on looking over a house, gave the occupants fifteen minutes to get out. There was no argument. The hapless owners would go around snatching up bedding and locking cupboards before heading off to neighbours for shelter. Our three-tonners would appear as if by magic and soon a hot meal would be ready. The crews of the fighting tanks, hidden in a protective ring, would soon be brewing up their endless char, and bedding down till dawn.

Now came the hour when, after a good meal and wines, we retired to rooms tossed for or commandeered, according to rank. Soon sounds of rending woodwork began, as drawers and cupboards were forced open. Weapons were often hidden and had to be found and destroyed.

The most extraordinary things turned up; ceremonial daggers, swords, medals from many wars, ancient shotguns, rifles and pistols.

And sometimes, good ones too. The thing which impressed us most of all was the Germans' fantastic preoccupation with things military. The books and, in particular, the pictures and photographs in these country homes, reflected this military background. Here, hanging all over the walls, was the physical evidence of a nation of war lovers.

Art and I developed a modus operandi – it took only one to handle the air traffic, so on the good flying days we took turns in the tank, and during unflyable bad weather we were 'stood down' and took our jeep to the nearest 'liberated' village, often still under gunfire. Here we'd find the local Burgomeister and demand he despatch boy scouts, girl guides or what have you to bring in all guns, swords, daggers, cameras and binoculars. Our interpreter took obvious pleasure in this order and added that the Mayor's head would be on a spike if all the above were not collected within the hour. There would be a frantic scurrying and soon the illegal articles started to roll in.

Art and I would sit in comfort and pick over the surrendered weapons, etc., old shot guns, some of them museum pieces, along with inferior modern rifles and guns would be lined up on the roadway and, if no tank were available, we'd use the jeep to run over and crush them. We destroyed hundreds this way. Cameras and binoculars would be given to the tank crews or any soldiers showing interest. In this way we got quite valuable personal collections and soon our tank looked like a pawnbroker's showroom.

The items 'liberated', to use the soldiers own vernacular, were all forbidden to Germans and as such, forfeit.

I was called over to the CO's tank and warned not to take too many chances in the execution of this chore. But it was like a drug in the blood and our forays became more and more daring. One wet day, Art and I approached a large farmhouse in no-man's land and some old bastard had a go at us with a shotgun. As we lay under the wet hedge where we'd thrown ourselves, we had some second thoughts but out from the house came a woman wearing a smile (albeit a trifle fixed) and bearing on a salver, glasses and a bottle!

She really sickened me – her grandfather I could admire.

Village by village we rolled on; everywhere white sheets were hanging from upstairs windows in silent surrender. Mostly the civilians smiled and fawned around – there is no other word for it. Sometimes, usually from an old soldier of World War I vintage, there'd be a surly acquiescence that was better to see.

'Here! Get this over the air quickly, Spud! It is most important that there's no cock-up!'

The message was strange. 'No air attacks on Road Saltau to Bergen. Repeat – No action whatsoever, map references N34, H9 and O42 inclusive.'

'What's up?' I asked.

'There's been some crazy approach by Himmler direct to Army HQ. They don't want any fighting near some big concentration camp in case the inmates escape and spread typhus,' was the reply. 'We're sending a representative to meet a Jerry officer and they're to follow this route by staff-car to a place called Belsen, for some sort of inspection.'

Soon the message was on its way and next day a ghastly report came back from our shaken man. The horror of Belsen was about to be revealed to a disbelieving world.

More and more I enjoyed the tank life. Our Comet monster rolled along and squashed things most satisfyingly. It could push over quite large trees, demolish brick walls and flatten cars effortlessly. Brierly, our driver was an excellent mechanic and maintenance man, but as a driver had to be relieved by his Number Two,* who was no good at maintenance but could turn our tank on a sixpence.

We were often shelled by 88's and we just pulled the lid down and hoped we'd make it to shelter. Shrapnel rattled off the hull, and machine gun and rifle bullets clanged away harmlessly. I had imagined a tank ride would be harsh, but in these monsters it was a gentle rolling, swaying motion and if there were to be another war, this would be my choice. But then, I wasn't in a fighting tank – ours was really just a thick-skinned radio shack.

Rumours were that we'd only be going to the Elbe River, where we'd meet up with the Russian armies. By this time I'd collected an excellent .22 target rifle, a magnificent .300 rifle and scope, a beautiful little 16 gauge over and under shotgun with a 9mm rifle barrel below. But my pride and joy was a double-barrelled 12 gauge shotgun with a 9mm rifle barrel below, complete with a powerful 'scope.

* Trooper Arthur Holder who emigrated to New Zealand and became a friend of Bob Spurdle.

One day, we liberated a POW camp and I spotted an RAF Sergeant pilot who looked in good order.

'Hey! Don't go back there! They'll fly you back to the UK by tomorrow! You'll be empty-handed. Here –', and rummaging among the weapons in the tank, I handed over a shotgun and a handful of shells.

'Take this and liberate that village,' pointing to a cluster of farm houses on the skyline. 'No one's done it over yet! Get going man, and get some souvenirs!'

Dubiously, the Sergeant peered at the distant houses and then loped off, shotgun at the trail. Too late I realized that with his blue-grey uniform he could be mistaken for an armed Hun. Too late, oh, much too late, I realised it was my best gun I'd handed over. It was the last I ever saw of either. Damn!

Art and I came on a large Schloss (castle) on one of our expeditions. An ancient retainer pottering about the courtyard showed us his pride and joy – a detached gun-room. Behind glass doors racks of museum pieces were lined up. The old man wept as we drove the jeep over their Damascene barrels propped against a convenient kerb.

In the huge garage a smart little Opel Kadet saloon was on blocks. Taking the jeep's battery out we soon hooked it up and found, to our huge delight that it ran perfectly. We towed it back to join the tanks. That evening, we decided to convert it to the 39th Canadian Recce Wing. The Canucks were almost a separate air force, a law to themselves. By painting Maple leaves on the doors and 'TAF 83' on one mudguard and '39 Recce Wing' on the other, we were sure we could pass through the many check points to Paris without serious challenge.

The 11th Division reached Luneberg Heath and we were the first into the big peace-time regular Air Force station. All the signs of hurried abandonment were there in the officers' mess. On a side table stood half-full wine glasses. An empty bottle lay discarded along with cast off officers' uniforms. Obviously a small staff had stayed to the last minute before disappearing into the anonymity of civilian life.

On the walls were three magnificent oils. Goering in all his fatuous finery smiled down on us, while Hitler's cold glare gave us pause. But

most compelling was the painting of Baron Manfred von Richthofen –
the Red Knight. Finding a knife I cut them from their gilded frames
and rolled them up. What a prize! And what a damned nuisance to
lug around in our tiny car!

We reached the River Elbe, our finish line. Here the British Army
had to cool its heels waiting for the Russians to arrive. The war was
as good as over. Art and I were relieved by a fresh crew and we set off
for Paris in our Opel for a well earned rest. We flogged the car off and
blew the money having a ball seeing the sights, ranging from the
Moulin Rouge and Folies Bergère to Napoleon's tomb and the
Louvre.

*

Dreading the visit, but determined to go through with it because
Demo had been an especial friend, I called on Madame De Molene
at her elegant Parisian apartment. She was as charming as I had
expected her to be and Art, with his excellent French, introduced me
and the reason for our calling. Yes, my letter, sent so long ago, had
arrived safely. Yes, she was delighted that we'd taken the trouble to
call. We were invited to luncheon during which my execrable French
made us all laugh. I regretted the wasted hours at college.

In my mind's eye, I could see Demo wrestling with the collapsed
skeet gun and hear his excited curses as the old dog-fox scrabbled
into cover while I banged away at it with my revolver. So many,
many dicey aerial adventures – so many hilarious parties and
laughs. Art translated these vignettes of our comradeship which
helped fill the voids in Madame's knowledge of her boy's life between
his escaping to Britain and joining the RAF.

Smuggled letters, heavily censored and necessarily imprecise,
were now linked and the many questions so long unanswerable were
now explained.

When about to leave the moment I had been dreading arrived.

'How did Jules die?'

How could you tell this mother of her son's smoking wreck
spinning down while he struggled, kicking, from his cockpit? Of his
hitting the damned tail unit with his head. How could I describe
circling the blood-soaked jerking body of her boy, my friend, as he
slowly floated down in his chute to drown in the hungry sea?

'Bravely, Madame – it was a mechanical failure. Jules was a crack pilot – it was one of the senseless, stupid things that can happen to any of us. It was very quick.'

For a timeless moment she held me with her eyes, then with a little cry she took my hands and wept. Art turned away and Demo was again with his mother and me.

I didn't want her to know a Hun had got him. Sorrow, not bitterness, would be easier for her to bear.

CHAPTER XVI

Farewell to Arms

On 28th April, I flew back to the UK by twin-engined Anson because there were too many goodies for a fighter to carry. The pilot, Flying Officer Clark, looked at me sideways – little did he appreciate the risks taken to secure the gear. He was a trifle nervous about landing at Manston, my ultimate destination.

'Put her down at Dunsfold, that's a good chap,' and so everything got whipped off and stowed away with friends at this backwater. Next morning we went on to Manston and Shirly who was delighted to have me back safe and sound from the front. The European War was over for me.

All manner of strange, fantastic things were happening with the Hun collapse. The Red Army was exacting a terrible revenge through the women of Germany. One after another the gang which had ruled the Third Reich were getting caught and jailed for war crimes or escaping their inevitable punishment by committing suicide. Hitler had his dog Blondie shot. He shot himself after marrying his mistress, Eva Braun, who died along with him. The nasty little Goebbels had his six children poisoned and ordered an SS officer to shoot his wife and then himself. Himmler, trying to escape detection, was caught in civilian clothes near Luneburg and bit the poison capsule hidden in his mouth. Later Goering took the same way out during the Nuremburg War Trials. And so on.

Day and night the German radio stations still operating poured out Wagnerian dirges. It was weird and horrifying. More and still more ghastly concentration camps were discovered – more and still more atrocities and massacres uncovered.

May 45: The War in Europe is over! With the death of Hitler his total control over the German people, enforced by their terror of his SS and Gestapo forces, ended. The Monster was no more and with his finish his horrible machine collapsed. The lights came on all over Europe; people started to rebuild their lives.

But for tens of thousands a new nightmare started. The Russians claimed their captured soldiers from German POW cages and also displaced civilians, forced to work for the Huns, to be returned to face charges of cowardice, desertion and collaboration. Stalin, the cynical despot, was not to be cheated of his pound of flesh and a dreadful purge resulted. Every 'liberated' country was embroiled in political power struggles; witch hunts by patriots to punish collaborators resulted in fearful travesties of justice. The unfortunate Polish army, that had fought so long and hard alongside their British comrades, was disarmed – Poland as they knew it had gone.

It was time to plan my next move – the Japanese were fighting every inch of the way; retreating island by island back to their homeland. I intended to get in at the kill – who was better qualified than I to lead a wing against this old enemy? I had myself posted to the Central Gunnery School at Catfoss to learn how to shoot accurately, something I should have found time for years before.

On 2nd August 1945, I climbed out of a Mark XVI Spitfire after an air-to-air exercise, and walked back to dispersal.

I didn't especially savour this flight, but then how was I to know it was the last plane I'd ever fly?

On 6th August, the first atomic bomb was dropped on Japan and with it my dreams were gone forever.

To be repatriated back to New Zealand, I was required to join the RNZAF. I protested vehemently.

'No way! I want to remain RAF until demobilisation!'

But it was pointed out that priority was to RNZAF personnel and that my family and I might hang around in the UK for months. Thus, the handful of Short Service veterans – the few survivors of so very many volunteers – were forced to acquiesce and leave what was, in our eyes, the best service in the world.

Shirly, Anne and I embarked on, of all ships, the very one I'd left New Zealand on, six years before – the *Rangitata*! As we steamed over the oceans' lonely wastes, sheltering in the shade of canvas awnings, our motley collection of aircrew swapped experiences. Some were bizarre and, in their telling, maybe we were unconsciously healing ourselves of deep psychological traumas:

Of the mess barman who, getting impatient at the long drawn-out revelries, got tetchy and uncooperative. He was grabbed and rolled up in a carpet, stood in a corner and forgotten. Next morning the unfortunate chap was found suffocated and stiff as a board.

Of the dreadful sight of two Canadians who baled out of their burning B25 too late. They hit Volkel's runway to bounce and then roll along parcelling themselves neatly into two blood-soaked twitching cocoons of silk.

Of the two Typhoon pilots scrambled off from Manston's runway. One or the other had a tyre burst just before becoming airborne and they collided to end locked together in a ball of flame. When the fire engines had finished, all that was recovered were two torsos the size of small suitcases.

And on and on and on.

But there were humorous stories too. At Manston one of the chaps was practising instrument-flying when some Me 109's strafed the 'drome. All of a sudden the Link trainer went into a spin and the pupil thought the operator was playing tricks. Eventually, after trying every remedy he knew the 'pupil' lifted his canopy to find the airman long gone and the Link with bullet holes in its airbags. As far as I know he was the only chap ever shot down in a Link trainer!

The days drifted away and at long last clouds over our homeland's green hills showed snow white in front of our bow knifing through the long blue swells. We'd made it!

Back in New Zealand an old friend of mine, Squadron Leader Williams, came on board to interview all the more senior ranks before disembarkation. He was very embarrassed.

'Spud, believe me this isn't my idea! My job is to see all you chaps and advise you, tell you, not to apply for permanent commissions in the Air Force! You'll only be wasting everyone's time!'

It was clear enough to me but a severe blow to some of the others who had pinned hopes for their futures on an RNZAF career. The cunning ones were coming out of the woodwork now danger was all over and were protecting their own futures. And so, by this shabby, miserable means, a cadre of very experienced first-class air crew were shunted aside. Sure, there were a lot of experienced air crew amongst the Pacific RNZAF air crews but nothing like the calibre of those experienced in the European conflict. It didn't affect me as I had other plans.

*

One day, climbing down a steep ridge while deer-stalking, I found my nerve gone and I had to be assisted back to the track. Worse, I found I couldn't watch a plane flying overhead. I had to look at the ground – it was a year before I could look up at the sky again and learn to ignore the pictures in my mind.

*

Friends ask me why I never flew again. Fly? What for? To fly a runty light aircraft chained by authority to follow submitted flight plans?

Never!

To cut this red tape, I'd need a Sabre's power. To hear my lost comrades' voices again, to find again the wonder and glory of sunlit spires and the deep caverns of the clouds, I'd need the magic of a Merlin.

APPENDIX 1

'74 Squadron and the Few'

Those 'Few' who flew operationally in the Battle of Britain with No. 74 Squadron were: (ranks as at the beginning of the Battle). Decorations not listed as some were in the pipe-line when the pilot was killed.

Killed during the Battle	Killed later in the War	Survivors
F/Sgt D. Ayers	F/Lt S. Brzezina	P/O W. Armstrong
P/O Buckland	P/O P. Chesters	F/O R. Boulding
P/O D. Cobden	P/O E. Churches	F/Sgt F. Burnard
F/Sgt F. Eley	P/O B. Draper	P/O D. Dowding
P/O H. Gunn	F/Sgt L. Freese	F/Sgt C. Francis
F/Sgt T. Kirk	P/O J. Howard	F/Lt J. Freeborn
P/O A. Ricalton	F/Sgt N. Morrison	F/Sgt C. Hilken
P/O P. St. John	F/Sgt E. Mould	F/Lt D. Kelly
F/Sgt J. Scott	F/O J. C. Mungo Park	F/Lt A. Malan
P/O D. Smith	F/O W. Nelson	W/O E. Mayne
P/O J. Young	P/O P. Stevenson	F/Lt W. Measures
		F/Sgt Parkes
		P/O Peace
		F/Sgt W. Skinner
		P/O A. Smith
		F/Sgt H. Soars
		P/O R. Spurdle
		P/O H. Stephen
		F/O H. Szczesny
		S/Ldr F. White

This list does not include those men who were injured and withdrawn from service. Nor does it include the dozens of replacement pilots who were killed, injured or taken POW in other operations with 74 after the Battle of Britain. 74 were sent to fight in the Middle East and returned to fight on in the UK and Europe after the collapse of the Axis powers in the Mediterranean Theatre

Squadron Losses

91 Squadron's Losses (incomplete) June 15th to August 25th, 1942

F/Sgt W. Sykes
F/Sgt Campbell
F/Sgt W. Orr
P/O Wildish (missing)

P/O E. Tonge
P/O J. De Molene (F/French)
P/O J. Edwards (missing)
F/Sgt Downer (N.Z.)

16 Squadron's Losses in the Pacific on their first tour.

F/O A. Hyams
F/Sgt L. Williams

F/O S. Duncan

80 Squadron's Sacrifice in Europe from 16th September 1944 to April 1945

P/O W. E. Maloney (Aus)
F/O P. S. Haw
W/O A.S. Williams (Aus) (missing)
Lt J. B. Gilhuus (Norway)
F/Lt J. Weston (Canada) (missing)
F/Sgt L. B. Crook
P/O N. J. Rankin (Aus)
F/O W. H. Long

W/O P. Godfrey
F/O R. H. Hanney
S/Ldr J. R. Heap (Ex. F/Cdr 80
Squadron)
F/O L. F. Royds
F/O A. W. McLachlan (Aus)
F/O D. S. Angier
P/O H. A. Horsey (missing)
F/O L. Smith

Record of Service

Most of the names and places and all of the dates have been taken directly from my log book. The operational sorties are countersigned as correct by the following Officers under whom I was privileged to serve. Ranks shown are those as pertained at the time of signature.

74 Squadron
Aug. 20 1940 to April 13th, 1941
S/Ldr A. G. Malan
S/Ldr J. C. Mungo Park
Ft/Lt J. C. Freeborn
Ft/Lt A. Bartley
S/Ldr P. A. Wood

91 Squadron
April 15th 1941 to May 22nd, 1941
S/Ldr Patrick Green
F/Lt A. Lee Knight
F/O Patrick Barthropp (for O.C. 'B' flight)

M.S.F.U.
May 25th 1941 to February 20th, 1942
S/Ldr L. Strange
S/Ldr G. W. Austin

91 Squadron
February 20th 1942 to August 27th, 1942
S/Ldr R. W. Oxspring
F/Lt G. C. Pannell
S/Ldr De Mozay (Nom de Guerre)
    (correct name Capt. Jean Morlaix)

116 Squadron
August 27th to October 24th 1942
W/Cdr E. Crundall
S/Ldr D. Woodman

NO. 2 TS (RNZAF)
Self as C.F.I. from January 1942 to May 1943

16 Squadron (RNZAF)
May 25th 1943 to September 1943
Self as Flight Commander 'A' Flight
No counter signature by C.O. (perhaps not required in RNZAF?)

130 Squadron
April 13th 1944 to April 28th 1944

80 Squadron
May 4th 1944 to 20th July 1944
Self as Flight Cdr 'B' flight
Major Björn Björnstad
Self as C.O. from 20th July 1944 to January 4th 1945

Attachment to 6th Airborne Division
February 20th 1945 to March 31st, 1945

Attachment to 11th Armoured Division
April 2nd 1945 to 28th April 1945

The Spitfire MK II Cockpit Check

1. On Entering the Cockpit

   Put on brakes. Check that ignition switches are OFF, undercarriage selector level in DOWN gate, indicator showing IDLE. Switch on light indicator and note that green lights come on. Note that flaps and landing lamps are UP. Check contents of fuel tanks. Test flying controls.

2. Starting Up

   Open radiator flap. Set mixture control to NORMAL and pitch controls fully FORWARD. Raise both fuel cocks levels to ON. Unscrew priming pump and give five effective shots of fuel. Screw down. See airscrew area is clear. Indicate readiness to erk at battery. Start Up.

3. Preliminaries to Testing

   Wait until oil temperature is 15°C min and radiator temperature reaches about 70°C. Note fuel pressure is 2 and a half to three pounds and brake reservoir pressure at least 120 lbs p.s.i. Put flaps down and up again. Set altimeter and directional gyro. See hood is locked open and set emergency exit door at half cock position. Set harness release in 'fixed' position. Proceed to run up.

4. Engine Testing

   In fine pitch, open up to rated gate, check that boost is + 9 lbs p.s.i., R.P.M. 2,750 to 2,850 and oil pressure is 60 lbs p.s.i. at NORMAL temperature. With pitch control fully forward check that magneto drop does not exceed 80 r.p.m. Keep throttle fully open and draw back airscrew control until r.p.m. drop to 2,400 (no further). Throttle down a little and notice that r.p.m. do not drop in spite of throttle movements. Return to fine pitch and close throttle. Wave away chocks.

5. Taxiing Out

   Check brake pressure. Before starting, release parking brake and see radiator shutters are open. Taxi out and get into position for take-off.

6. Final Preparations for Taking off

   Check rudder setting. Set elevator about one division nose down from neutral. Note that mixture control is back in NORMAL. Place pitch control FULLY FORWARD. FLAPS. Check they are UP.

7. Take Off and Climb

   Become airborne. Gather speed and raise undercarriage. Note that red light comes ON. Wait for speed to become 140 m.p.h. A.S.I. and then start a gradual climb. Reduce boost to + 9 lbs p.s.i. and reduce pitch to give 2,850 r.p.m. Accelerate to 185 m.p.h. A.S.I. at 9 lbs p.s.i. boost and maintain this speed. Note that oil pressure is 60 lbs p.s.i. Fully shut emergency exit door and then cockpit hood. Do systematic cockpit check.

8. Cruising

   (i) +7 lbs p.s.i. boost and 2,650 r.p.m. in NORMAL mixture, are the maximum (normal) continuous cruising settings.

   (ii) the greatest cruising range can be obtained at 200 m.p.h. A.S.I. with airscrew pitch set to give 1,700 r.p.m.

9. Approach and Landing

   Stow maps. Open hood. Check radiator shutter setting: lower undercarriage and see that green light comes on. Ensure that mixture control is back to NORMAL. Place pitch lever in fully FINE. FLAPS: Lower after turning in to land. Glide at about 120 m.p.h. A.S.I. without engine. Land.

In an operational 'scramble' most of the foregoing was done automatically after leaping into the cockpit. One did what one could while taxiing out for take off.

If not in the air and formating within three minutes of the Klaxon's blare one was in for a blister from the Controller!

Bibliography

Clouds of Fear, F/Lt R. Hall DFC, Bailey Bros. 1975

Spitfire Command, Group Capt R. Oxspring DFC & Bar AFC, Wm. Kimber 1984

I Fear No Man, Douglas Tidy, Macdonald 1972

A Clasp for the Few, Kenneth Wynn, Published by the Author '81

Tiger Squadron, W/Cdr Taffy Jones, MM, DSO, MC, DFC, Allen 1954

Bounce the Rhine, Charles Whiting, Leo-Cooper 1985

V2, Maj. Gen, Dornberger, Hurst & Blockett 1954

The Narrow Margin, Wood & Dempster, Arrow Books 1969

Lonely Vigil, Walter Lord, Viking Press 1977

The First and Last, Gen. Adolph Galland, Schneekluth 1955

RAF Biggin Hill, Graham Wallace, Putnam 1957

The Hurricats, Ralph Barker, Pelham 1978

Reach for the Sky, Paul Brickhill, Collins 1954

Eagle Day, Richard Collier, Hodder & Stoughton '66

The Big Show, Pierre Clostermann, DSO, DFC, Chatto & Windus 1951

The Battle of Arnhem, Christopher Hibbert, Batsford 1962

The Catafighters, Kenneth Poolman, Wm. Kimber 1970

'Flap', 39 Recce Wing RCAF, 1945

Mr Bob Cools, Burgomaster of the City of Antwerp, Belgium

'Tee Emm', RAF Training Memorandum

74 Squadron Operation Records Book

91 Squadron Operation Records Book

16 Squadron Operational Records, NZ Records Office, Wellington

80 Squadron Operation Records Book

74 Squadron Combat Reports, Public Records Office, Kew, UK

80 Squadron Combat Reports, Public Records Office, Kew, UK

91 Squadron Combat Reports, Public Records Office, Kew, UK

16 Squadron Combat Reports, NZ Records Office, Wellington
and with special references from Sir Winston Churchill's *The Second World War*, Cassell, 1951.

Glossary

AA	Anti-aircraft
AP	Armour-Piercing
AOC	Air Officer Commanding
ASR	Air Sea Rescue
ATA	Air Transport Auxiliary, formed from civilian pilots and airline crews
Boffins	RAF slang for scientists
Contrails	streamers of condensed water vapour created by extreme pressure and the right degree of humidity
DF	Direction Finding. A RT call to base activated a reply giving a course to steer home
De Wilde ammunition	a type of .303 bullet which exploded on contact. Not very lethal in effect but useful in indicating correct aim and as an incendiary if fuel was leaking from the damaged plane.
DI	Daily inspection; a series of routine checks done before each day's flight.
Drogue	A hollow tapered tube of canvas shaped like a wind sock. This was the target towed a couple of hundred yards behind another aircraft and 'attacked' by the novice marksman.
DRO	Daily Routine Orders
FDO	Fighter Directing Officer
GCI	Ground Control Interception
GSU	Ground Support Unit

LAC	Leading Aircraftman
Link Trainer	A crudely shaped 'aeroplane' supported on air bladders controlled by compressed air. In its covered-in cockpit a pilot practised flying by instruments. Almost any flying condition could be simulated and the pilot's ability checked by an instructor seated at a separate console.
LMF	Lack of Moral Fibre: a serious charge and not taken lightly. I saw only two cases of this in six years which involved British air crew.
Mae Wests	Lifejackets so nicknamed after the popular American film star with big 'knockers'.
Marsden Matting	interlocking steel plates forming a firm landing strip
Oberfeldwebel	equivalent rank to our warrant officer
OTU	Operational training unit
P39	Bell 'Airacobra', a mid engined single seat fighter
Rhubarb	sortie by one or two aircraft hunting for targets of opportunity, over the Continent usually on days with very low cloud cover.
RTO	Railway Transport Officer
Smoke trails	caused by condensed water vapour from the aircraft motors
Sweep	later codenamed 'Circus' when used in conjunction with a small group of bombers. A trouble-seeking foray by strong fighter formations to force the Jerries into combat. This helped the Russian front by making the German Air Force keep a large fighter force in France.
Tadpoles	short vapour trails
TAF	Tactical Air Force: fully equipped and serviced wings and groups formed to operate independently on the continent;
WAAC	Women's Auxiliary Army Corps

Index